TIME TO TIME

BY

RANDY SPENCE

Time To Time

(Illustrated)

Copyright © William R. Spence 2011

Canada

All rights reserved

ISBN: 978-0-9876915-1-4

For Nan, Sam and Nick
Bed time stories

Acknowledgements

With warm thanks to Chamnongsri for advice and inspiration, Mark Czarnecki for the marathon, Wendy for the great leap somewhere and Ed Carson for kind and expert advice. This book also owes a great deal to Ed and Fran, Rohinton and Marie-Claude, Janie, Mark - and to Krista, Timo, Michael and Alan Spence and their families for panache. Thanks to Barry Norris for adept editing and to many friends in many countries for illuminating the world. James (Jake) Fowell and Simon Greer did the illustrations and cover - musician-artists flirting with fiction.. from time to time.

Listen
Labyrinth
Rudiments
Sanctuary
Inferno
Submerged
Assassination
Desperation
Spacelift
NOA
Nuclear
Rhetoric
Ensemble
Netwar
Cameo
WMD
Ascent
Portals
Pinnacle
Junction
Aftermath
Presentiment

Listen

影 Shadow is the name I was given. Others will write this segment of place and time in their own tongues and images. My rendering starts with Merimbula, but from there it goes back as well as forward. In the end, there is no beginning.

Kat stopped and studied the image that stared back at her the day that time stood still. It was hard not to notice her reflection in the long pool leading up to the entrance of the deep-space listening station. For the small crew gathered Down Under to listen to the universe, the months went by like a story remembered, a flood of images.

The end of a long evening had the feeling of expectation, the distant hunting horn of an early summer squall ringing up the valley through the open sweep of the deep listening arcs. On the horizon, the sun dipped into a vast orange bowl formed of rugged purple hills. Echoes of the zephyr died away and a fine silence descended like a gentle shower.

People and objects loomed into view, larger than life for being unexpected. Flame trees and purple jacaranda, twilight reflecting on the pool, beauty almost comical in its perfection, the agony of beauty's death just below the surface. Next door lay the ocean, where fatality stalked the beds of coral as surely as it haunted the bluffs they commanded or the rising bush land of the outback behind. We're like the sun fish, Kat thought. There might be a warning, a silver flash before the end. Might.

To the real inhabitants of Merimbula, the crew at the listening station were alien, their behaviour like the birds that surrounded them, the comical creatures that strutted, searched, nested, stored, survived, and died when their skill or luck ran out. To the old landed families of Oz, they were the eccentric sky watchers, to the original inhabitants, lost spirits, to the Asians simply impractical, wasting time.

They were far enough from the growing settlement to feel alone, a family grown introverted. There were few secrets here for those who listened, but there were sinuous currents of deception, a microcosm of masked emotions, for those who by choice or blindness failed to observe. Cast away on a transcendent coastline just north of Eden, a wild sail north from Tasmania, they were choking on unfulfilled expectations. Time was passing without progress and they boiled in the desire for any breakthrough, any hint, another intelligent message from the stars, something they could understand.

As she studied her reflection, Kat's thoughts wandered back to another time, somewhere just beyond the veils of childhood. This was happening too often these days. Frustration breeds fancy and boredom is a window into memories. In her mind's eye, a gale battered the Minch and the waves sprayed the houses, even far up the shore above the low cliffs that framed the harbour. A tiny sail appeared and disappeared in the waves beyond the mouth, dancing in the tirade, making it to the mouth, but injured. She ran down the long path to the harbour, while men set out in the motor dory. When they brought him in, she saw he was young and wild and half-dead. She nursed him to health, and they found time for the meadows that summer while he healed, moments of freedom, explosions of colour, now gone. Memories changing with the years, gently imprisoned in time.

A shift in time. The land of Oz was a vast expanse with magic in its beauty and its past, a world away from the old magic on top of the cragged crown of the Scots empire facing Cape Wrath and the Butt of Lewis. But not entirely different. In both domains, life hinged on the naming of reality, on identity and clarity, for good or evil.

Phil interrupted her mind's wandering, his face popping up on her wristcom. "Back in ten." How had that happened? Time skips ahead, in and out of fast-forward, a slave of our selective memory. In a hospital recovering from combat, a moment ago, now married, a mother, in no time at all, no malice aforethought, no stage fright, no *single* regret. Stay in the moment, a voice reminds her through the gulf of time and place between the then and now. Stay in the moment, October 2032, All-Saints just ahead.

If you listened only to the growing crop of detractors, humanity was still at a complete loss to understand the first brief waves of intelligent deep-space transmissions that had brought them here to Merimbula and shocked the human psyche to its core. NOT ALONE, now suddenly listening to 'others,' trying to understand what they said, whoever or whatever they were. The transmissions were no more than patterns, but intricate patterns, deeply unsettling, impossible to comprehend or to ignore.

At Merimbula, they analyzed the Visitors' transmissions for the thousandth time, looking for meaning of any sort. Are you taunting us? What are you planning? Two years is an eternity when it is filled with nothing. They reminded each other, too deliberately and too often, that they had made headway, developed whole new technologies for tackling these imponderable communications. But time and tide reminded them that they'd learned nothing important, living now on a hope and a dare, global patience drained, attention seeped away. Politics as always had redirected the world's focus to the here and now. The Visitors soon slipped out the bottom of the lowest common denominator. Silence. ALONE AGAIN, the only intelligent species in an infinite uncaring universe. Humanity's loudest cynics declared that the messages had come to Earth from a now dead species, that humanity could wait millennia or forever before it knew. There was even the hint of a hoax, that the Visitors transmissions had been sent somehow from Earth.

But the world had changed, even as it lost faith in the reality of the Visitors. Although some reasonable people and some fanatics dismissed the whole episode, it was out of the question for most to walk on without looking over their shoulders. In the end, only the hermits and ideologues could retire comfortably into denial. The galactic plot had thickened.

Even for so-called scientists, they were a strange lot, those who persisted in the belief that they could decipher the transmissions or might soon get another instalment from the universe. Not a bad bet, for that matter, if you waited long enough. Beneath the beauty, Merimbula had an other-worldly air and some dark shadows, a warning that few of the cast here assembled were precisely the characters they sought to portray.

Beya moved with the unselfconscious grace of the savannah, the undulating vertical wave of the giraffe she often described. Though they'd seen her attack when confronted, she was most often in balance, not fully aware of her power. You couldn't be around her long without falling in love — men, women, children, dogs, cats, old, young, everyone did. Béatrice at birth, in the foothills of Mount Meru, with Kilimanjaro in the evening sky. Beya had stuck. Beneath that mellifluous exterior ran strong currents. Her spirit was marked by the death of her brother Kilifi two years before, caught in a crossfire serving with the peacekeepers of the African Union. Killed for believing in peace. And her balance was not one of peace, but of powerful forces knit in a tightly wound equilibrium. Her spirit was strong, sometimes off the scale of Kat's normally reliable sixth and higher-order senses. Trained in psychology and diplomacy, Beya injected a quiet strength into their ambition to match speed with the Visitors.

Phil had gone around to Nguyen's for the late-shift round of cappuccino and biscotti. He was perhaps the only one here without dark corners concealed. Team leader and comtech specialist, pretty good detective and periodic entrepreneur, there could be no greater gift for Philamon Rush than the Visitors' messages, no challenge so exciting. They were a winning lottery ticket arriving in the night like an infant left at the door.

Phil also provided perfect cover for Kat, she recognized with a guilty shiver, some protection from her past, a firewall against the people who knew she had intuition, analytical skills and operational experience. They weren't wrong, but they knew only part of the story, like everyone's story, known in glimpses, woven together, interpreted, rewritten. It was eons ago when they'd met in Canada, with moonlight on the snow and the air so cold it could shatter, married before the arrival of the Visitors' signals. How they'd jumped at the chance to run the deep-listening operation at Merimbula, clear the path for discovery, record their names large in the history of humanity, meet another sentient race!

Canadian to his work boots and plaid shirt, Phil was apologetic, curiously attractive, and often whimsical. Somewhere along the line he'd become an inspired father. What more could a woman ask? Could she ask for more? Too many questions, too many long moments of inaction and contemplation here in paradise. Was Phil the only one here hiding nothing, or did she know him too well to be able to see those contextual areas of ambiguity that surround us all?

With the persistent rumours that 'some' of the listening stations would be closed, attrition was beginning to take a toll. They were lucky still to have all the local staff. Losing Ewan Wesson to Wellington next week would be a blow to the mathematical research.

Kat looked across the hall at Sandover, a hard maze to read. Aspiring economist and technologist from Yunnan, Singapore, and the Ivy League. By her receding standards he was young, thirty next year, and he seemed driven by the hope that the messages from space would reveal new paths to peace and prosperity. But the next moment he could be gone, lost somewhere in time or thought. Under an idealist exterior was a highly tuned observer, strung like a Fender, yet gentle in that enigmatic way some Asian men possess. With some encouragement, he was irretrievably smitten with Beya. You couldn't take anything for granted, Kat thought, but if he didn't have good intentions, he was a very good actor.

In the last moments of old time — pre-Orion, as it came to be known — Ellis Holland was chatting with Sandover, gesticulating, pushing some new theory. Ellis was the code and encryption guru, intense, startled but friendly, a shock of sandy hair and stern glasses partly hiding a boyish face. There were occasional clues to his convoluted view of the world: a nerd in wolf's clothing, decent, sometimes hilarious, treading water, commenting on the dependably human irony of the present state of limbo — purgatory, as he described it, dancing on a pin in case the Visitors noticed or cared, slowly descending in the quicksand of perfect uncertainty, unable even to get their attention.

Mathias Abbott approached them along the circular walkway around level two, hardware wizard, tall, awkward, born-again American, eerily ambitious, determined, fanatical.

"Too confident by half," Chuanli whispered to Kat as he came along side. "He's backed by Golgotha and the new Christian Right."

Chuanli was Sandover's friend, like Sancho Panza to Don Quixote, and a master at pattern recognition. There the metaphor ended, Kat realized, Sandover was no tilter at windmills nor Chuanli just a skilled sidekick.

"They're trouble, all right!" Kat agreed.

"Bunch of thugs and killers, if you ask me, Kat. Gone from the frying pan into the hellfire since the tame old days of Reagan and Bush!"

"Your heroes, I can see."

"Lord forgive me if I offend any rednecks, but Abbott wants to chat with the Visitors, for Christ's sake, fall on his knees before the agents of God, speak through them with Jesus and the Almighty."

"Good luck! They're as likely to exterminate the lot of us as they are to connect us to The Top Dog."

"You can't change these people, Kat. He's hard-core creationist, obsessed with being first, finding divinity, bathing in the power and the glory of the Lord. God help us if he turns out to be right!"

Jean-Christophe Moreau chose that moment to grace the assembly with his presence, casting a disdainful glance across the sixty-metre bubble of clear crystal that was hunched beneath the arcs and mountains beyond. Obsessed by the wetware, he led their sorties into artificial intelligence, vain attacks upon the vastly complex architecture of the Visitors' patterns. On the surface he was a charming young Parisian with blue eyes, thin pale hair, and a cultured air of boredom. Underneath? Muddy, but you could bet your grandmother's stamp collection that if you knew J.C. better, you'd have to call Abbott well adjusted. Somewhere he was insecure, angry, likely vicious. Kat had learned to read the signs. A damaged soul alone, trusting no one, unpredictable.

Frozen in the moment, gathered at their nightly pageant under the stars, they were listening to the silence of the receivers and watching the whispers of the dying light. With the squeak of a styrofoam cup, Kat's attention snapped back to Beya, following her line of sight toward an image that had just appeared on the main monitor. The sound from the speakers didn't so much break the silence as come to life in the heart of the room. It took a moment to register. Phil strolled in with an armload of pastries, expecting a hero's welcome, only to find a petrified forest of astonished statues.

Abbott moved to the displays, stared, raised his hands in a gesture of entreaty, headed for the receivers and slipped in behind the racks of electronics. Minds began to focus. An incoming signal was being recorded digitally and conveyed in audio by the trained software arrays. It was coming from the central speakers, which implied, they all knew, from far out in the galaxy. Abbott reappeared.

"From the arcs," he said, and a collective gulp echoed through the vault. Phil set down a tray of cups and a bag of goodies as he scanned the screens of a dozen monitors with jaw-dropping intensity.

"Not possible." Kat was reading his lips as the signal continued to fill the room with that clarity you get from the best equipment. No meaning, but a cadence in the signal that was not unpleasant and a sound like speech that had been scrambled, garbled but fleetingly familiar.

Something nudged a memory, and Kat looked at Beya, immobile and alert, like a deer in the headlights. Sandover watched her with an intensity that could send a spike up your spine. People and relationships came into sharper focus as everyone exchanged glances, the solitude of J.C., the yearning of Abbott. A moment of truth stretched into ten of silent attention, silent speculation.

When the signal stopped, there was silence for a heartbeat. Collective exhalation.

"Eleven minutes even," Abbott breathed, "I'm starting a full check. Got it all down."

In seconds they had a digital transcription of the signal. Improbably, it translated almost flawlessly into groups of phonetic sounds, like words but jumbled words, meaningless in any known language. By 23:15 every instrument and recording had been checked. No malfunctions or tampering could be detected, at least on the first pass.

All available evidence indicated that an eleven-minute transmission had been received from the direction of the constellation Orion, in some jumbled phonetic language. Their decryption systems offered no other xeno-cultural or technological matches. Phil called friends at the other listening stations; all had received the same message, were equally dismayed, and in the same panic to understand the meaning.

The media were minutes away, an hour at best. Kat saw Sandover speaking quietly with Beya, then Phil, before heading in her direction.

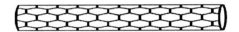

By moonrise, most had drifted off to homes or bars to absorb the shock and watch the world's reactions or face the public. Their experience confirmed that anyone who wouldn't sell or give a story to the media had their privacy stolen by the paparazzi just the same. J.C. hung around, angling to be included in conversations. Beya was having none of it, and he finally skulked away with some thinly veiled current of anger directed at Sandover. A long moment passed as they gathered on the clear-walled observation terrace, looking past the arcs to the star-lit skies, a moment one remembers. The meeting was Sandover's call, so Kat waited for him to break the silence. Phil and Beya apparently had the same thought.

""I have the deciphering code for the message we just heard, the Orion message."

Silence.

"At root, it is an association of pairs, a word for a phonetic sequence, each pair unique, each required to be known in order to translate the message."

More silence. None expected the next words.

"I deciphered the message, very securely, while you were all shifting around trying to get rid of J.C. It says it is from Phil and all of us, from the future."

Blow us away with a straw!

"I've set it up on my com so it will self-erase on conclusion. I keep one copy. You would like to hear the message?"

Phil's expression was an odd mixture of curiosity and excitement with an icicle of the fear they all felt. Kat wanted badly to know why Sandover had the code, but that could wait.

"In for a nickel."

"Here goes."

"*Philamon Rush, if you are hearing this, you are hearing yourself, or me if you wish, in November 2041. First things first. We have a plague, nanotech plus organic and artificial intelligence. NOA for short. It will eliminate human and other forms of life unless research that was started years ago could give us a way out. What we know about the plague agents follows.*"

Sandover's next words came at a guess from microbiology, chemistry, nanotech, and cognitive sciences. Kat recalled intros to all these subjects in her training, but beyond that she had learned only what was needed for missions. Nothing was coming to her mind beyond mild disbelief with a chaser of severe disbelief. Sandover looked oddly relieved as he resumed, jolting them out of their daze.

"*You will understand the basics, but you will need to find specialists in bio, nano, and A.I. to chart the research strategy. Locating the right people is crucial. Be very careful and tell no one. There are those today who caused the plague, those who have much to gain, if it doesn't annihilate us all, and those who will save themselves at any cost. All of them have militias at their disposal.*

"*We are transmitting by a combination of what you would call black holes and worm holes. Black holes slow time infinitely at their centre. With the ability to create nano-sized black holes in laboratories, we have created environments where time and space are compacted, so that divergent segments of place-time that are very close to each other. If you hear this, we have succeeded in creating a 'worm hole' or interconnection between place-times. These are not physical connections, but we think they will convey code, messages. We are aiming at you and the other deep-space stations which are listening intently for just such a code.*

> *"The following data will help you develop inter-place-time communication technology. While stopping the plague comes first, this interacts with inter-place-time. We are aiming these broadcasts as best we can at the last days of Merimbula, but the margin for error could be high."*

Sandover paused to take a breath. More strings of technical terms followed, all even further from Kat's training and experience. Math, physics, cosmology, who knows?

> *"Parallel developments in temporal and relational physics suggest that a connection between two segments may cause damage to the nearby 'fabric' of place-time, anywhere from minuscule to cataclysmic. It is the nature of place-time to be self-healing. The symbiotic whole begins immediately to reconstruct a new reality and block further disturbance.*
>
> *"Consequently, we think there are parallel universes in the same 'place,' but only briefly. 'Briefly' on the cosmic scale is very hard to define in terms of days and months, because of scale and measurement error. Our best guess is that after place-time is traumatized, by communication from one place-time to another, it becomes fully healed by the time the 'latter' place and time are reached. Both may have changed by a little or by a lot in the process. Thus, you may face the plague much earlier than we. The schism and healing will speed the convergence of our worlds. How much? We don't know, but you may not have long."*

Kat was able to smother a spike of fear. Bad news in the midst of a nightmare has a tendency to roll off your back. As if echoing her thoughts, the message continued in Sandover's calm voice.

> *"When place-time heals, the power of the cure follows directly from the power of the schism. The amount of damage to everything in the vicinity depends on how much vibration there is between the two ends of the string — most importantly, on how many intelligent entities are involved, how many lives and causal chains have been altered. This means again that you must be very careful to tell no one, for your sake, but also crucially for everyone's sake. Telling the world about this message might look like the best way for humanity to be prepared for the plague that is coming. Unfortunately,*

we believe that revealing inter-place-time communication would ensure human destruction more surely in the end than the plague itself.

"You may be relieved to hear that you and the inner four are all alive and well at this moment, or more accurately, these moments. We are in this adventure with you, with essential roles to play at this end.

"You should be able to communicate back to us. The past is an open book from where we stand, unless and until the sequences of time and place are changed too much by their interconnection. Many events will be immediately altered by this message, and our past will diverge from your future. But they may stay close enough to talk for a while. So leave a message for us in the classified ads of The Sunday Times. It has survived to this day and is searchable for us online. Put the word 'Portobello' in the message, and direct us to some unused media archive that you can access.

"Be careful. Others in our time are watching us. Tell us what you are learning and doing. Don't use this code again, nor any other from Sandover. Kat is the best at deception. Trust her. Following is what we've been able to learn about critical research facilities in your time."

This part they all understood, a long list of names, organizations, and research programs.

"People will covet and pursue the source of this transmission, just as they have with the Visitors' patterns. They may initially think this is from the Visitors, that our extra-terrestrials have observed humans and may be testing us again with more familiar symbols. People will fight and kill for the technology and wealth they believe is hidden in the message we are sending to you. In one form or another, you will be leading the anti-plague and place-time technology developments. You will become targets. Beware. You will need money. Here are investment suggestions from a reliable perspective. Each of you should invest separately so as to attract as little attention as possible."

Kat heard names of companies, stocks, bonds, funds, and dates. Sandover paused with a sheepish don't-blame-me look, as if willing them toward something unclear. If any of this was for real, they had just dropped through the rabbit hole into a land that looked decidedly more hostile than the droll world of Alice.

"We believe that the possibility of inter-place-time connectivity is known only to us, yet it could become known to others. While distant from current advances in physics and cosmology, it is not an impossible jump if you are looking for it. It would be terminal in the hands of terrorists. If we live through the plague, we will have to try to survive the consequences of place-time connection. We are working on this, initially to mislead others from the path.

"The plague arose from the race to develop smart medical nano-organisms, driven by enormous profits and fears. The creature that may kill us started in a safe corner of medical research before its business and military possibilities became clear. Ambition trumps morality, as the pharmaceutical empire of Édouard Moreau has proved in spades.

"If all goes well, the world will be different, and you will be here. If you are hearing this, the process has started. For you it may take years, for us months or weeks. What happens when you get 'here' is anybody's guess. Theory supports intuition that the central agents of the schism are the most highly vulnerable as divergence collapses. Should you survive and arrive, we and our past will have been replaced by you and yours. You may yourselves face such a choice one day. Go well!"

The silence was palpable, a meal they all had to digest. It looked like a long night. Kat's instincts distrusted the message. There were more questions than answers by a long shot, if they had that long. The first question was where the code had come from, and how Sandover had got hold of it.

Labyrinth

Kat looked into the night, hoping to find some perch for her floundering hold on reality. The arcs were framed by a moon just past its peak. Behind rose two storm fronts angling toward each other, tangible forms of her fear and anger, battling over the fortress walls. Saints and fools accept with indifference whatever life hands them. Kat was neither.

This boded little but ill. The broad patterns were clear enough to her. Phil would already have gone through fifty scenarios in that emotion-free analytical mode his mind slipped into. The fact that one runs off the roadmap of logic into uncharted territory was not to him a possibility. The paths she saw ahead were all treacherous, uncertain, everything she most hated and most needed. Everything had changed. Phil would resist, do his best, suck it up, accept what came. Noble, ultimately right headed, but also very dangerous. Logic and instinct are ascendant as partners but fatal as enemies.

"What about the cipher codes, Sandover?" Phil was first to the punch, saving Kat the trouble. Sandover looked sheepish but resolute.

"I created this code after I came here, to Merimbula. It's based on random word pairs, selected from different on-line dictionaries. For words that are used a lot, multiple pairs are included. The words are also scrambled phonetically among each other, using another random generator. As a result, the code is virtually impossible to break without a copy of the word pairs and the phonetic generator. I keep only one copy and I keep it behind rock-solid firewalls. As I was listening to the Orion message, this code came soon to mind. I wasn't sure until I ran it."

"Could anyone else have got a copy?"

"I don't see how."

"A message from the future is hard to believe."

"I know, it's a lot, to ask you to trust me. I know you may not. It may help to know that I was asked to prepare this unbreakable cipher."

Now they were getting somewhere. Facts open a window for trust.

"Who?" Beya said it for all of them.

"My father. He is now retired from the business and power structures he navigated throughout his career, though still connected to high places in Asia and beyond. He asked me to make the code and keep it absolutely secret."

Silence. Was he telling it straight or was he a convincing performer. They needed to know. That Beya trusted him said a lot. Phil looked at Kat.

"Analysis?"

Kat nodded. Nothing ventured, nothing gained.

"Either Phil learned the code in the future, before the message was sent, or someone hacked Sandover's files and used the concordance to send the Orion message."

"Are you saying Orion could have come from here and now?" Beya's confusion was not feigned.

"Four possibilities in all," Kat corrected. "Orion was a tech trick Earthside, a transmission from a distant satellite, a message from the future, or another message from the Visitors."

Beya looked at Sandover as she voiced a collective enquiry.

"Why are you telling the three of us?"

"The message referred to Philamon and the inner four," Sandover reminded them. "Phil and Kat must be two. I know the code. Of the rest of us here at Merimbula, the fourth had to be you."

Phil was the first to see that they needed time to think and to find out if the message could have been faked to look like a deep-space transmission. All the stations would be working on it. They swore to silence on the cipher. It went without saying, but some part of each of them wanted to hear it said. They also needed time to find out what and who lay behind the directive that had led to Sandover's cipher.

Saturday passed in a blur; they met again Sunday morning on the beach near Eden, thirty-seven hours post-Orion. Beya looked pale as Sandover shifted a tall beach umbrella to shade her from the glare. The silence began to last too long Kat summoned a voice that had slept for as long as she cared to remember.

"What do we know, Phil?"

"Our colleagues at Manitou and Kilmarnock, Rio Gallegos, and Guiyang have all tested their equipment. No bugs. The transmission seems to have hit all the dishes *as if* from deep space."

"And?"

"If it's not a hoax, we're responsible for the future of our species and completely unequipped for the job, if you ask me, which you did."

Phil had seen Sandover's body language tighten a shade at the word "hoax."

"Sorry, Sandover, I don't think you would lie to us, but it *is* one of the logical possibilities. You could tell us that the message said anything."

"That doesn't explain how it was sent," Beya argued.

Kat watched carefully. Sandover continued to look serious but somehow more at ease, somewhat disengaged as he paused to frame a reply. He was gazing up the coastline with a faraway look, but she sensed he was also registering every factoid of his surroundings. Mystery wrapped in enigma.

"We'll know soon enough if it was a tech trick done Earthside. Is that possible?"

"I would have said no," Phil answered, "but we have to be sure."

"Who's the best technician in the business?"

"On software? Probably Ellis or Jean-Christophe. Abbott on the hardware. Ellis is our best bet, for sure."

Kat couldn't help agreeing.

"I wouldn't trust the frog prince with a dull spoon, and his buddy Abbott is a self-appointed martyr who should never have been reborn. Might as well ask the bankers to regulate the banks or toss the ring to Mordor."

"We can't just be silent," Phil added. "Everyone will be asking the same questions. We'll look suspicious if we don't ask them, too. We can focus our own investigations on technical matters, steer away from any hint that we understand what the message says."

Four heads nodded agreement.

"OK," Sandover resumed, "but among us we need to get to the bottom of this. If Orion came from a satellite, from humans in today's world, the questions arise as to who and how and why. And why the four of us are fingered."

"The only reason I can see," Beya volunteered, "would be to get research started on bio-nano and AI, anything that might cause global disaster in the future. That would make sense if the senders were ahead in technology and saw trouble coming. On how, I have no idea."

"Someone had to go to a lot of trouble," Phil brooded, "getting a satellite out to somewhere around Orion without anyone noticing. Is that possible?"

"Yes." They all stared at Kat.

"I thought of that, did a pinch of research. There are enough anomalies in near-space annals, the facts and fiction as told by the major powers over the past decade or so, to have covered a few satellite launches. Maybe even an invasion or two by the Visitors."

"But who would go to so much trouble even if they could?" Phil mulled. "Political or religious groups with plenty of money? Philanthropists? And who could have taken such a jump ahead in comtech? China? America? Some consortium or cult or conspiracy?"

The Illuminati, Kat thought — Phil's favourite cult classic from decades back, the essence of all conspiracy theories tossed into one deliciously mad recipe. She watched as Sandover and Phil traded lobs like tennis players warming up for the match.

"As for who might have higher technology across the board, it could be extraterrestrials just as well as people. The third possibility."

"Benevolent, it appears."

"So far."

"Our Visitors?"

"That would have to be the best guess."

"Then they would have to have learned your cipher. Somehow."

"True, and that seems very unlikely," Sandover admitted, "unless they are actually here among us, or at least a lot closer than we think."

Silent thoughts. The obvious question came involuntarily to all.

"What if the Orion message is what it claims to be?" Beya asked. "The fourth option?"

"Well, there's the rub," Phil sighed. "If any of what Orion says starts to materialize, the technologies it reveals or the money it promises, we'd have to start believing that communication across time is possible, that the messengers could be ourselves. Which means our first priority would be to follow the directives that have been sent to us and only us, or so it would appear."

A dark premonition ran through Kat's mind, tinged with all the terrors of the past. On her own or with Phil, she could face anything. Life is a crapshoot. Those who say otherwise have never been shot. But the kids, she thought, Jesus and Merlin, what of Dylan and Lara? What if she couldn't protect them from plague or worse?

Sandover was very quiet again, staring down the beach. Kat imagined pictures from the next years and decades erupting from his mind like thought bubbles in a cartoon, images of peace and war, people, moons and stars. His voice drifted gently back into the silence.

"Aliens are a tempting explanation, but there's no way of knowing if they don't want us to, so that's the explanation of last resort. That leaves us with humans, present or future or both."

Where Phil darted among the parameters and patterns of a puzzle, Sandover jumped from one deduction to another until he had circled the issue and reined it in. Resuming command stance, Kat signalled Sandover to continue.

"We need to find out if Orion was sent using known technology. Phil's the one for that. We need to know why I was asked to prepare the cipher and who could have stolen it. I can pursue these questions with my father."

"Even if no one but us knows this language now," Phil rejoined, "if someone else learned it at any time in the future and could transmit across time, *they* could have sent this message from the future as easily as any of us. And aside from one of you teaching a third person or having it dragged out of you, excuse the bluntness, some of the world's best minds will be examining the Orion message and trying to discover the code. We can't rule out the possibility that someone will unravel it."

"The message said we were all OK in the future," Beya added hopefully. "None of us gets tortured to death."

"Don't make book on that," Kat snorted. "Whoever sent Orion would have said that even if it weren't true."

Their heads were now spinning. They needed a break, but the need to avoid fatal mistakes kept them all focused as best they could.

"So, one or more of us may be captured and tortured or forced to send the message. Cheery thought!"

"Indeed, Beya," Phil acknowledged, "and it can get much more bizarre, even if you don't admit the possibility of inter-place-time communication. People are already relating Orion to the Visitors' transmissions. They may think to ask if the Visitors' patterns are also human fabrications. It's like an ever-expanding riddle."

"Getting back to reality for a moment," Kat suggested, "it's very unlikely that we'll know the whole truth any time soon. So we'd better learn about bio, nano, and cognitive science, find friends in high places and leading edges - and look for enemies."

"What if we went public with the cipher?" Beya asked. Kat had a gut feel and a flash of precognition that she was right. On the other hand, the Orion message had given them very clear instructions to the contrary.

"I'd vote to wait," Phil offered.

Sandover and Kat nodded, she visibly more reluctantly. Beya followed suit in the end.

"We need to start exploring inter-place-time communication, too," Phil sighed. "I'll start on that but I'll need your help. We can't trust anyone we don't know intimately, platonically speaking."

"Getting rich won't be so bad," Beya smiled. This would do a lot to validate the Orion message, Kat realized, but better to be poorer if it meant escape from plague or worse. Living in fear is easily overrated.

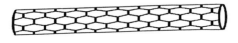

For the next three months, time swirled around them, rushing their boat downstream, now and then pinning them in the eddies of daydreams. Word came that Merimbula would be shut down by the end of the year — there wasn't enough money. Desperate for funds to respond to the droughts and ravages of climate change, the folks in Canberra reached the fiscally prudent conclusion that anything important from space would be picked up by the other stations. Best be a free rider. In practice, they were likely to be right and everyone knew it. The formerly temperate countries had more money these days and could be counted on to keep the vigil.

At the same time, the world was jolted once again by the Orion message into gathering its wits and forces to meet the Visitors. Analysts of all descriptions poured anew over the Visitors' patterns and the Orion reception. Security agencies redoubled their efforts, searching in random and tandem for signs of tampering, or some reasonable *earthly* explanation of Orion.

Kat and the others watched the demise of Merimbula with more than a little panic and some fascination. Any hopes for a last-minute reprieve proved wishful thinking. In public, they concentrated their outward energy on investigating how the listening stations could have been deceived, distancing themselves from the swirling bubbles of conjecture about Orion.

Though it was hard to bear, they had little time to grieve. Aside from their day jobs and the media, they were all hunting for the next paycheque and happy to have a roof over their heads a little longer. On the annoying side, everyone at Merimbula knew they would be dispersing like petals to distant destinations, so the pressure redoubled to squeeze them dry of media interest before they left. Interruptions came from every corner, the press, governments and spooks of all persuasions.

Nor, despite their imminent dismissal, did the demands diminish for results on the content of the transmissions. Orion perched on their shoulders like a one-tonne parrot repeating 'dimwit' over and over. Still nothing. Inexorably, they became old news beside the theories proffered by leading pundits, code breakers, cognitive specialists, xeno psychologists, political bag men, religious zealots, and just plain nuts — in short, everyone the story-hungry media managed to identify, inveigle, or invent.

As they supervised the packing of equipment and mothballing of Merimbula, Phil and Kat were asked to join Manitou. The Great Lakes appealed to the banshee in Kat. She'd seen pictures of the deep-space listening setup there, an exquisite structure on windswept granite. Their home-to-be was out on a short spit of land in the North Channel of Georgian Bay, where water and horizon meet the eye on every side but one, wild and treacherous, rich in ancient spirits.

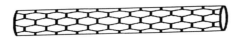

The marriage of Beya and Sandover was a bit of magic in an otherwise anxious time. Beya had no family except Kat and Phil, but Sandover's father and mother came from Singapore. Lee Eng Kai was a sharp-witted, gnome-like man with a smile that lit up a room. Meiling's grace and energy added the final touch to the small beachside ceremony. They kept the party to nine, including Dylan, Lara and Chuanli, an act of exclusion that did not go unnoticed by Abbott and J.C. Eng Kai let them know that the cipher had been requested by powerful friends for reasons he professed not to know but promised to investigate. Sandover did not tell him it had turned up in the Orion message. Kat watched as their collective agitation deepened on dozens of small fronts. Living a lie was a complex business.

Sandover got his appointment at Cambridge and Beya was recruited by the U.K. office of Women of the World for a research and writing assignment based at Cambridge. The four musketeers, as they began to think of themselves, pulled together what finances they could and made some cautious investments. They began to prosper a little, enough to make them wonder again where the tips in Orion had come from.

The end of summer heat and dust were soporific as Phil burned the midnight oil, his refuge and his cross. All four worked with the other stations to track down the Orion message. Each foray turned up a few more questions but no answers. To all appearances, Orion was generated by more familiar technology than were the Visitors' patterns. It had come in an incredibly tightly targeted beam from somewhere between Orion and the Pleiades — the Rain Stars, Beya called them. The tight-beam technology looked profitable, so many communications labs were in a sprint to understand and copy it. The far more alien quality of the Visitors' patterns remained inscrutable in terms of tech as well as content.

Phil had left theoretical physics in university, dismayed at whiteboards filled with symbols and integrals unrelated to anything. If you lost the trail you were toast, and he had lasted only four weeks. It had troubled him more than a little because he loved science, more deeply influenced than he admitted by his uncle's boss and research team's winning the Nobel. He'd been twenty-seven when he went to Stockholm for the award ceremonies, a procession of receptions, lectures, banquets, royalty, and Verdi wafting down upon thousands of dinner guests in the grand old City Hall.

Now he was back at the grindstone of theoretical treatises and expert interpretations. No dreams of glory drove him now, just adrenaline and a strong pinch of terror. Mixed with physics were forays into the contours of biotech, nanotech, and their evolving mergers with artificial intelligence. Lists proliferated, ideas and contacts, experts to track down. He became their project leader de facto, even if they didn't know at first they had projects. He planned strategies, Kat helped in design, and they all set pieces in motion.

In their last days at Merimbula, they gathered together as often as they could, inventing plausible reasons for their continuing interaction. Suspicions surfaced. Jean-Christophe, before heading for his family home in Bordeaux, took every chance to corner them, especially Beya, sometimes to imply they were hiding things, other times just, it seemed, to underline his family's pre-eminence in the councils of power.

They responded with care, warned by the Orion message. J.C. and Abbott formed a Merimbula sub-committee on everything-Orion, dragging the rest into interminable discussions in-house or, worse, with the media. Between the two of them, acuity warred against avarice, with an absence of generosity so complete on both sides as to revolt everyone around. Abbott's inner colours came to the surface, self-styled voice and hand of Jesus on Earth, a fitting companion for Jean-Christophe's inner rage and vacuum. They were becoming a pair of symbiotes who could empathize only with each other. Dangerous if they combined forces, Kat knew, but luckily there was not a shard of trust between them.

Ellis pretended to follow the advice on his screensaver: 'when all else fails, lower your standards.' Underneath his sardonic asides, he looked as determined as Phil, running all the jumbled patterns of Orion endlessly through self-learning decryption models. His often ferocious attention summoned to Kat's mind a premonition of super geeks hunched over coms and wrist tops, hacking global communications, ruling the world.

Phil remained the most upbeat. Guided by the Orion data, he found research labs studying new comtech at Imperial College in London and the California coast south of Half Moon Bay. The others helped where they could, becoming a repository of knowledge and watching his back, lieutenants with a lot to ponder and a lot do. Time paraded as a friend. We have lots of time, Kat told herself as she raced against something, someone, but not yet against time.

Although anticlimactic, the last hurrah in Merimbula was enchanting in its own way. They knew what they were leaving behind and the odds against finding it again. Not innocence — they weren't that green — but a rest stop on the way, a time of firmness under the feet until the next shoe dropped. Night after night, as if to mock them, a mountain-sized gold-red sun settled regally into a purple ring on the horizon. One night, an unexpected whiff of cool air turned the sky to crystal. Kangaroos came and listened, curious about the commotion and sensing their inheritance. What did they hear? Did they look up at the night sky along the big arc? Did they also seek some sign from the heavens?

Kat's old instincts knew that a war had started, as sure as if they'd been attacked by armies or aliens. They couldn't share their secret without losing the war. But it felt massively wrong and vastly lonely, hard to hold, hard to focus. Plague and place-time seemed one moment like fantasies, the next like unbreakable curses. Saving the world or playing out someone's whimsy, it appeared, was going to proceed in small steps.

At the same time, Kat knew she had skills not practised and friends not seen for years. It was time to think carefully. In the field, that always meant time to act. Neither ideas nor men, God bless them when you have a moment, were going to keep her children alive. She might, and she knew people who could help. That and a good shake of the dice.

Rudiments

Kat felt the pent-up fear, the impossible balance of gratitude and foreboding. A ray of early morning sunlight stole through the eastern window and danced playfully on Phil's shoulder. A gentle hand began to trace a figure eight on her back, the sign of infinity, edging ever harder into the overwrought muscles of her neck and shoulders. A jolt of pleasure shot through her as she folded happily into his clever massage. Fingers pressed her spine upward as they worked out the knots of tension. Lips brushed her ear as she rolled on top, moved with the rhythm of his hands, kneading their bodies together, engulfing them in warm waves of relief. Thankful muscles merged with the sounds of the awakening day, receding into a universe of the moment, slow and certain harmonies released, hearts and bodies at peace, united in the hope of respite, willingness to believe, a lack of any good alternatives when you got right down to it.

She wanted nothing more than to disappear in this warm embrace forever. Unfortunately, life was knocking at the door. Tomorrow is another day and the future lies ahead. Perhaps.

The kids would soon be back from a sleepover at Danielle's, like the three musketeers when Dani's daughter Amélie was wedged between. Fifteen-sixteen-seventeen, what a time of life! Discovery, the end of high school portending decisions, opportunities, dangers, foolish risks, and moments of incomparable joy. Thank the mages of old for Saturday. Home and hearth beckoned, both too much ignored in recent days. There was always the next schedule to draw up and discuss with the Manitou team, but not today.

Sometimes, when the sun caught the orange lilies along the shoreline, Kat felt a pang of regret for the rolling Australian hills. Recollections would scurry away across the back porch, gone with the fall gusts. The Ojibwa spirit of the wind aroused her Celtic ancestry, at home in this dramatic wilderness, always changing, sometimes violent. Winter was coming, an anxious word in the true north strong and free, full of frozen promises and memories for those who had grown up here, memories she could almost feel. Autumn had been stunning, with every kind of brilliant orange and red in dazzling parades along the shorelines, yet it had dredged up other memories, too, dusty halls, schoolgirl fears, measuring up, doing it right. Winter would bring powerful winds, temperatures of 30 below, intimations of immortality served up in a frozen dish by Ms. Nature, mother and destroyer. Imitations of immorality flashed through her mind, calling forth memories of Jean-Christophe Moreau and Mathias Abbott.

It was hard to imagine Merimbula deserted. A stray image crossed her mind of their ghosts, their future selves, ricocheting through the arcs in some different reality. The Orion transmission had not been repeated, and they began to fear they would hear nothing more. Sandover had posted innocuous messages in the media, as Orion had suggested, but if these had reached their future selves or anyone else, they received no sign in return. No one they knew had mysteriously vanished, which surprised Kat a little, as did the calm that surrounded them like a fine net.

Underneath, though, the artificial serenity gnawed at her gut, summoning memories of pre-op briefings. Beya and Sandover were too far away in the halls and towers of Cambridge — that was part of it. They needed to talk more often. Outside, as if to mock her complacency, the great lake and landscape congealed to a calm before the storm, darkening into a deathly still horizon, gathering to explode in fury. Tempests were coming from every direction, even the future, but it was still possible to wish, postpone, deny a little longer.

In the late afternoon light, she sat with Phil on the back deck, looking out over the mounting gale, whitecaps crashing in over shoals in the wide sweep of skyline arcing south to

Wreck Point and the remains of an ancient gambling boat smashed one night on the reefs. Lara and Dylan circled out on the rocks, examining a crayfish shell, then a skittering skink. Her banter with Phil swirled in eddies, like the gusts that drove the breakers onto the shore.

All that lay before them was nature's work, biotech and nanotech constructions, nothing in sight man-made. Phil took that reality to one extreme, with the mantra of the scientist. Science trumps religion, reason trumps faith. Kat knew better, but listened once again with a sceptical eye that he couldn't fail to notice. No point, she mused, in giving him any encouragement.

"OK," he ventured, visibly assembling his arguments, "after ten billion years of slag, simple elements combined to form many compounds, like water from hydrogen and oxygen. This led to the first, very simple living organisms, cells and bacteria, by far the most plentiful forms of life on the planet. These life forms were created by lightning striking the basic atoms and molecules enough billions of times to separate them out and group them together into new forms. After eons, one form brought together the four nucleic acids we call adenine, thymine, guanine, cytosine — A, T, G, and C."

"So far, so good."

"After an almost endless series of accidents, several billion nucleic acid molecules became linked by tiny phosphate hooks to form strings of deoxyribonucleic acid, DNA. On each DNA string, combinations of the A, C, T, and G acids became codes, genes, about three million of them on one string, not counting the ones we used to call junk-DNA before we learned their role. Very significantly, these first bacteria, with their enormously complex data and programming capabilities, were able to reproduce by dividing. It is hard to overstate the importance of this capability for survival and evolution."

"And awesome if not miraculous that it could have happened through countless accidents."

"Yes, but wait a moment if you really want miracles! A single human cell today has exactly the same structure as the first bacteria. The model is a few million codes on each of the DNA strings in each of twenty-six chromosomes within the nucleus of a single cell. Nature is a very clever packer! And the DNA strings unwind and wind in millionths of a second. Nature can move unbelievably fast."

"Sometimes very slowly," Kat countered.

"Indeed, this is the story of evolution, blinding speed within the cells, but interminable experiments, checks, and balances in the evolution of the gargantuan system of bio and nano tech some call Gaea."

Phil flipped an image onto his monitor, from a kids' guide to biotech by the look of it.

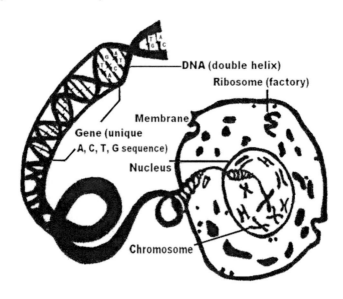

Meanwhile, back at the cell, with the genetic codes and DNA came the production of RNA, ribonucleic acids, in little factories in the nucleus of the cell. RNA strands were the loners, while DNA strands lived in pairs, winding and unwinding in the blink of god's eye."

"Aha!"

"Just a metaphor — I didn't mean *God*. So the RNA hung out in the cell's body, or ribosome, and became the synthesizer of proteins. They, too, contain millions of codes. Then, somewhere late in this series of eons, these single-cell entities learned to *cooperate,* to join forces."

"Hold the phone, Dr. Scientist. How did we suddenly get from a DNA string to a whole creature with its factories, codes, and programs packed in a case? I know, don't tell me! Another series of countless accidents? Sounds like a very tall story to me!"

"Well, maybe, Mrs. Sceptic, but that's not all. The proteins are visions of beauty in their intricate structures. These divine creatures are the workforce of the life form, forty thousand strong in the case of *homo sapiens*. They are the messengers that carry out the basic functions of the collective as it survives, develops, and reproduces. They constantly direct the millions of higher functions going on in us all the time, right now, as we speak."

"Accidents."

"Maybe, and keep in mind, Mrs. Doubt Flinger, that for decades now, scientists have been shooting lightning continuously through what they think was primordial slag. They haven't got DNA yet, but they *have* recreated some of the building blocks of life, including the nucleic acids. And don't forget, it took ten billion years to get from slag to a living cell. Ten billion years is a *very long* time. We've had two millennia since Christ, so try to think about a thousand of these millennia instead of just two. Now think about each of these thousand-millennia *eons* as just one *chapter*, and imagine ten thousand of these chapters. It's a very long time."

"OK, Dr. Logic, but this study fills a much-needed gap in our knowledge."

"Mark Twain."

"Samuel Clemens, yes, but you avoided with only a passing glance the most dubious part of your story. The atoms and then the compounds and then the cells 'got together,' and their programming and control systems learned to cooperate to form larger organisms — plants and animals, flora and fauna, amidst a growing sea of bacteria, lest we forget."

"Exactly, Kat. And viruses — don't forget about those little critters, the single-cell creatures that can't reproduce, so they embed themselves in the cells of anything that can. Feared and revered are these ubiquitous symbiotes with their startling powers of adaptation and destruction."

"Red herrings, perhaps."

"Planted by the KGB?"

"Not likely, Phil, they died out in my youth."

"All right, Lady Divine-It-All, I know what you're going to say, and I am forced to admit that an awful lot has happened in the three or four billion years since the first forms of *life* appeared, even if it was almost an infinity ago. And yes, every accident that worked well for survival and development and reproduction tended to stick. Messengers and messages were developed so that the cells and their offspring would repeat successful responses. So, too, the complex arrays they formed, the stems and leaves and seeds of the plant world, the skin and bones and organs of fish, amphibians, birds, and mammals. Incredibly complex structures with spectacular operating systems, to put it very mildly. And it's not always the strongest species that survive, nor the most intelligent, but the ones most responsive to change."

"Charles Darwin."

"Yes, though my interpretation."

"But once again, Professor Far-Fetched, you digress. The bottom line is that these accidents just sort of became entities that are conscious of themselves."

"They may all be, Kat — all living entities — what do I know? The structures and mutual activities of all life forms may make for a kind of collective consciousness, an unfathomably complex composite entity. But I hear what you're saying. An understanding of the entire organism *by itself*, in the case of humans, is no longer beyond our wildest imaginings, despite our having exceptionally wild imaginations as a species. We actually know a lot about how life works. We know thousands of times more than people did even a century ago. We probably know the basics even if we still have a good way to go. The whole story may turn out to be finite or in all practical terms infinite. Time will tell."

"So, to summarize your composition, Professor Tree-Without-Forest, the only known highly complex and intelligent life forms took five billion years to go from slag to egregiously multifarious organization, then learned to think and pretty much figured themselves out. By accident!"

"To be fair, a legion of uncountable accidents, survival of the fittest."

"But this is slag we're talking about, Phil. What in God's name is it doing competing with other slag to survive? Something *additional* perhaps?"

"Now don't go all creationist on me. But, OK, we really know nothing about *why* this all works, although we do know the gist of *how*. We know so much that every new discovery cures another disease, regenerates an organ. The stakes are sky high, so it's hardly surprising that the global bio-nano-AI industry has weathered the economic storms and blossomed in the booms. It's a far cry from the jackets-and-genes ventures that poached scientists from the universities back in the eighties and started the commercial development of biotech."

"Hold on an instant, Mr. Evolution-Oil-Salesman, you stray again. Let's finish the vanishingly tall historical tale before skipping to industrial conglomerates. You claim that your 'accidental tourist' view of life on the planet is a credible story. Speaking for myself and probably a significant share of the world's population that thinks about it at all, I find the last few billion years of this story particularly implausible, if not fanciful or downright absurd. You're saying that, while the whole universe was slowly *devolving* after its Big Bang, which I hope it took time to enjoy, stuff on Earth was getting more and more organized — *evolved* — to the staggering point where it figured itself out?"

"I do wonder occasionally, if the truth be known, but I'm not quite ready to ditch Darwin and the whole evolutionary drama quite so fast. If you have a better idea short of religious doctrine, please be my guest."

"You don't need doctrine to imagine that there might be some 'impetus,' let's call it, in the direction of complexity and life — some forces we don't fully comprehend."

By now, Phil was giving her that disparaging look he reserved for people with insufficient grasp of the obvious, her exact criticism of him. Being intentionally annoying made him almost cute. Outside, the wind had picked up again, the bay gathering into compacted passion. Feeling the fury, Kat plunged on.

"I'm not talking about religion or God, Dr. Out-On-Limb-Of-Tree-Without-Forest, just a little doubt that it all happened by eternal accident, by countless deaths, failures to evolve fast enough, countless creations of something *better*. A little doubt should be easy for us to accept when we still understand so little about ourselves, the most conscious living entities in the universe, or so we think. What constitutes a person? Why is a person completely different from her clone? Why are we still so barbaric and inept at survival?"

"Fair enough, but don't shoot the messenger. I'm just the scientist, I don't know everything about God and man. I don't go around blowing people up if they don't agree with my stories of creation and destiny. Fools and fanatics are always so certain of themselves, wiser people so full of doubts."

"Bertrand Russell?"

"Impressive, I thought secret agents didn't read philosophy."

"They made us take soft courses to keep us human."

"You're lucky! Think of the fanatics who will never recover from the twisted dogma they were force-fed as children. What makes us so pliant in the hands of crazed visionaries and their murdering minions?"

"Gods only know, Philamon Rush, and the gods of my forefathers aren't telling. Violent repression has a tendency to work. And we appear to be rapidly collecting all of them as enemies, the most pernicious race of odious little vermin that nature ever suffered to crawl on the face of the Earth!"

"Swift?"

"Impressive. *Gulliver's Travels*. I thought scientists read science fiction."

"My mother studied lit and biology. Odd combination. She's was always the most persuasive person I knew, by a good margin. I read everything from Shakespeare to Proust and Dostoyevsky to Faulkner."

A pause in the conversation lengthened into a reverie. Phil and Kat huddled in the last patch of evening sunlight on the deck, snug in the lea of the wind. Lara and Dylan skipped across the deck, whisking the shadows away. It was impossible to be serious for long in the face of so much enthusiasm. Dylan was starting to get inquisitive about things around him, a worry because of his quick grasp of ideas and people. It was a mother's blessing to see his protective stance with his little sister, another small triumph to see her own talents and independence. Dylan looked like a rascal raccoon as he peaked around the corner.

"Remember those stories you used to tell us when we were kids?"

Heavens, Kat thought with a jolt, when your kids call themselves kids, they're no longer kids. Not that she didn't know this, just that they change so quickly. Phil raised an eyebrow in reply.

"You mean the Gang and their trusty spice-drive space yacht?"

"Just so," Dylan winked. "Well, we were thinking you could tell us another one — I mean, if you want."

"Instead of discussing world affairs?"

"Why not both?" Lara enquired, in character as diplomat and mediator. "Knowledge comes in many forms."

"OK, here goes," Phil begrudged, "no interruptions!"

Both kids giggled, as though they had been transported back a decade, wide-eyed youngsters intending to interrupt at every opportunity.

"So, one night, the gang were lounging around the spaceport when they got a red alert from Alpha Prime and blasted off toward Jupiter."

Phil always started a story in a loud whisper, shifting into lulla-voice when, as kids, their eyes began to close.

"The spice ship was humming and Kung Fu Dylan was eating beans."

"Uh-oh!"

"Suddenly, from out of nowhere came a whirling pinwheel the size of a supernova."

"How can something come out of nowhere if it isn't anywhere?"

"Pilot Lara asked the right question. They were about to find out!"

"How big is a supernova?"

"Some say it's infinitely small at the start, just a little Big Bang, but it gets big very fast as it blasts through space. This pinwheel was the size of from here to the moon. They veered around to check it out, but failed to see a spiral arm racing at them from behind. As it flew over the spiceship, it whipped them around."

"Did they barf?" Dylan asked with a malicious grin.

"Happily, they had remembered to eat lots of carrots and drink lots of water, so their stomachs were strong and their eyes were peeled."

"Yuck."

"The next thing they saw was Stanislaw Lem. They concluded they were in a time loop."

"Who's Stanislaw Lem?"

"He was a writer who found memoirs in a bathtub. He wrote about time loops, where you could meet yourself going the other way. The next thing they saw was Stanislaw Lem. They concluded they were in a time loop."

"You said that."

"Ah, but they were in a time loop. How could they know they were in it? How could they get out?"

"Didn't their watches work?"

"Yes, but they didn't remember what time they'd said it was before. Or after, for that matter. Fortunately, just when they were about to meet themselves going the other way, Kung Fu Dylan could no longer contain the gas which the beans had manufactured in his digestive tract."

"Blaster!"

"And he blew the spice ship right out of the pinwheel."

"The time loop."

"Precisely, just in time."

"So what is time anyway?" Lara asked.

"Nine-thirty, look at that! Way past your bedtime!"

They were now fully devolved into their characters of a decade before.

"Nooo, you know what I mean."

"OK, time is something that runs through everything. Like mass or energy. Mass is full of energy. Your fist has enough energy stored up in its atoms to run our house and car for years."

"Is that what the crobies do?"

Dylan watched the repartee between Phil and Lara with a practised eye.

"Exactly. They're like super-tiny creatures that harvest the energy out of mass without blowing it up. They can give us all of the energy we need, but they're dangerous, too. Every now and then they get a little out of hand and start nibbling on their chains."

"But what about time?"

"Right. What about time to go to sleep? No? OK, back to energy. There is a huge amount of energy in mass. Albert Einstein figured out how much. It's like thirty-five billion times the amount of the mass you started with, which is a BIG number."

"How big?"

"Four times as much as all the people in the world. Time is something else. Albert also explained how time is different for people moving at different speeds relative to each other."

"Do they have to be relatives?"

"It helps. But here's my hypotenuse. Maybe time is like energy. Maybe if it got out of control, we could have time bombs. Or maybe we could make time crobies that would harvest bits of time from mass or energy!"

"So, what would happen if you met yourself going the other way?"

Lara had Phil locked in a stare both expectant and evaluative. Kat covered a nervous smile. How much did they sense, how much would Phil spill?

"That's not the way to put the question, if you ask me. It's like saying 'nothing can be absolutely right!' and then your friend says 'you're absolutely right.' The real question might be whether there could be different versions of reality, and whether they could influence each other."

"Is that your hippopotamus?" Dylan asked.

"Maybe, but I know it's a tall story! I think Stanislaw was using time loops more for entertainment than anything else."

Thin ice, but that seemed to deflect their curiosity for the moment. The story concluded, the cabal broke up, and the gang made off in their separate directions. College Boards for Dylan in the morning, Kat remembered — so soon, too quick, empty nest around the corner. Phil came back from the kitchen looking tired.

"We should do more of those, I miss them."

"That one was pretty close to the bone, Phil. I really wonder what kind of crap the future is going to dump on them. Don't you have visions of their bodies mutilated by plague? I don't want to see them die, it's the worst horror, but I don't want to go first and leave them alone. either."

"Now don't jump to contusions. I'm terrified, too. But the kids, as you call them, are almost adults. Not that this changes the horror of what might happen to them, just that they're going to be part of the drama. They may end up protecting us, for all we know. As for me, I was programmed to deal with uncertainty by attacking it with reason and determination. Take the offensive! So that's all I can do, learn everything we may need to survive, drown the fear and impotence in thought and action, suck it up. I know it's a basic character flaw. I'm emotionally bottled and amputated, but it makes the days go by. Some days I even think there's hope."

"OK, enough, but must you always fill their heads with visions of star ships and universes?"

"Merely a pedagogical tool, a delivery system for knowledge and insight."

"A delivery system for something more smelly!"

"Probably harmless, and I don't think they see any real connection to our lives."

"Don't underestimate their insight. Trust me on this, Phil. The shape of a secret is perfectly defined by what is unsaid, unexpressed, left out where it might be expected to come in, by the borders of its non-existence. Not surprisingly, the people who can see these borders best are the people who have grown up observing you and learning to navigate you. We know ourselves the least of all and the people who know us best are our children."

"Makes sense, I'll be careful. But the sci-fi isn't so bad. They know it's fiction, just fun to toss around. It might make them a bit weirder than most kids, but I'd say they started with pretty strange genes. Can't imagine where they might have got those! Anyway, it gives them some things to think about."

"I don't see them reading much sci-fi."

"They probably got enough in the bedtime stories. Everyone to their own taste, I say, however misguided. Anyway, the best of science fiction is very good adventure, romance, mystery, science, the future of humanity and all that. I never understood how people could be uninterested, to tell the truth, even accounting for different tastes."

"Is it well written?"

"Like every genre, some is magic — Tolkien, Azimov, Clarke, *Dune*, *Hyperion*, *Ender's Game*, or *The Speed of Dark*. Lyrical and deeply moving, prophetic and fiercely ethical, familiar and profoundly human."

"Ha, you read that somewhere!"

"Well, I borrowed a bit, but it's mostly true, anyway. Face it, this race is on the brink of going out into space or stumbling at the frontier and dying of mortification."

"Isn't that a tautology?"

"Total or partial, it's a dead end to turn away from the most obvious frontier, to accept meekly that a large meteor could destroy us all while we wait meekly on our planet. I'm with the people who want us to take a chance instead of wasting all our resources trying to stuff more and more people with their insatiable appetites onto a ball of rock that's already too small. And damaged."

"So what do we do, Herr Saviour?"

"The pathways to redemption, my child, lie at both ends of the spectrum. The dive into nano and beyond was started in the middle of the last century by a physicist who said 'there's plenty of room at the bottom.' By the eighties, biosciences and technologies were figuring out how living organisms work. Then came the jump down to nano, a billionth of a metre, the size of a few atoms, a thousand times smaller than the smallest forms of life. Nano boomed in the aughts and teens. By the twenties, technicians were building inorganic substances from atoms and molecules, and now they have a good start on building organic constructs that live and breathe. Soon they'll make food and energy, a cob of corn or a litre of ethanol. Molecular manufacturing is nano's holy grail today, not to mention the space elevator."

"You think that will fly?"

"Funny. It's started for sure. It's driving the big investments in carbon nanotubes. Construction is feasible if you have something light and strong enough to make a big rope that flops out into space from Earth like a string from a spinning ball. The idea's been around since the 1890s. Crawlers move up and down the rope. Solar energy is harvested on a large scale and excess heat returned to space. The optimists and promoters say it'll be finished in half a decade."

"I know the security implications, that's my field, but I never looked at the technology. Will it pay?"

"Probably, Kat. There's a lot of room at the top, at the other end of the spectrum, off-planet, manufacturing in vacuum, space exploration, harvesting near-asteroids. If an asteroid anchors the elevator at the other end, the rope can be a lot shorter and lighter. The asteroid provides the carbon for the braided rope, so they can 'spin' the elevator cable out from the asteroid and down to Earth by gravity and light propulsion.."

"The rope is made of these carbon nanotubes?"

"Yes, a natural form of carbon, along with graphite, diamond, Bucky balls and the rest."

"Whose balls?"

"Easy there, Kat. They're pure carbon molecules with sixty atoms in the shape of R. Buckminster Fuller's geodesic dome. Nanotubes, by contrast, have their atoms in a cylinder."

Phil flipped another image onto his screen.

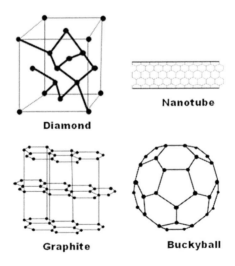

"Scientists have strung these nanotubes together up to hundreds of kilometres long, but only a few billionths of a metre wide. They are the perfect braids for a very long rope, *very* light and *very* strong. Scary, too. Way worse than asbestos if they get into the environment and food systems. So the elevator is possible but risky, and I doubt that the powers that be will allow anyone to propel an asteroid toward Earth any time soon."

Kat nodded as she replied.

"Everyone will continue to oppose until enough countries possess the means to destroy or deflect the asteroid. After that, from a security point of view, the danger from the asteroid is neutralized."

"That isn't far away, Kat — months, I'm told. Then the consortium will proceed. Propulsion engines are being installed on the two chosen asteroids — Fuller and Bucky, as the media have dubbed them — to push them toward Earth."

"Still, enemies won't give up, Phil. Some will make plans to sabotage the elevator. Maybe no one will try to crash Fuller into Earth, but the spooks can't rule it out. There are maniacs as well as zealots. You can bet that the personnel on Bucky and Fuller will be screened with nano-toothed combs. You can also take it to the bank that one or two will slip through. Everyone has ample time to plan."

"What about after, if the elevator gets up and running?"

"Still a big problem, I'm afraid. If the rope separated from Fuller, it would wind itself part way around the Earth's surface, cutting a swath of destruction — but nothing compared to Fuller hitting Earth."

"I'd still say the spacelift will get built, Kat. Our future takes us into space."

"I'll tell you one thing, though, if anyone starts to develop black hole technology, no one will allow it Earthside or on Fuller. It will have to be Bucky. So if you're thinking of resending the Orion message in the future, you're going to be on a small rock looking four thousand miles down.

"I'm not against an occasional vacation from the home planet, Kat. Would you come? There's got to be a lot to learn out there in Planck time and space, where the curtains over the history and nature of the universe may start to be pulled back a little at a time. It would be nice to think that we might even find better ways than space ships to discover the universe. The elevator is a start, lots of room at the top, out there in the galaxy."

"What about communication across time?"

"I don't know, Kat. I don't believe it most of the time. I wish it was science fiction, but it will turn out to be either science or fiction."

"Maybe you should read something else," Kat suggested, "when you're working so hard on stuff most people would consider pretty far out to begin with. Try a good mystery, brush up your detective skills. Choose from my selection of fine vintages. Follow the Buddhist path, capture the universe from within."

"No time for escape?"

"No escape for time."

"Touché. How do we manage?"

"I'm very tolerant."

"Well, there is that, and some shared hopes."

"Beya's full of the same passion, Phil. Sandover, too, but he sees the world getting better on account of analysis and management, logic and ideas. He's driven by the same forces as you, but he has shadows in the corners of his eyes. Beya feels the foreboding more like I do. She faces it with faith, where Sandover puts his faith in reason."

"What about the Visitors, Kat? What insight does that wizardly ancestry of yours suggest?"

"I think I'm too biased by pride and vanity to truly *see*, Phil. I don't want to believe in far-superior beings. And yet those intelligent patterns are still just plain alien in nature, intricately unfathomable to us. So I believe the Visitors have to be extraterrestrials if they still exist, if they haven't died out in the great morass of space and time since sending their transmissions."

"Space is big!"

"George Bush?"

"Dan Quayle, actually. A man of remarkable ability to find great depth in the perfectly obvious."

"Well, I know I shouldn't look down my nose at the new cults or the Church of the Ultimate Moment, but it's hard to take them seriously. The posturing of the big religions and governments is another story. We're frozen in time by the wish that nothing more will happen. Behind the facades, my heart and history tell me that artillery pieces are being moved into position, stalking the stillness of the mirage."

Kat wanted to go on, to tell Phil how paper thin was the ice that kept his cheerful view of the future from falling into the void. She wanted him to understand the sheer power and ruthlessness of the forces lining up against them. She wanted to tell him about Dylan, but it wasn't time and two wrongs don't make a right.

Sanctuary

Beya felt her memories drift to a time long gone. There were lions in the village. A few rays of candle light crept under Uma's door and caught Kilifi's big white eyes as he grimaced in glee and terror. They squirmed under the bed, knowing the lions would not come in, but they did one time, a mother who spared them but took food.

Enough, she thought. Why does my fickle mind go on vacation so often without notice? What is happening to us? Where is the innocent girl that I was, unaware, except for Mzee, who told us stories of the capital, and Heleni at school with the world on the Net. Why do I feel drugged, lost in drowsy lotus perfume? Baba would say 'Think girl, tell me the story that you see.' But I see many stories. The same story repeated becomes two different stories. Sandover says four, in the case of economists, two for each hand.

Sandover's parents would be back soon from exploring the delicious grounds and diversions of Cambridge. It was easy to see Eng Kai's influence on Sandover, both positive and reactive, pushing him onto a different course, the world of professions and ideas. Eng Kai knew that Sandover's understanding of economics was already greater than his own, but he, too, was a fast learner.

Meiling had told her more of Sandover's childhood — adopted from a family of cousins in China and raised in the best of Asian family values. She said the early years in China had marked him, set his course, prepared him to sail through tough schooling with ease, pushed him now to master everything in the tangled dancing spheres of power and wealth.

Spring was in the air at last, though more a hope than a genuine appearance. Sandover wanted to talk. There was a lot he could hide, but his body language gave him away more than once in a while. Beya had wanted to talk, too, in good time, when he was ready. He'd start on a tangent, she knew, angling toward what was really on his mind.

"What do you think, Beya? I've reached the conclusion that the International Women's Alliance is here to stay, the revolution is over, women have won."

"Hmmm. Maybe. We do want it all. No kids dying, no hunger, disease, insane wars, or violence against women. On the positive side of the ledger, opportunity, justice, peace, prosperity, love, children, music, and an astronomy course with field visits. What about you?"

"Nothing much, Beya. I'm a practical man, I'd like a world free of scarcity, no more economics. But you'd need more than dynamite to get me out of Earth's atmosphere in spite of my extraterrestrial ancestry. Would you really go into space?"

"In a nano-second. Like the twigga. What do you mean, extraterrestrial ancestry?"

"My forefathers in China were farmers, Beya, very poor. But in one generation, a man and his wife changed their fate. They had eleven children. He was the letter carrier for the village and had learned to read. He studied and talked to people and found out how to raise ducks and snails together, mix strong plants with rice or vegetables to keep away insects, and use biogas from pigs to light lamps for reading. After years, the family was well fed and happy. None of their neighbours copied them. They didn't want to work so hard. They laughed and called them aliens, just for a joke, but it stuck. Today they would be honoured. A raft of officials and foreign dignitaries would visit them daily and point to their accomplishments."

"I can see you're a little more terraformed I. Where I grew up, in Tanzania, we couldn't tame the land. You couldn't always count on it. We had to have other foundations for our dreams."

"And so you dream of the galaxy?" Sandover asked.

"Only after peace and prosperity."

"Of course, but don't hold your breath. Progress, as many have said, is like driving a car with a blacked-out windshield, with only the rear view mirror to see what unfortunate human beings have been bumped off the road by the advance of civilization."

"Do you think we should be working with Phil and Kat more? Postpone our personal ambitions a while?"

"I don't know Beya. We keep thinking in the same circles. We can't all live in the same place and work together without a lot of risk. We're the backup team for now. We don't control anything much beyond our own noses. It gets frustrating."

"But fascinating, too."

"The snippets from Phil and Kat are certainly extraordinary, like jigsaw pieces as they assemble, a small army of enemies and adversaries beginning to take shape. What an arcane world of inventions, companies, governments, secret services, buccaneers, and freebooters. I had no idea how it worked before, competitive to the point of cutthroat, held together in the end with money and brutality by a handful of corporate bandits. Dog eat dog, greed in the driver's seat. And look out for the splinter groups whose zeal boils into insanity at the drop of a microbe!"

"Even worse, love. I've been studying Pharmacon, the conglomerate at the helm of the nano organic empire," Beya said. "It's easily as scary as the lunatic fringe. They'll kill for fun or profit, preaching all the while. They're a pack of cutthroats and egomaniacs who scorn all laws because the world owes them power and immortality. Among them are racists and fools ready to genetically enhance themselves and their armies to go for supremacy, pockets of nano- and bioterrorists starting wars that may not end for generations. J.C. and Édouard Moreau are at the top of the dung heap. Terrepharm has enough clout to bully the Pharmacon

Council. They're in close cahoots with people you don't want to know about, let alone meet."

"There are some bright spots, too."

Sandover's inclination to emphasize the positive was familiar ground for Beya. Glass half-full. It wasn't naivety, just an incessant optimism that Beya admired but couldn't quite bring herself to share.

"Are they worth the price?" she asked.

"Health is improving almost everywhere. Biotech's promise is being delivered even to the poor. There's a lot of room at the bottom."

"It's still a mixed blessing to me."

"I can't argue with that, Beya. People are getting the goods they need but production is run by a gang of robber barons. The risk of systemic failure is way too high and the consequences far too horrible. Pharmacon is holding the reins."

"The reins and the guns, with Terrepharm's finger on the trigger. That could easily be J.C. They've had to make deals with the powerful nations, but there are still too many dozens of countries with governments that can be bought. The breakthroughs keep coming, health and hope, so we turn a blind eye when it serves our purposes. Until it's the biogenetic enhancement of people to be smarter, faster, and stronger than us."

"Or worse, Beya. We could all be terminated by some accident."

"Maybe we could start a global movement for smarter, gentler, and more tolerant people instead. Who am I kidding?"

"The military and security side of bio-nano must be almost impossible."

Sandover knew a lot about the spooks, Beya knew, more than they learned from Kat. She assumed it came from his "family," but he was guarded about his sources and she didn't push it.

"Kat says the spooks have the best tools and the most dogged determination. They call all this stuff nanorg and pretend it's under control. Behind the facade, the corporate congloms do what they want in rogue countries. When the liberal nations try to move against them, they can shift their ops and militias almost overnight."

Beya paused to smother a flood of fears that jumped unwanted into her mind. Soldiers, spies, ruthless congloms, mad scientists, maniacs, and mercenaries. Always sensing her tension, Sandover offered a counterfactual and a shoulder to lean on.

"On the brighter side, Beya, there are lots of responsible companies in the progressive countries that use nanorg for health and progress as well as profits. The campaigns against genetically modified foods go on, but when it comes to health, we want the cures in time to save ourselves and our children. We think that genetic engineering in our own body is just personal, that it won't endanger the globe. We haven't learned much in fifty years, since the first big fight in the U.S. courts over the transplanting of genes into human beings."

"What happened?"

"It was in the eighties, two decades before we were born. The case was about a young girl with a terminal disease. The scientists were opposed to using a genetically engineered drug and warned the court about potential disasters, unknowns, and incalculable risks to society. But the medical profession prevailed, in the heat of the debate, when a prominent doctor explained that the alternative for most of his patients was certain death."

"Looks like you've been reading up on biotech."

"Not like Phil, Beya. Mostly I read just the smart commentaries. You can't help getting interested in the big prizes they're after. I wish I'd paid more attention to physics and chemistry in school, less to economics and the social sciences."

"Biotech always seemed too complex for my brain," Beya confessed. "Our teachers discouraged us, too. Math and science is not for girls."

"And then there's nanotech, Beya, the inorganic side of reality's coin, from the tiniest structures made of atoms and molecules to the stars and galaxies. Cell-sized machines may soon be built from component parts, programmed to reproduce. Their forerunners are already at the heart of the current generation of computers. Soon they'll be able to take anything apart, atom by atom and build whatever we want from the pieces. Molecular manufacturing is at hand, making a paved road or a kilo of hydrogen from atomic scratch. In the end, everything around us is just an incredibly complex formula, finite and knowable."

"I thought that was a lot less true for the higher forms of life, where there is some kind of an essence or entity beyond the structures that can be mapped. If you make an eagle out of atoms, wouldn't it act very differently from the original?"

"Could it even fly? No one knows, Beya. Cloned birds can fly, but they're alive, produced organically. With nano-manufactured replicas, they'll find out soon enough. If they make a peanut and it tastes right, that'll be something to bet on."

"If we could construct a virus or a human being from atoms and molecules, could it go rogue or go into some new realm of consciousness?"

"Beam me up, Scotty, but keep your stunner ready!"

"Laugh while you can."

"You're right, Beya, it's not that funny. As if that weren't enough, it's sort of the same picture in cosmology. They say in twenty years they will know exactly what happened in the first billionth-billionth-billionth-billionth-billionth of a second of the universe. They'll know it at the physical level of a billionth-billionth-billionth-billionth-billionth of an atom. But they may still have absolutely no idea 'why.' On the other hand…"

"That's three hands, Sandover Lee."

"Good point. You'll have to lend me a hand. Besides nanorg and cosmology, development is accelerating out into space. Back around the end of the nineties, the head of NASA said that a Coke-can-sized probe would reach and land on a passing asteroid two years from Earth launch, then use its DNA-based biomimetic system as a blueprint to evolve, adapt, and grow into a more complex exploring and thinking system. We're not quite there yet, but we're close."

"What about Phil? Can he find enough allies without being prey for the crazies?"

"I wish I knew, Beya. You have no idea how much I wish! Kat and mouse. At some point soon, they'll need more help from us. Four heads are better than two. If we need to move closer, could you do it?"

Sometimes luck and the Lord are with us, Beya saw with a sigh of relief. This was what they needed to talk about.

"I ran into Angela Nealand at a meeting at Trinity on Thursday and she asked me about joining them at the International Women's Alliance in New York. She's awesome, brains of the movement. Saba Luanzi, too, of course; she walks on water."

"You think the IWA will keep growing exponentially?"

"Nothing grows exponentially forever San, you know that from economics. Still, you'd have to bet on it going on for a while. There was a gargantuan political space that women hadn't occupied for a long time — forever, in fact, with only minor historical gaps."

"Matriarchal interludes."

"Very few. As we move into that space, you can be sure we won't move out any time soon. It's nice here. No big incentive to apply for exclusion and persecution again. Men woke up too late in most places, thank heaven. Don't get me wrong. I'm not assuming women will do brilliantly all the time. But it would be hard to do worse than men have. What about you? No more studies soon, the end of childhood, you'll have to go back to work for a living. I'm sure you could get a job you want in New York."

Meiling's laughter filled the vestibule. Her entries were full of grace and colour. She had scarcely arrived in Cambridge before she and Beya began exchanging fashion ideas and accessories. Beya looked hot in the Chinese *cheongsam* and the Vietnamese *audzai* Meiling had brought as gifts. Meiling looked fabulous in the African *kangas*, though she hadn't got up the courage to go public yet.

"Are we interrupting?" Eng Kai asked.

"No, we were just winding up a conversation," Sandover chuckled.

"The evensong was extraordinary at Christchurch, with the colours of the setting sun."

Eng Kai fell easily into evocative mode. He would paint his vision of the evensong, though his portraits were his real strength. Beya kept adopting appropriate poses, hoping he would notice. Sandover found this amusing and said, not to worry, Asian men were culturally sensitive to others admiring something they have.

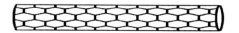

Sandover raised his glass to Eng Kai and Meiling. The dinner at the Roseate Swan had been exquisitely simple. They sat in an old stone chamber above a high arch, wrapped in woollen pulls against the damp embrace of the evening.

"Mother and father, to your visit! You have no idea what pleasure you bring. And to the rest of your voyage. We will return the favour if you will permit us, when you have settled back on Fern Hill."

"To your return to Singapore," Eng Kai responded. "And will you stay in Cambridge next year, or is it too early to know?"

"It is good if we can ask your thoughts on this, father and mother," said Sandover in what sounded like family-formal mode. "For myself, I am not an academic in the end. I am too eager to be involved with changes in the world."

"What is the end of that road?" Eng Kai inquired.

It was easy to see how Sandover came by his verbal parsimony, Beya thought, as he paused to consider. She knew he had asked himself this question a dozen times in the past month.

"Head of the World Economic Organization. I think that is the top job in the field. Someday I hope to have a shot at it."

"The WEO has an appealing mission," Eng Kai mused. "But isn't it very conservative, still dominated by the right wing of America?"

"Not so much now, father, and I think it has to change more. America may never give up being top dog, in spite of the hammering it has taken so far this century, but lately it has been more restrained."

"I'd say restrained by its own citizens more than by the rest of the world."

"Whatever the reason, the results are promising. The real development agendas are resurfacing, the investments in people and technology, smart management, real competition, honest government, and first-rate public service."

Eng Kai was gathering breath for an interjection, so Sandover paused and waited, head bowed slightly.

"I am thankful to the Americans, my son, as are you, for championing individual freedoms and democracy in rhetoric if not always in practice, particularly abroad. If we didn't have them, we would be have to invent them. Singapore might not exist. We might nevertheless wish to reinvent a less violent champion if we could, more civilized. Their criminally large export of weapons continues only slightly abated. Certainly they are not alone in this, yet they dominate the global machinery of carnage and apocalypse today as much as before."

"America holds sway in many halls of power, father, legitimate and otherwise. The market fundamentalists may never understand that ultra-right-wing American policy shafts the world and wounds America as sure as the red sun rises in Beijing. Beya wants to help Saba Luanzi to make sure they aren't in power."

"I admire her cause," Eng Kai said, "the word before the sword. At the same time, we need to be free of physical and military repression as well, to have counterbalancing forces, something I have been studying."

The after-dinner brandy had by now settled in for the night. Meiling was nodding. Beya was thinking of thousands of little munitions plants in America, with millions of people marching to work every day to make mines that blew legs off farmers in forsaken corners of the Earth.

"I think Americans have understood that the world is moving on rather quickly, father, hopefully enough Americans, and better late than never! They've ratified the global alliance for arms control and are slowly disarming. If you're cynical, you would say it's just a new way of reasserting dominance. In their favour, they finally committed to the international human rights and law accords. They're behaving a little better in technology, trade, and finance. While we have to make our way ahead with them, I hear what you are saying. Raw power prevails at critical moments. Let us keep in close touch on those counterbalancing forces."

Meiling looked like she was dozing as Beya kept drifting off, too. She wanted to know if Sandover would answer his father's questions about his plans after Cambridge.

"Spoken like a Singaporean," Eng Kai reflected. "Where would your next steps be, on this lofty career path?"

"I had been thinking of Canada," Sandover replied. "They seem to know the elephant and the donkey better than anyone. But in the end, to make a long story short, I think Washington or New York are better choices. They offer the full play of international relations and finance. I've made some contacts, a few irons in the fire."

Sandover would get job offers annoyingly easily, Beya knew. He interviewed like a dream, with his quick grasp and chameleon instincts, winning over prospective contemporaries before they caught a glimpse of his real resolve. Like a time-bomb, she thought, startled full awake by the notion.

"One more thing," Eng Kai resumed. "I will speak with Weisheng. Beya, you should hear this. The sea on which you plot your course is not altogether a friendly one. Not for your friends in Canada, either. Yes, I know of them in some detail. Weisheng has friends who will keep an eye out for you and for them. Though you know a lot about the players and the game, please do not underestimate the lengths to which some of them will go to win, or just not to lose."

Eng Kai and Meiling left on Saturday morning. Beya missed them and thought longingly about a winter escape to Singapore in the coming months. After they'd been alone again for a few days, her level of anxiety had jumped another notch and was showing no signs of retreat. They had some basic matters to decide before they left Cambridge in the summer, and Beya thought she knew what the answers were going to be. Obsessive merged with compulsive, flooding her mind with the repercussions of the mistakes they might make, the opportunities lost.

"I heard from Meiling today," Sandover called as he rounded the stairs, fresh from a seminar at Trinity.

"Are they still happy with your career plans?"

"Eng Kai will be fine. He has his first son nearby in Singapore for building the family fortune. The second son should build reputation and respect. Professions and public service are perfect for me."

"What about Weisheng's and Eng Kai's warning?"

"Well, I do think we're in over our heads in a pretty basic way here, Beya. We're a bunch of literati, let's face it — academics, scientists, activists, researchers, the chattering class. We're excruciatingly thin on street smarts and unfamiliar with the powers we're getting tossed up against. We have to learn fast, that's our job. But we'll need some muscle, too."

"What are we talking about?" Beya had a sinking feeling.

"There's a joke in my family, Beya, that if you delve deeply, everything that is unexplained can be traced to the Chinese mafia. Probably not the Big Bang, but that's also a possibility I've heard mentioned."

"You swing from ominous to jocular so quickly that I can't tell which you feel."

"Both Beya. Mostly ominous. I think we need to take security precautions. Now. Weisheng most definitely possesses muscle, but this is a family arrangement, given to us without questions, a matter of honour. They stay alert and respond fast to any of us."

"Really, the Chinese mafia?"

"No, I don't think so. But I don't know exactly, and that's the point. It's an arrangement made by others, based on allegiances and debts going back a long way. The less we know, the safer we are."

"But why is Eng Kai so concerned about our safety? Yours I can understand."

"I don't know, Beya. Although he has a large collection of powerful friends, he never shares details with me. He is supposedly retired, but I know he's active in international coalition building, a relatively old art now being practised on the global stage. He's been engaged off and on for years, ever since Bush-Cheney and the neocons drove the U.S. and the global economy over the edge of the cliff, teetering only a hair from total collapse. Eng Kai says they did more damage than anyone in the history of humanity."

"That can't be! Stalin? Hitler?"

"Lots of historians agree that the numbers of dead are higher for the whole period of market fundamentalism and more people had their lives destroyed as well."

"But they weren't malevolent people."

"Maybe it's just that they had power over a bigger stage."

"I still don't understand how the Democrats squandered their lead after '09."

"That's just America, Beya. They have that inborn tendency to find scapegoats in a political system that's still dysfunctional and corrupt."

"That bad?"

"You'll experience it firsthand soon enough. In spite of reform attempts, what gets done is what has the most money behind it. Almost every vote in both Houses is for sale. You look sceptical. I once accompanied Eng Kai to Washington for discussions about coordinating financial sector regulation. Eng Kai's coalition wanted fairer treatment of foreign banks. We were told that this would require three crucial votes from committee chairs and members, this being a hot issue, and the costs of each would be in the tens of millions."

"But that was thirty years ago, surely it's changed!"

"You'll see. I hear the prices of votes are a lot higher. After ineffective attempts by the Democrats to put a stop to the overbearing power of lobbies, the Republicans reinstated the free-for-all. The unions and citizens' groups had no choice but to play. Some argued it wasn't a bad system, efficient, whoever paid most got what their hearts desired. But the legislators quickly devised ways of artificially multiplying the number of decisions and votes. The Democrats tried to stamp it all down again. Maybe only half the votes are for sale today. Maybe that's low enough to have the public good actually count sometimes."

"Which is why we have a chance on bio-nano-AI control?"

"Exactly," Sandover said, "though we're still in a partial vacuum of power and morality, a long way from having an honest sheriff on that side of the world."

"And Eng Kai is involved in some way?"

"I think so, in efforts to fill the vacuum. He is also worried about new rumblings he hears over the Orion transmission."

"New information?"

"No, the opposite, nothing new after two years. We're all dressed up for the Visitors, with nowhere to go. Intelligence agencies are pushing harder into ways the Orion message could have been of human origin. One member of the staff at Kilmarnock was abducted and grilled by professionals because she had made some thoughtless remark about tampering. She apparently knew nothing interesting and was released. Her captors left no useful clue as to their identity."

"Who exactly is Weisheng?" Beya asked.

"He's very wealthy, rumoured to be a kingpin in many covert organizations, both real and fabled. It's very hard to separate myth from reality. At one time, he was a mafia boss, then moved on to bigger things. Father mentioned talk of a pyramidal structure of triads, built down from the top by a score of powerful accomplices worldwide. More mythology perhaps, but there could be some truth. In any case, Weisheng has powerful friends with all kinds of interesting capabilities."

"Isn't it dangerous to accept their protection without knowing more about them?"

"Yes and no. We haven't asked or accepted anything formally. On the other hand, I haven't opposed father's intervention. Phil and I are agreed on pushing ahead and learning as we go along. The downside is that others will think to ask why we are being protected. Or there could be demands on us in the future, under threat of withdrawing their protection. It's a big risk either way. If we refuse, they'll probably protect us anyway and we'll just be more in the dark about who they are. We need friends but we can't afford to become hostages."

Beya didn't know quite how to ask the question that had been building in her stomach. But it was getting to be time. She decided to come at it on her own tangent.

"How does this work? I mean, how do you make contact with Weisheng?"

"They watch us. So far they have contacted no one but me, by com, never in person. I told father that the four of us are in it together, so we'll each have a shadow soon. We don't have to be physically together. I know you were wondering how to bring it up."

What a lamb, Beya thought, so much like the brother she had lost. She wanted both ecstasy and fraternity. Somewhere she knew it wasn't reasonable. They were both smiling as Sandover continued.

"We should stay together as long as we can, Beya, for security and everything else. We're the only four who know what the Orion transmission said. We are going to stand out to everyone looking closely. The easiest way for our enemies to gain our knowledge would be to extract it from one of us. It would be foolish to be careless."

"We need a magic wand."

"I found you the next best thing, a rainstar sapphire with a reputation. Don't underestimate its value."

It was the most beautiful object she had ever set eyes upon, tear shaped, with blazing points of starlight in blue-black space. She put the ring on her finger and felt she would never be without it. They might go separate ways some day, but fate is fickle and maybe they could have their way.

"We should go to New York, Beya, Washington one day, but for now we need to be where all nations meet. We need to be near Phil and Kat. I need to be with you and we need a home for our family."

Inferno

Beya gazed out the window of the floatplane. Everything looked normal, like a picture book, as they touched the rippled surface of the bay and taxied in toward the long dock, set on old log cribs that marched out across the water from the boathouse. Pines and rock, moss and wind. It seemed their pilot took a different route each time they visited Kat and Phil in this never-ending pageant of creation. "Two billion years ago," he'd announced through their headphones in the new, high-tech Twin Otter, "this land was a mountain range higher than Everest."

Now it was carved with the beautiful patterns and colours of silica, granite, iron, and exotic substances that rose from the original stuff of the planet as the mountains collapsed, a vivid tapestry of its history and pain. Pain felt odd amidst this grandeur, but it lived here, too, in the vast expanse of nothingness and solitude imposed by the sheer scale of time and erosion. "Put aside your petty squabbles over land and water," the First Nations say. "You are here for only a second. Your children and your nation are here for only a minute. Make the most of your time."

Justine yawned from her bassinette as they watched the floatplane depart amidst hugs and the warmth that flows among friends and fellow travellers. Kat broke the silence that descended as they hiked up to the house, over the brilliant embroideries of nature and God.

"You look elegant, so metro! New York is settling into your souls. Welcome back to wonderland. She's so beautiful, Beya, so peaceful. Motherhood suits you!"

"She's always been adaptable, Kat, such a blessing! But you're the lucky ones. I can't believe how soothing it is here, outside the churn of the wheels of power. Overlooked and free. New York was madness even before Justine."

"Let's talk while she's napping, Beya. Our kids are busy putting the boats and docks in order for the night. They love to look for adventure this time of day as nature is getting ready for bed."

A moment later they were toasting the unfolding sunset and listening to the forlorn ballad of a pair of loons out looking for a last late meal. Kat was much more tense than a few months back, anxious to be closer to the front lines and almost unaware of how much she was already doing. She was uncannily good at asking the right questions, a gift that had already righted their course several times. She also had military training and field experience, though she never talked much about those days. On very rare occasions, Beya saw a glimpse of something primal, a kind of feral fury.

To each her own burden. Beya was already swamped by the speed at which the horizon was expanding and changing. From Phil and Sandover came a world of nature's creations whose sheer audacity caught her by surprise. Bacteria in the ocean that absorb tiny bits of iron and silicon to manufacture a minuscule compass that reads the Earth's magnetic lines and keeps them in ocean depths where they can survive. Or the search for other genetic masterpieces that life and the divine hand have conspired to create, bacteria with propellers, the fast-healing cells of sharks, microbes that turn waste into energy overnight. On the near horizon were nano-sized membranes that filter hydrogen out of water or air in the search for a 'free energy' economy. Underneath it all was the story of elements, molecules, proteins, genes, and DNA.

They lounged for a moment on the deck as the sun slid behind the pine-lined horizon west of Manitou. As the last traces of light flickered on the bay, clouds began to congregate far off on the south horizon and a dry half-moon eased above the treetops. Sunlight and moonlight lay together on the water, the always-present spirit of the wind registering indelibly on their souls. On their minds, by contrast, was what to do next, whether they were on the right track and whether they were moving fast enough.

It was three years now since Merimbula and the Orion reception. The U.S. elections were coming fast. Beya was working with Saba Luanzi, a political dynamo and a force of nature. Beya and Sandover met Phil and Kat as often as they could. Together, they sent 'reports to the future,' or so they fancied them — a log to whoever had sent Orion, placed in the dead archives of the Library of Congress. Because they expected no answer, the silence that followed their updates came as no surprise. While no news might be good news, they were edging ever closer to 2041, the purported date of Orion.

A pause grew as they each pictured a different reality, their future selves sending a message to the past, desperate in a world convulsed with nanorganic plague.

"If Orion was sent from a remote satellite," Kat began, "its senders would be watching for our reports. As we're telling them everything we learn, they have perfect data at no cost."

Phil was the first to venture another view.

"I can't help thinking we're going to feel naive up 'then' when there's no inter-place-time communication and no plague."

"I feel like that sometimes," Kat agreed, "but there's something big afoot. We're talking about a transmission whose source remains a complete global mystery. We need to make what sense we can of it."

The storm front had been growing in size with remarkable speed and suddenly pounced. Lightning struck nearby, an ear-shattering sonic boom a split second after the explosion of light. It was suddenly very easy to feel small, to taste the frailty of the structures that sheltered them. A silent prayer ran through Beya's thoughts, a thank you for this shelter, please let it last.

"We have some strong clues," Sandover suggested. "We're all getting richer. That means Orion came from a superior source of knowledge and prediction."

Phil raised both palms in a gesture of acquiescence. Time stood still again.

"It's too quiet."

"Something feels very wrong."

Phil and Kat ran for the front deck. Beya took one look and went for Justine. Lara and Dylan were sprinting over the rocks toward them when they reached the deck. Ferocious spectres of dark clouds barrelled toward them, forms taking shape in their bowels, sharpening in definition like eerie birds of prey. The osprey blocked the way of the vulture and froze in a moment of truth. Then all hell broke loose as the night rang with detonations of thunder, lit like visions from Hades by vast sheets of lightning.

Kat was the first up when the tumult stopped. The shapes were melting and the clouds recomposing.

"Lord almighty!" Beya cried out. "What was that?"

"One was protecting us from the other," Kat growled. "It felt like they held our future in the balance."

Sandover turned from scanning the dark horizon, removed an earphone they hadn't noticed before and barked out a string of orders.

"Listen carefully, we're under attack. We have to make it to the caves at the base of the cliff, half a kilometre. If we're separated, we meet at the cliff's edge. We'll have help if it hasn't been disabled in the dogfight. Move!!"

Beya ran with Justine. A shadow crossed the edge of her sight as she plunged across a field of uneven boulders, too frightened to shriek, daggers of lightning showing a path for a split second, darkness reaching up from the chasms among the rocks. She heard Sandover behind, and smiled inwardly. Phil cried out, stumbled, and went down just ahead. An explosion, no, a deafening crack of thunder, up again, staggering toward the cliff. A glance back as a firefight erupted behind, Kat at the rear, firing into the melee. Of course she'd have artillery, Beya realized without a conscious thought. Then silence, the cliff's edge. Sandover raised the top end of a rope ladder that hung over the precipice, anchored to a giant block of granite.

"Go, Phil, Beya with Justine, Lara, Dylan, Kat."

"I'm last," Kat snapped. "Best shot."

Sandover whispered something in her ear. She gave him the machine pistol as she turned to the cowering lot before her.

"Phil, now!"

The sky lit up again, much closer. Stay calm, Beya reasoned. Tie Justine in. Acrophobia froze her until Kat shook her lightly.

"Focus on your hands, on the rope, every movement."

Swinging in nothing, the sound of waves crashing below, one hand missed, she couldn't reach the rope, strength ebbing in the hand that held, swinging in limbo. Then a brush, a chance, two hands again, focus, slow and sure, feet on the rock, thank God, Phil ushering her to the water, a small arrow-shaped boat.

Dylan and Lara caught up as they climbed in, then Kat, who looked up at the cliff. A sleek aircraft flashed overhead. Beya's heart fell as the rope ladder tumbled down to the rock below. The curt voice of their helmeted driver rolled over them as they sped into the black storm waters.

"Heads down! He'll be safe."

Beya clung to that desperate hope as they dodged the powerful lights that searched from above. She caught a glimpse of an aerial platform as they boarded a small submarine in the murky darkness. Where was Sandover?

"What did he say to you, Kat?"

"He said 'My op, covered'."

"What does that mean?"

"In the jargon, it means he was running the militia that protected us, not just a player. It could also mean that he was in the best command position. Covered means he expected to survive, but people say that sometimes when it's not true, to motivate the others to save themselves."

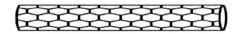

Jean-Christophe leered at the figures stampeding toward the cliff. Mice in a maze, they ran, tasted freedom, fled into his claws. They let their guard down like fattened fools, floating on the fantasies of their feeble minds. They knew nothing of power, nothing of pain, the baptism of creation falling upon them from the sky, their gods gone missing, their pretty thoughts drowned in the blood of their futile screams, gored by the prey they dared to hunt, deranged lovers in his sights, target locked, whispering their pathetic prayers, their time spent. And then came the moment he had lived a thousand times in his dreams: Sandover caught in his trap, the abyss behind him.

"We meet again, Sandover Lee. It seems you have nowhere to go but down to your death on the rocks below. We have a pleasant night before us now that your puny force is beaten. This time you will tell me the truth about Orion or you will die. It would be a shame to lose what you know, but your death would give me the pleasure of capturing your African whore and prying the truth from those lovely lips. No doubt she will learn to cooperate for the sake of her precious whelp."

"There is nothing to tell, J.C. You know what I know and you have seen the last of me for now. Farewell, we'll meet again in hell!" With a mock salute, he stepped backward into the night.

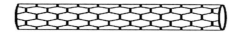

Beya felt consciousness slipping away, the strength and balance she displayed to the outside world all but gone. Like an egg, she thought, one crack and everything spills out, the inside empty, the fraud exposed. Something hot and liquid appeared before her, Kat and coffee, a blessed relief. The world returned. In the blink of an eye, the kids passed out in the fore compartment, Lara carrying Justine, comforted by Dylan. They were safe. Kat studied the face of the man who appeared from the pilot's cabin up front. East Asian, smiling.

"Welcome aboard."

"Chuanli?"

"Yes, my dear, surprise. Friends of the family asked me to keep an eye on you. I have been here for several months. The blitzkrieg came out of the blue. Our air cover suffered heavy losses to disable the enemy. They were Angels of Death, cream of the corporate militia, linked with Pharmacon and Terrepharm, Édouard and J.C. Moreau. Sandover has run into a patch of trouble but his com is alive. I failed to rescue him. This will not sit well with the family, but we have hope. We will stay hidden until the coast is clear."

Chuanli bowed in Beya's direction. Kat looked her way and smiled.

"I should knock you out for the night, Beya. Standard procedure when there's nothing more to be done."

Beya wanted to be awake, to hear any news, find out what this madness was about. As if reading her thoughts, Kat conceded.

"OK, rest tomorrow. Situation analysis. We've got all night. Chuanli, who's behind this very high-tech equipment?"

"Don't look at me! I'm told what I need to know. My employer is Seaway Enterprises, based in Shanghai, underwater exploration and development. I was asked by Sandover's family to take this job, to learn the depths of the Great Lakes. Georgian Bay is quite shallow, a hundred metres at bottom, so we are travelling very carefully to avoid detection. As soon as the coast is officially clear, we will pass into Lake Michigan and U.S. waters, headed for Benton City, north of Chicago. I am to accompany you to New York in Seaway's private jet. Sandover will join us when he can."

Beya flinched at "when he can."

"I've seen enough ops to recognize an exceedingly formidable enemy with leading-edge tech and surprise," Kat assured. "If it was anyone's fault, it was Seaway's tacticians or their masters."

Her words trailed off as they tried to imagine who those masters might be. Someone was going to a lot of trouble for their sake, someone who also had breath-taking technology.

"If we're scuppered on Seaway's tab for the moment, I could fill you in a little more on comtech's latest evolution," Phil offered. "It connects with what just happened."

No one objected. Curiosity might kill the cat, but the cat had nine lives.

"I met Ben Singer in Palo Alto, at a conference where he was speaking on physics and advanced communications. We had several talks and I was able to drop a couple of hints regarding tight particle communication. I was very careful to make sure he thought they were his own ideas. That was July. In the last few months there's been a lot of new activity in their labs on the coast."

"You trust him?" Beya looked sceptical.

"I didn't mention inter-place-time, of course. We need to keep that idea away from his thoughts until much later, if possible. His training and intuition in physics is going to lead him there eventually. After our discussions, he asked me to join the board of Pinpoint Technologies, just set up to develop commercial applications. I'll be able to see if the technology performs and if we can trust him down the road."

"Well, there's the nail in the coffin of the Orion message's being false," Kat sighed. "We still have no real idea who sent it, but it's given us personal wealth and now new comtech."

"The tech is much cheaper and more precise than today's wireless," Phil added. "The upfront cost is high, to get a reliable network built out, so it will spread slowly at first, faster as fibre and wireless towers wear out. Sandover has a better idea about the economics."

Awkward silence. Kat jumped in.

"Pinpoint communication is also a lot more secure than wireless, isn't it? What I mean is that idiots can breach security with any technology, but aside from people-error, this pinpoint technology makes 'just listening in' on other people's conversations about as easy as finding a needle in the universe."

"You're right, no existing surveillance technologies can 'find' pinpoint conversations. They exist only at the two ends, sent and received via paired particles."

"You might think intelligence agencies would love this because it's almost perfectly secure," Kat observed, "but unfortunately, it's perfectly secure for the enemy, too. Goodbye to everyone's best source of counterintelligence!"

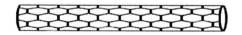

Maurizio Torbido watched as J.C. screamed at the cowering marine who stood before him.

"You have not found his body? Idiots! Look in hell."

A single shot pierced the night shadows as they fled before the sweep of the searching lights.

"You didn't have to shoot him, *mon ami*. You could have waited to see how he intended to obey your order. Looking in hell is an interesting challenge. Knowing the loyalty of your men is of great value."

"No matter, Maurizio. When we see where *this* fool's body falls, we will find what is left of the chink!"

"I fear not, Jean-Christophe. They had stealth, we have traced it. They had men on the ledge beneath the cliff. They were ready. We missed a step but we're back on his tail."

"Don't fail me again, *consigliere*!"

"I am no fool, *capo*, I will finish him myself."

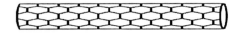

Kat carried on the flow of conversation, more to distract Beya's thoughts from other perches than to solve the mysteries they faced.

"Each of us is a security asset of huge value, Beya, so also a security risk of equal value to the enemy. We are, in short, a prize catch if it happens that we know anything important, and thus a disaster to lose to the enemy. If we know nothing, too bad, we're easily expendable. The progressive powers protect us to prevent us falling into the hands of their enemies. Don't assume that they care about us a bit beyond that. And most of them just failed us."

Beya was beginning to fade back into a state of shock. Phil looked ragged but determined. Chuanli brought more steaming coffee from the fore cabin. A muted soft green light gave their sunken cave an eerie intimacy. Kat pointed a finger.

"Snap out of it, Beya! That's better. I need your help here. Our personal security problems pale beside human xenocide by nanorganic plague. While Phil's had his head in science,

I've been studying the players. Terrepharm is changing. Édouard Moreau still holds the reins, but J.C. is marching to the beat of his own drum whenever it suits him. Torbido is happy to go along. It suits his brutal tendencies and it's hard in any case to control the boss's son. In public, Édouard remains the prominent French baron, perhaps with some limits to his greed and lust for power, his Byzantine right-wing ideology, and his disdain for the peons of the world. Unfortunately, neither J.C. nor Torbido has any such limits. Torbido is a highly effective operator with access to strong means of persuasion, carrot and stick. He has used some selective executions to instil fear among Pharmacon's scientists, some of whom had the audacity to squeak about the dangers of new technologies in the wrong hands."

Beya cringed inwardly, the cracks in her armour threatening to reappear. She'd seen enough of J.C.'s vicious arrogance Down Under.

"After Merimbula, J.C. taught a year at INSEAD, a classy business school in Fontainebleau for the favoured sons and daughters of Europe. Then Édouard made him VP, a mistake. He quickly began end-running his father. According to the tabloids, J.C.'s family is a textbook case from the 'aughts - Édouard a self-styled mogul incapable of close relationships, his wife hurt for decades by his emotional absence. She finds close relationships elsewhere, according to the paparazzi, her privacy protected by Torbido's commandos and the threat of reprisal. You can fill in the rest. J.C. will never have Édouard's love. He hates his father and is deeply hurt by his mother's pain. He can't see how close human contact could lead to anything but injury."

Kat sounded like she was reciting from a file. Beya wondered once again about the sources of her knowledge.

"J.C. has stayed in touch with Abbott, now a rising star in Golgotha and the U.S. Christian Right. Golgotha has been watching us and our movements more closely over the past year. Where countries and conglomerates stand on the use of nanorg technologies gets rather interesting and complex. There's a scale running from 'no holds barred' all the way to 'ethical' and even philanthropic. When you add in the military and terrorist dimensions of nanorg and the political spotlight now on nano and sub-nano-sized creations, confrontations are always a blink away."

"What are they most afraid of, Kat?" Phil asked what they were all thinking. "I mean, what is so valuable or so destructive that you can't let the enemy get hold of it?"

"It started with the crobies, the little secret that slipped out when their inventor gave the patent to the world. The crobies turn crop waste into oil in a day instead of a millennium. They're bacteria modified by genetic material from fast-healing life forms and the growing lines of 'boutique' genes. After the public outcry that followed the nightmare vision of escaped crobies gobbling up the planet, they had to develop a terminator version that absolutely can't reproduce. On top of that, each crobie has a 'killer buddy' that destroys both, if their containment is breached."

"But how does this involve big Pharma, if the crobie cat is out of the bag?"

"It's the next wave they're after, Phil. Pharmacon has learned its lesson: control the labs and patent the tech immediately. With the patent for crobies gone public, anyone can use them *provided* they agree to make their own discoveries available to everyone else on the same basis. Everyone who can build a crobie facility, meaning just about *everyone*, is crazy not to do it. Cheap, clean fuel is only a year away."

"Sandover says the changes in the global economy will be huge," Beya ventured. "Mostly, they'll be positive, but not for the oil-producing countries. It'll hit the desert countries hardest. They get struck twice, by oil's demise and by not having much biomass around to decompose. It's going be a huge blow for the progressives and a lot of ammunition for the fanatics, just when many were modernizing."

"They'll at least get low-cost fuels from imports," Phil suggested, "but that's going to be very hard for them to swallow. Nano-hydrogen may save the day, with the extraction of hydrogen from water at lower and lower costs. It's standard chemistry and nano-size membranes, levers if you like, to break the highly charged chemical bonds."

"That brings us back to our problem with the nanorg plague."

They all knew what that meant, coming from Kat. More trouble.

"Back to reality?" Phil smiled.

"Nice place to visit," Chuanli snorted, returning to their small circle, "but who would want to live there?"

"Sometimes I wonder if I do," Kat mused. "Our kids are a lot more real to me than this maze of pinpoints and nanorgasms."

"Nanorganisms," Phil corrected, "nanorganics is a growing landscape of sciences, technologies, small firms, Pharmacon, and the other congloms, alongside the panoply of government agencies, religions, ideologies, and concerned citizens' groups. The branch I'm watching most closely is being dubbed Danomics, after Isaac Azimov's humanity-saving robot, R. Daneel Olivaw. It involves sending nano-sized constructions into human bodies. They cause the body to do something — produce healthy liver cells, for example, and replace damaged ones. Biotech had already done this with stem cells, but it was always hit and miss. The nano constructions add a lot of precision at a fraction of the cost."

Kat asked the question on all their minds.

"What exactly are these *constructions*?"

"As close as I can tell," Phil squinted, "they're complex molecules put together after mapping the differences between the damaged genes and the undamaged ones in, say, a person with liver disease. The molecules signal the cells to produce the good genes and dispose of the bad. The trick is in engineering the best molecule possible. And that's where the 'R. Daneel' part comes in. In order to get there and do their job, these little 'robots' have to have a degree of adaptability. So they have a small artificial intelligence component, organic in structure but non-living. They are intelligent in a purely *adaptive* way."

"Oop!" Kat exclaimed, involuntarily. "That's worse than terrifying. What can they adapt into, and is it really that easy to sit down and whip these things up?"

"No, not really. I mean the nano benches are everywhere now. They only cost a couple of million, but only a few labs have the knowledge. They have a new brand of atomic scoping microscope and a bunch of 'tools.' The microscope shoots out a stream of electrons, much smaller than atoms, to map the surfaces of the atoms and molecules it hits, like sonar. The digital pictures are stunning, from single hydrogen atoms to carbon Bucky balls. The tools can shape and manipulate the building blocks of matter and life."

Playing God, Beya thought, as Phil continued.

"There are some very good cognitive scientists involved, so primitive artificial intelligence is entering the picture. As to what these simple bots can adapt into, it's a very good question. They've been injected into animals for over a year now. Human trials may come up for FDA approval by next year. So far, they've had great results and no disasters. The old biotech argument stands: the alternative for many patients is certain death. Though the AI has been kept extremely simple, the odds that nanorg bots will *never* escape are probably zero. The damage could be impossible to control."

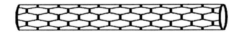

Sandover was frozen. A voice reached him as if from a great distance.

"You must go through the tunnel, Doctor Lee! I have been briefed on your claustrophobia. There are divers waiting to help and more at the other end. I will knock you out and take you through if you don't go, but the odds go down. Swim, look straight ahead. When it gets narrow, focus on the flipper in front of you. Five seconds."

All his systems balked. What if he got stuck? He couldn't face that, couldn't go out that way. Time was up.

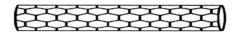

Maurizio tugged Édouard's arm. "We must go, *capo*. The Seals are coming fast."

"We lost him?"

"He got to the water, went under, into a cave that is being blasted to dust as we speak. Bid him adieu, we will not see him again. *Andiamo avanti, capo*, take your time quickly!"

Submerged

Beya struggled to stay awake. Exhaustion comes when you don't want to take it any more, not when you can't. In a dream she nestled into Sandover's shoulder, flashes of lightning sending fleeting pictures of his face, now worried, now more serene. Arms tightened around her, leaving behind the pain that his suffering awoke. The storm melted into a symphony of power and sound, moving in time with the music, no separation between them but the thinnest edge of the night. Then all was silent, floating, drifting into perfect harmony.

Morning came too early. Justine awoke hungry and they were soon up with hot drinks and new hope. The kids went up front with Chuanli. Sandover's com was still active but there was no response and no other news. Time was stretching, becoming too thin, not on their side. Kat took up the conversation once more to drown out the quiet.

"I want to know how complex these nanorg bots can be made. And how obedient. I grew up with those predictions about nanotech turning all life into green goo and all dead matter into grey goo. A world of slime and asphalt. This was dismissed as too apocalyptic by your generation, Beya, but it's back, a real possibility with this new line of nanorg bots. They could ultimately kill the patient they're designed to cure and spread until they kill everything living."

Beya wondered if green goo could have a collective consciousness. Odd thought. Probably not. Would she live to find out?

"There are countermeasures being developed, of course," Phil hastened to add, "beyond the containment systems and the killer-buddies. The bots are now being tested in labs on most types of plant and animal life to see what damage they cause. The testing is very expensive, so there's lots of debate about how far it should go — birds as a group or hawks or sub-species like ospreys."

A rumble like thunder crossed their subliminal awareness. Surely not depth charges!

"Seismic," Chuanli barked from the bridge. "Could be nature, could be oil or mining exploration probes looking for us. We'll sit a while."

Kat glowered at an unseen enemy as Phil hurried on.

"The effect of the killer-buddies on living organisms is being tested at the same time. So far, so good. Countries may decide differently, and some may risk smarter bots, but we have some time before anyone can build elite AI and integrate it with the nanorg."

Beya shuddered.

"How much time, Phil?"

"The powers that be want a very cautious path. Unlike crobies or nano-hydrogen, the science and knowledge in nanorg isn't open. It's owned and protected to the death by Pharmacon."

"That's our plague," Kat spat. "Someone produces nanorg bots that are intelligent enough to escape."

"Looks that way," Phil admitted. "One branch of Pharmacon is making bots from living materials, another is trying to manufacture them from component atoms. The second is a much harder path but the result would be a very finely tuned weapon for ill or for good. Obviously, a lot could go wrong, even with the best intentions. It gets a lot worse, of course, if the bots can reproduce."

"One big mistake and, presto, cream of yesterday's life!"

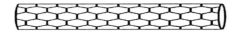

Sandover blinked. A distant red point of light danced on the edge of his consciousness. Alive. Unable to move. Don't lose it, he prayed. Alive is the worst possible outcome except for all the others. Ha ha, like democracy, don't laugh, no room. Others must have survived. Keep busy, figure it out, plan your revenge, this will end. Time is finite, time can be controlled, a good time will come, all in good time

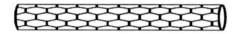

Beya's focus returned at Kat's next question.

"What am I hearing about you and Saba Luanzi?"

"She's got a chance, Kat. She's going to be Kenzie Moore's running mate in November, two women running for president and VP of the U.S. of A. Although Harbison may have the advantage of the incumbent, with the inevitable errors of the modern presidency, being incumbent isn't what it used to be."

"They're weak now," Kat surmised.

"In the end, the Republicans haven't delivered, too busy fighting everyone and each other. The Visitors remain unfathomable and prosperity is rising. Dog-eat-dog predictions and scare tactics aren't working. Moore could win. Sandover's done some work for her on the economic platform. If Saba becomes VP, we'll have powerful new ways to keep tabs on nanorganics."

"You've been busy!" Kat exclaimed. "Saba was nowhere in sight a year or two ago."

"Well she was, really, not at the national level so much, but she'd done everything else. She just decided it was time. She recruited me early this year through Angela Nealand, bless her soul. And she contacted Sandover after looking carefully through the professional staff at the WEO. We get along well, Maybe I've been opportunistic, but so has she.

Common Swahili roots help, though in fact our ancestors fought. She's a force to behold, charismatic and just plain 'in charge.' So far, she's got everything she's set her eyes on."

"What about Sandover's spectacular rise in the World Economic Organization?"

"He hasn't hit the inner circles yet, Kat. The WEO's a slow beast, like all the international financial institutions. It's still imprinted with the cultures of its newly swallowed antecedents, the World Bank, International Monetary Fund, and World Trade Organization. On the good side, their studies show we are all getting rich together. With growing global affluence, we don't have to keep repeating the barbarism of the past."

"'Don't have to' and 'won't' are entirely different matters," Kat retorted. "Some will go on fighting for greed or glory, arrogance, fanaticism, or just plain entertainment. What will poor humanity do if its taste for violence isn't fed? Will new frontiers be enough? Will we evolve or kill each other off as our primal instincts adapt too slowly? Don't bet the farm on people changing that fast, that's my advice. Maybe evolution has to speed up when a species faces extinction, but nothing I know tells me it's likely to happen."

Phil deftly changed the subject

"So, what are the corridors of power saying about Orion and nanorganics, Beya?"

"Having eliminated a hoax or a tech trick, they've come down squarely on the remote satellite explanation. To be fair, they don't have any reason to think of inter-place-time communication. And the Visitors remain beyond investigation. So, the story goes that someone invented pinpoint communications earlier, maybe in the twenties. Whoever it was sent a satellite out toward Orion. When it got far enough away that no one could tell the difference, it transmitted the Orion message. You could do all this and never be detected at this end, once the satellite was up and away. That's the beauty of pinpoint."

Phil's expression was dubious.

"Why do they think anyone would go to all this trouble, Beya? Could anyone really do it, and who might that be?"

"All of spookdom is obsessed by exactly these questions," Kat interrupted. "They don't know what language is being used, but they know the sender does, and they believe it's some faction here on Earth. Without knowing any of the content of Orion, they concentrate on the usual suspects: the powerful nations and their alliances, corporate consortia, religious blocs, powerful coalitions of thinkers and activists. Any of these might be prepared to intervene in world affairs by means of a deep-space transmission if it were in their interest. Spook-scenarios include either starting or stopping a global plague among likely motives, so all of the nanorganic technologies are being dissected with sharp scalpels. In terms of satellite launch capability, the elite military intelligence services are the main suspects, but no one rules out any powerful party, given how many launch facilities there are and the ethics of some of the owners."

Beya thought of the attack on Manitou. J.C. was there, evil, deranged!

"Sandover will be OK, Beya."

"I know he has contacts that spookdom knows little about, Kat. Chuanli is one. Pyramid could be the sender of the Orions, but I think it might be the right hand for another power."

"Why? What power?"

"American paranoia says the Orion senders are connected with one of the anti-Western military pacts. The Europeans see veiled leagues of powerful transnationals behind every lamp post. Whoever it is, their motive isn't apparent. What is clear is that the Orion message has served notice to humanity and cast a powerful shadow over world affairs. The spooks presume this was done to achieve some objective, either humanist or destructive, or maybe just to protect their position of technical superiority."

"It's an interesting theory, Beya," Kat reasoned, "but for the four of us, it falls apart unless someone could have learned Sandover's codes. If someone did, it probably means they hacked his system just after he created the cipher. The time between that and the Orion reception was too short to have launched a satellite and sent it far into space. Maybe they sent a satellite out right after the listening stations sprang up in '27 and '28. Maybe the listening stations gave them the idea — that and the Visitors' patterns."

"If you want to be mischievous," Phil suggested, "and you believe that a communications satellite was launched, there's no reason that an earlier one couldn't have gone out and sent back the Visitors' transmissions. You said there are enough gaps and anomalies in global records to cover a clandestine launch or two. I'm guessing this is another thriving field of spooktivity."

"Yes, but far down the list," Kat signalled. "Most people still think the Visitors' transmissions are alien. There is some spooksensus on the version of reality that includes real extraterrestrials, but attributes Orion to some powerful human faction. Maybe they were contacted by the Visitors, maybe even hooked up with them."

"If present-day people are behind Orion, they might conceivably succeed in keeping it to themselves."

"Not likely, Phil. Three people can keep a secret if two of them are dead. Worse than that, for everyone who didn't send the Orion message and thinks we might understand it, their only options are to assist or oppose us. Capture, kill, torture, or influence in more subtle ways. Witness the attack we just went through."

Sandover teetered on the edge of insanity, muscles screaming in panic, claustrophobia overpowering his will, the worst nightmare. At last his mind wandered.

Nothing to fear but fear itself. Good one, Winston. As if that weren't enough! They will find me. We have the edge, but not if I die. Put your mind in another place. Think back. We worked into sunset on a hill by the stream that fed the bamboo when it rained and soaked the land for the fruit and rice. Tending crops, fixing the pumps, books after supper under the dim light, the piercing stare of Na, mother of a generation, keeper of the light. Teh said 'listen, there is something vast on the edge of the night.' Na said 'you are the one chosen by the light. Your brothers will protect you, formed of the same plan. You are special but you cannot survive the prison of your mind. I will show you how to vanish.' Farewell if not goodbye. Hurry, my brothers, there is much left to do.

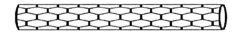

"So, who's pulling our strings?" Kat's question was gentle for a change. They were once again edging closer to the brink of exhaustion.

"Occam's razor," Phil theorized. "'Don't increase, beyond what is necessary, the number of entities needed to explain anything.' The most obvious explanation is the best: inter-place-time communication. From the leads in Orion and the science we've been able to digest so far, I think it might become possible. I say it has to be our base case until some piece of it falls apart. If the pinpoint or nanorganic technologies presaged in Orion don't keep panning out, that would be the deal breaker. So far, so good."

"So far, so bad," Kat challenged, "and what's the counterfactual? How much of pinpoint and nanorg was going to happen anyway? The spooks' version could also be right. It doesn't have any holes in it, either, even for us who understand Orion. In that case, among other things, the 'reports to the future' that we've been dutifully filing would be reports to someone listening for them now, somewhere on the planet."

"Maybe near-space, too," Phil corrected, "but that's a conversation for another day."

"If you ask me, which you did," Kat scowled, "we're getting our derrières kicked all over the map to help play someone else's hand. Set aside your visions of heroism. We're a comedy act on a tragic course unless we fight back. The shooting war started last night. Sandover has powerful friends. We might survive long enough to figure out what we're up against and how to regain control."

"Like the spooks," Phil answered, "we seem to be fixed on the remote satellite explanation for Orion. I won't argue more. I can't help speculating, though. There are intelligent satellites already, for example. The Visitors could be some maverick artificial intelligence that got lonely out there in the universe and wanted to talk. Ditto for the Orion senders. Meanwhile, back at the world, everyone waits and expects and fears to understand their memo, to meet them or talk to them or hear something we can understand. It feels like Narnia in overdrive. If you're particularly psychotic, many other variations are possible."

"We need to find out how Sandover's code got into Orion," Kat injected. "That's the key. We need to do it in the midst of a whole mess of scrutiny around every step we take. After today, whatever cover we had is blown to bits. We'll be under guard or surveillance 24-7. No normal lives for our children, either, no more poking into pinpoint or nanorg like innocent bystanders. On top of that, Beya's heavy into American politics at the highest level now. A heavy U.S. security blanket will cover us henceforth. If that's a huge asset, it's also the last exclamation mark on the tombstone of our privacy."

"What do we really know about our rescuers?" Phil asked. "Sandover must have said more, Beya."

"Sandover's contacts had told him to be very careful, just recently. We didn't move fast enough. Now, if we use the coms they've offered us, they will have direct access to most of what each of us knows and a lot of control over what we hear. I'm not saying they would play us foul. They just saved our lives."

Kat finished the unspoken thought.

"But who the hell are they?"

Beya's heart leapt into her mouth as the fore cabin door opened. The smiling face of Chuanli grew larger as he pushed his way toward them.

"We have no definitive news, but we have information. Dr. Lee met Mr. Moreau, the son, at the top of the cliff. Your husband dove over the edge into the waiting arms of our soldiers. They got to a cave entrance under water, but a high-pitched explosion followed. Then silence. One of our birds that came in low under their radar sent a seeker at Moreau."

Beya held her breath. There had to be more.

"Sandover had the high-tech kit, Mrs. Lee. The water isn't so cold this time of year. We're still searching. They either got caught in the explosion or they went deep, to the bottom of the bay. It's what I would have done. They'd have come ashore at a place they thought was safe, then stay in deep cover until the coast was clear. Either way we'll find them."

"Either way" was not much to hang on to.

The rest of the day passed in nail-biting silence, punctuated by Justine's routine and everyone's kindness. Sleep came to Beya at last. The next thing she heard was the sound of gears shifting. She opened an eye.

"Welcome back." Kat's cryptic voice didn't hide her relief. "We're in Bad Axe, Michigan, a hundred kilometres north of Detroit in a lorry. No sign of pursuit. You passed out. We gave you a sedative for good measure. You needed sleep."

It all came back.

"They found him Beya, we're all headed for New York. He's in a coma or something like it. He was trapped in a collapsed cave, lucky for him just above the water. His state is like hibernation. He needs to be brought back. After that, we'll all be in New York under heavy security. Prison's just another word for all that's left to lose."

Beya didn't care. Sandover was alive, she could bring him back, anything was possible! Kat launched a distracting volley of new information as Chuanli retreated.

"Our protectors, we are now led to believe, are a venture sometimes called Pyramid. It's triad in structure, with a rumored but invisible inner council or Pinnacle. They operate mostly through trading companies internationally. Local operatives like Chuanli connect only to their triad cell. They've made it known widely that protecting us is a family affair. No one really believes this. Beyond that, there are a lot of gaps in intelligence circles about Pyramid."

"We have allies in the big civic coalitions," Phil added. "They have intelligence without muscle. Free IP and Crucible are manned by independent scientists. We'll need them both. Another job on our list."

"Scientists are an idealistic lot, thank God," Kat agreed. "Unfortunately they're no match for the congloms. Abbott's as dangerous as JC. Obsessed by the Visitors, he's preparing the faithful to join with them if they are friendly. If not, the true followers will be the first of all humans redeemed by the apocalypse. Likely the only humans. It's a much too exclusive vision for all but the fanatical, but that's a growing crowd, a smoldering alliance of the old style divide-and-conquer back room military industrial complex of money, religion, power and politics. Even Ellis is involved."

"Surely not Ellis," Phil implored, "he never seemed vicious."

"Ellis is different," Kat conceded, "weird for sure but also very smart and completely obsessed by pinpoint and all the deep-space transmissions. He's leading a group of self-appointed virtual revolutionaries and 'liberators" who are able to work on the Nets pretty much without detection. They're the top global consultants on digital security — in effect, its ultimate masters. They've even managed to influence world events by slipping ideas into confidential conversations."

"The near-thaw in Arab-Israeli relations?"

"A gradual thaw over many months, by one account, deftly developed by small nuances introduced into diplomatic communications. The deceptions got noticed eventually, of course, and the thaw froze again, but some good was done. Ellis and his merry band have been dubbed The Imputers by friends and foes. Everyone searches the Nets for their footprints, yet it seems they can travel almost at will. It looks like they meddled in the South Asia accords, not to mention Tibet. We need them as friends."

Kat paused to inhale while Beya and Phil absorbed this news. The only certainty Beya could see was a lot more to do. No rest for the wicked, no time to celebrate a death evaded, the last vestiges of blissful ignorance dashed and drowned in the Great Lakes.

"Danielle Gauthier is one of Ellis's inner circle," Kat added, "our friend at Manitou. There's some local gossip that they share more than talk. She's a kinder person than he, surrounded by her family while he lives like a hermit. Maybe she can help us with the ripening of Ellis Holland. I've worried about our kids seeing a lot of her daughter, though, so we've been careful to keep everything about Orion away from Lara and Dylan. Kids know at some level of course, they always do, by the shape of what goes unspoken."

"Still, as long as they don't know the specifics, we're all much safer."

"Maybe, Phil, but secrets have a high cost. Living a lie is hard. Most people don't see that. In any case, Dylan is probably close to guessing some of it. They both have to be asking why their mother and father are under attack. They need more help from us. And we need Danielle's help, too. She's a software specialist with a towering reputation, blindingly quick and digitally invisible. She shares Ellis's obsession for cracking the deep-space messages."

"Is that it?" Phil looked hopeful in a resigned sort of a way.

"There are, of course, many smaller security interests and 'initiatives'," Kat concluded, "not that dangerous by themselves, though they could be treacherous in combination or as random elements in a close battle."

"Scares the hell out of me," Phil sighed, "but not as much as the science itself. While we've been constructing nanorg bots, nature's been rather busy, too. She keeps throwing up new diseases as fast as medical biotech fights the old ones. The silver lining is that our fear funds the research and development of treatments and cures. There's even a silver lining to climate change in the transformation it's caused in energy and lifestyles."

"Small consolation if it kills us all," Kat snapped. "We're perilously late in removing carbon from the atmosphere, and the longer we delay, the faster we have to do it later to avoid complete disaster. We were beyond stupid, criminal, not to cut emissions a lot sooner. Precious time lost, precious chances missed."

"Amazing greed."

"Amazing ideology over intelligence."

"Amazing arrogance in North America."

"Amazing trash, Phil. America wallowed in 'reality' while the planet burned. Everyone had a shot at media fame. The world moved on. Terrorists mostly stopped targeting the U.S. Why bother, with the politicians and half the population doing it so brilliantly on their own?"

"On the upside. Kat, the most ambitious project in the world theatre managed to get a start: the space elevator. Once the asteroid is in place, the carbon for the cable will be partly harvested from the air, the way trees and plants do. Developing enhanced photosynthesis is a huge industry. The lab trials have already achieved big multipliers on the conversion rates of plants, absorbing carbon-dioxide and emitting oxygen. They're building the first pilot for the carbon-harvesting modules that will go on the near end of the Lift."

"Cartoonists are having a pretty good time with that one," Kat snorted. "A big ball in orbit with a second one coming, attached to a large dangling appendage that gets hot and becomes longer and firmer as it spouts out a stream of carbon nanotubes from its tip."

"Nonetheless," Phil insisted, "with all the major countries on board, the consortium has a good shot, so to speak. Unfortunately, making it too difficult or costly or unattractive for terrorists to target is a problem not yet solved. Sandover told me once that he'd never go near it, Beya. Said he has a recurring nightmare about shooting out the top of the elevator into space."

Beya smiled. Only hours now until they were reunited with Sandover. Where had he gone, his mind and spirit? How could she find him? The rainstar remained impassionate, unmoved.

Assassination

Kat pulled her wrap more tightly around her. New York was crisp in its big-city, still-comfortable-but-definitely-gloves-and-earmuffs, late fall way. Election fever was, in Phil's words, oot and aboot on the streets. The Federal Security Agency had put them up in the old Helmsley Hotel on Madison Avenue. Kat's higher senses caught a faint whiff of ancient scandal in the corridors, the image of an ancient queen of mean. Notwithstanding, the rooms were deliciously decadent and the views spectacular over Midtown and the UN. It was a short taxi ride down to Flatiron and Tribeca, where a *pied-à-terre* had been readied for Beya and Sandover.

Even with twenty-four-hour security, a penthouse to themselves wasn't bad. Phil and Kat met Beya often, ringed by security, travelling back and forth between the Helmsley, Beya's elegant flat, and the hospital. Sandover was still out cold but his bodily processes were more rapid.

Tonight, the hospital again. Dylan and Lara would welcome the quiet at home, Kat thought. It was tough on them to be so isolated. On the bright side, school looked like it might be possible. There were enough kids in New York with protection from FSA and other national security agencies to justify keeping three high-security schools.

Roberto escorted them down to the waiting vehicle while Oscar guarded the door, coms on, alert. This was a good pair, with no clear idea of why this family mattered to FSA but unambiguous orders to keep them out of harm's way.

They needed secure communication now, Kat knew — the coms that Pyramid had offered them via Sandover. Mobiles were useless, easily monitored. With Sandover out, the only safe course for the moment was to meet in person and be sure they weren't heard. Not easy with the range of super bugs and eavesdropping devices available. Not efficient, either.

Once across the Roosevelt Island Bridge, the FSA detail at Coler-Goldwater Memorial ushered them in to Sandover's room. Beya looked forlorn, but brightened a shade at their arrival. Hugs, there can never be too many hugs.

"Evening, Kat, Phil. Wish I had better news. It's like he's locked himself in but didn't tell anyone where to find the key."

Into the room at that moment strode Sally Strauss, British MI8, in full hospital regalia. Kat hadn't seen her in twenty years.

"Nurse Sullivan!" Beya exclaimed. "Please meet my dear friends Phil and Kat."

"Pleasure." She didn't bat an eyelid on seeing Kat. Clearly well briefed.

"I've done some research," Sally continued. "It's why they keep me around here. There are several ways in which human hibernation can be reversed, according to East Asian wisdom. Intimacy has the best reputation. My duties call me to emergency. If your friends would be so kind as to stand guard, they could just tell anyone who comes along that Mrs. Lee is taking a moment alone to pray for her husband."

"There are other ways?" Beya enquired.

"Yes, you never know which one will work."

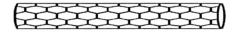

Lianshen looked across the street and up toward midtown at the apartment of Sandover and Beya Lee. She was not careful, but then again, she had tasted violence too recently to make her truly wary. Zi Ong 'Mike,' prowled the nearby streets on his delivery scooter, always in range. Good kid, good at looking different every day. The transmitter planted in his com made it easy to follow him on Lianshen's pinpoint handset. The technology was leading edge, dangerous for Beya and her friends to have, but Chuanli had told Lianshen to give them handsets anyway, that they must never be out of contact Always options, always risks.

Lianshen's thoughts drifted back behind the veils of time. After the birds died, he and his brothers were taken to a camp where Zhŭ taught them science and politics, the first time the World was more than chickens and rice. Once bitten… Then Shanghai, astonishing, jazz all night, working for Yang Jibao. Now New York, where he found the flat for Beya and rented a room across the street. Mostly he steered clear of the big picture as ordered, but once bitten... He used his cover well, took pleasure in it, talked with the shopkeepers and citizens. In quiet moments, he did tech and finance specs for Shandong and East Asia, on the Internet late at night. He passed messages when it was safe. Trouble skirted the field of battle as he waited and watched, hidden, each biding their time.

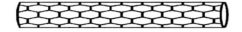

Kat had just resumed her pacing when Beya burst out of the hospital room looking a dishevelled shade of radiant. They all rushed back in. Sandover was propped up on a pillow, eyes open, foggy, trace of a smile. Beya's ring drew everyone's attention, the rainstar sapphire brightly glowing.

"Look, it's a tiny pyramid," Phil exclaimed.

"There's a coincidence," Sandover croaked.

"Got to talk," Phil rushed on. "Let's get you out of here before they find out you're conscious."

"You don't have to worry about Nurse Sullivan," Kat interjected. "She's MI8, an old acquaintance clearly here to get my attention as well as to help Sandover. Don't be fooled by her motherly appearance, she could put your lights out before you saw it coming."

"So," Phil chided at Sandover, "what brought you back?"

"I have no memory," Sandover pleaded, as a cheeky look crossed his brow, "but if I did, I'm quite sure it would be lovely."

"Beya?"

"In the words of Nurse Sullivan, you never know which remedy was the one that worked."

"Speaking of the good nurse," Phil added with a glance in Kat's direction, "can you ask her to help us get out of here?"

"She will have prepared. Speak of the devil."

"The devil you know," Sally added as she rounded the corner toward them. "This way."

As they stole off quietly into the night, Phil asked Kat if Sally Strauss would be grilled about their departure.

"She won't be hanging around. On paper, Nurse Sullivan will have been transferred to an upstate hospital right after we're back in the hands of FSA. From there, she will vanish. But my past will call again soon enough, don't worry. I owe them one. I'll keep you posted."

They went straight home, back to prison. No offence to New York, it just looks different when every move has to be planned and accompanied, when you are the animals that go out in cages with handlers to pass through the panoply, like Land Rovers on the Serengeti, watching a hundred thousand realities but intersecting with none. FSA treated their homecoming like a mother greets a lost child returned, joyful and furious all in one breath. It took a day to answer their questions and convince the hospital that Sandover did not need further attention, that their care had been the determining factor. Staying on the good side of the medics is a rule Kat had learned quickly in field ops. By nightfall, they were looking across the skyline of Manhattan, gathered on the balcony at the Helmsley as the kids watched a movie on the ViD downstairs.

"Where to start?" Phil ventured.

They all looked at Sandover.

"Pyramid!"

"OK, OK. But you're going to be disappointed. Chuanli gave me one of their new comsets before we travelled north to Manitou. That's how we escaped the firefight and how they found me in the rock pile. When the attack came, they told me to get you down the cliff. The rest you know."

For Kat it didn't quite add up, so she risked a query.

"I don't mean to be impudent, Sandover, but the resources being devoted to our well-being are enough to keep a small country safe. Doesn't that go a bit beyond family?"

"No question. But I don't know if it's because of me or all of us."

Still something missing, unspoken.

"OK, but we need to know more, and you're the only one they might tell. Let's move on from notable friends to prominent enemies. Two days ago, Terrepharm pulled off a hostile takeover of Pfizer and the European subsidiaries. If they get their hands on the Johnson-Bristol constellation, the chances of controlling the development of nanorg begin to evaporate."

"The research consortium we've been helping quietly to foster is taking shape," Phil countered. "I think you know most of the Crucible network at least by name, top nanorg scientists from the universities with an international board of laureates and open-minded leaders. They're getting good at predicting nanorg developments and telling the world. Their work on the laws of nano robotics has been influential."

"As in Azimov's laws of robotics?" Sandover smiled.

"Actually yes," Phil responded. "These new nanorg bots can initiate actions, adapt to a degree, and reproduce if allowed or enabled. So it's crucial to have global agreement on what rules govern their behaviour and how to enforce those rules. As you know, Azimov had three laws. First, a robot may not injure a human or, through inaction, allow a human to come to harm. Second, a robot must obey the orders given it by human beings, except where such orders would conflict with the first law. And third, a robot must protect its own existence, except where such protection would conflict with the first or second laws."

"That's elegantly simple, or simply elegant."

"Azimov's fictional R. (Robot) Daneel Olivaw deduced a 'zeroth law,' implied by the other three, that a robot may not injure humanity or, through inaction, allow humanity to come to harm. 'He' (Daneel) succeeded in steering humanity clear of disasters in the next stages of Azimov's galactic diaspora and empire. But R. Daneel had an exquisitely advanced positronic brain, which we're probably two decades or more from developing."

"Unless this is another field where someone's jumped ahead undetected," Kat retorted

"But how do you stop a sub-microscopic nano-organic robot with little intelligence from injuring a human or causing injury?" Beya asked.

"Well," Phil conceded, warming up to one of his favourite subjects, "Azimov's robots were hardwired to shut down at the prospect of disobeying any law, or in case of irresolvable indecision between laws. This isn't technically feasible for the nanobots, at least not yet, but *shutting down* and *self-destructing* are the right ideas. Unfortunately, no one has been able to specify clearly enough the conditions for shutting down. So the default system is that a simple and powerful destruct mechanism must be built into every bot, with a trigger that activates the destruction unless it continues to receive a critical substance or signal that only humans can provide. Dead-man's switch. Fool proof but not idiot proof, as the critics say. Subject to tampering."

"Is it enough?" Beya was clearly looking for an affirmative.

"No, but it's the best we've got and the basis for the security systems being used in the testing of nanobots in the human trials. Similar systems have been used in crobie development and in animal testing of the nanorg bots. Because these bots are not intelligent enough to comprehend the consequences of their actions, the 'laws' governing them have to be very simple and easily enforceable. The laws are basically 'protect people' and 'obey orders.' 'Protect the immediate environment' would be the next law, but for the moment, the first and second are the only ones that can be implemented."

"How does it work?" Beya looked very sceptical. Sandover, mostly recovered, listened intently.

"The nanorg bots are designed to help people and obey orders," Phil explained. "They have simple mechanisms for monitoring changes in their host. If the changes trigger their sensors, they stop and await orders. Their creators can also issue orders at any time, to shut down or make adjustments. If all else fails, the dead-man's switch destroys the bots the instant they stop receiving input from humans. That and multiple containment systems may be enough to stop accidents. It's the same approach as Azimov's. Without the hardwiring, however, it's a ballpark or two more risky. For one thing, it won't stop humans using bots as destroyers."

"What if the bots are made with more intelligence?" Sandover asked. "Does that make them more or less controllable?"

"If the bots are made smarter, so they can be more effective in healing people, they get easier to control but more lethal if not controlled. It's a race against time and competing visions. Some deeper set of laws and enforcement protocols comes into play. Even with the fairly dumb bots we have now, getting some set of rules agreed globally looks like a long shot. A treaty on containment and dead-man's switches would be a huge gain if enough countries signed on. This would open the way for inspection and some collective judgment on how humans use nanorg bots."

"This is starting to get hot at the WEO," Sandover offered.

"It's bubbling up to the surface in the election campaign, too," Beya agreed. "The battle's blazing over who controls the intellectual property in nanorg. By law, Pharmacon's patent applications have to disclose the knowledge and technology involved. In reality, when the prize is big enough, they never tell it all."

"FreeIP watches new patents," Phil volunteered in a hopeful tone. "They warn us about anything in nanorg that looks like it could be dangerous."

"What exactly are we looking for, Phil?" Sandover enquired, "and is it likely to show up in a patent application?"

"Probably not. But we're learning the inside corridors of nanorg's commercial world, and that's worth a lot. Crucible is our other main source right now. As Beya gets more and more access to military intelligence circles via Saba and the Democrats, our surveillance gets a lot sharper."

It felt all too slippery to Kat, but she knew they didn't have a lot of options. Until they found the needle-bot in the haystack, the question of 'who was using them for what?' would no doubt remain a mystery.

"Some good things are happening at the WEO," Sandover offered. "With energy prices falling and WOW in full gear, there's real progress again in human development and poverty reduction."

"Saba's a fan of development as freedom," Beya added, "freedom from hunger, disease, violence, insecurity, exclusion, and freedom to learn, earn, express, innovate, and participate. Attaining freedoms people value depends on their capabilities, people and communities, principles of social justice enshrined in constitutions and laws, informed public debate, and harmonious social choice. Freedoms carry the responsibility to care for each other and renew the planet."

"Democracy?"

"Maybe, but democracy has big troubles in countries where there's a close balance between two opposing power blocks. Whichever one is in power, the other is a *large* minority that can be unhappy or excluded or oppressed by the majority."

"Religious and ethnic states exclude minorities by design," Beya declared, "but thankfully the number of hard-core religious states is on the decline."

"Ideological states are just as bad," Sandover countered. "Look at the last fifty years in the US, the free-market binges interspersed with the free fall of failed markets. You would think we would learn."

"Human nature changes slowly," Beya sighed. "A generation needs to break free from its negative roots. If you think it's too slow here in America, it's not even a snail's pace in some parts of the world."

"That's changing, too," Phil contended, ever the optimist. "Mobile phones were the Trojan horses. Before the millennium, it was possible to live a life on this planet with only one view of the world, the one dictated by the mullahs or the privileged, whoever was in power. But global communication was pounding at the door, threatening the age-old monopolies. Burma knew it, North Korea knew it. All the powers that controlled access understood perfectly what was at stake. Many fought back."

"It takes time," Sandover added, "for the world to be able to survive freedom of thought and expression. Everyone can speak, but who is listening, making sense of it, getting agreement? We haven't yet found a substitute for hierarchy of one kind or another. Still, Phil's right: free communication is an essential ingredient of every successful country's recipe. Think of the people you know and the issues they're passionate about, from MADD to the G27, from the environment to space migration. The countries doing well make it easy for everyone to be part of the debate. They get things done efficiently. Of course, they do it in very different ways politically, from benevolent autocracies to social and liberal democracies. Your country, Phil, does quite well."

"Maybe, when we're not quashed by some weary introvert's vision of what is right for everyone. Don't get me started on Canada."

Beya rubbed her eyes and heaved a sigh.

"While the ideologues are fighting for control of the world, we've still got immediate concerns to attend to with Pharmacon, extremists, spooks, pinpoint, nanorg, danomics, the Imputers, Crucible, and FreeIP. Shoulder to shoulder or atop the heap — Pyramid. Have I missed anything?"

"Don't forget the Visitors," Phil suggested, "or the future, for that matter. But, yes, Pyramid looks to be the key to understanding the rest."

Days passed like soldiers in uniforms. Kat was getting better at seeing the jigsaw puzzle, finding where new pieces might fit. Phil made two trips to City College in the heart of Harlem, a great learning centre grown from modest roots. 'Visitors and friends, for more than 180 years, the City College has been a landmark of diversity, opportunity and academic fire, powering alumni success stories ranging from Ira Gershwin to Jonas Salk to Damien Benedykt.'

On a clear October afternoon, Kat looked back at the old grey stone towers of the college from across St. Nicholas Park, Phil was looking for a cab, traces of cloud hanging high in the sky, a ridge of fantastic gossamer figures stretching back over East Harlem and Roosevelt Island.

FreeIP headquarters was here. Kat had come to meet Claudia Lorca Cortez, a Colombian-American lawyer who'd worked in tough neighbourhoods before becoming famous in conflict negotiations around the world. In the end she ditched the elegant private offices to become an advocate of openness, a different way of doing business. With a mastery of IP law and communications, she'd taken the lead in FreeIP, backed now by a large global network of lawyers, economists, and other professionals who toiled on the many fronts of keeping knowledge open. Most worked *pro bono*. They became the target of scurrilous attacks from Pharmacon and the other industry congloms, so they had to be doing something right.

To Kat's surprise, Claudia knew exactly what Phil was looking for, though not exactly why. They shared anger over knowledge hoarding, for different reasons — hers more principled and noble, Phil's from the cold fear that what you didn't know would probably kill you. Phil was by now quite well versed in pinpoint and nanorg technologies, and Claudia was particularly ardent that these not be subverted.

Claudia introduced them both to Damien Benedykt, a Nobel laureate with a striking physique and a Willie Nelson sort of voice that made you want to call him Jake. He headed the biomedical school, specializing in nanorg and robotics. They talked about technologies and agreed to meet again at the end of the week.

For Kat, the drive back from Harlem was a trip down memory lane, the beautiful east side of Central Park, past the Reservoir, splendid Guggenheim, and the stately Metropolitan Museum of Art, along the East Green to the Pond and south through Grand Army Plaza into Midtown. As they passed a Takashimaya retail tower at the bottom of the park, she thought of Sandover's story of Singaporeans naming their own grand-elegant Takashimaya the Ministry of Shopping.

At home, Phil went off with Dylan and Lara while Kat caught a moment by herself, a chance to take in the grandeur of the city through the glass walls of the Helmsley penthouse. Big night coming in the Big Apple! Big night for Beya and Kenzie Moore.

As evening approached, Kat and the kids sauntered among the trees on the side of Bryant Park. The Crystal Palace flashed across her vision — 1853 and the first American World Exposition, a remembrance from some book or a scent of the living past. In her mind's eye, the ghost of the palace filled the park. Above and all around them was the clash of gothic and modern buildings, giants with dizzying grace.

A cloud moved across the sun and the scene shifted, but the Crystal Palace image remained in Kat's reverie, a shadow cast on the magnificent optimism of a scientific age long past, a monument to yesterday's magicians. Could they imagine us now, she wondered, foresee our wizards with the power to cast spells far more powerful and evil, altering life and the near universe? Humanity was cursed, she knew. This power came a fraction too early in the march of history. Another decade or two and the world might be civilized enough. Wishful thinking. Grow up fast, she thought, or die out faster. Whoever designed this chapter of human history certainly had a sense of humour.

Lara and Dylan reassembled masterfully behind the bench that Kat had occupied, trailed closely by bodyguards Roberto and Daniel. Transport arrived and they set off for Gramercy and Stuyvesant Square.

"So, I've been thinking," Dylan began as they inched their way south toward the Empire State Building, between swish Murray Hill and the Garment District. Having a son who is thinking usually presages some draconian dilemma whose horns need untangling.

"What have you been thinking?"

"OK, here's the thing, the crobies can digest stuff fast, and the Visitors must have had crobies for a long time because they're so far ahead of us. So they could have made crobies that would digest us all and let them have our planet."

Interesting, Kat thought, the young are as hypnotized by the Visitors as anyone.

"OK, Dylan, so what are they going to do, having granted us indigestion? Could they still turn hostile?"

"They haven't said anything for a long time," Lara ventured, "so they must be up to something. Unless their spaceship failed or had trouble and they couldn't come closer. Then we'll never know. Maybe they're waiting for a reply. Maybe they don't want to meddle, like on Star Trek — you know, the Prime Directive."

Lara's voice dropped half an octave as she recited.

"As the right of each sentient species to live in accordance with its normal cultural evolution is considered fundamental, Star Fleet personnel may not interfere with the healthy development of alien life and culture, including the introduction of superior knowledge, strength, or technology to a world whose society is incapable of handling such advantages wisely. Star Fleet personnel may not violate this Prime Directive, even to save their lives or their ship unless they are acting to right an earlier violation or an accidental contamination of said culture. This directive takes precedence over any and all other considerations, and carries with it the highest moral obligation."

"Well, a lot of people at my school think that's what the Visitors are doing," Dylan added.

"But they did send some messages," Lara reminded, "and that's a big intervention. So if the Visitors have the same prime directive, they would have to be righting an earlier violation or accidental contamination. Probably contamination, if you ask me, because no one's noticed any earlier violation. Or talked about it, anyway."

"Yeah, well, maybe they have a zeroth law, too," Dylan persisted. "Like, they can't intervene, but they can't let us destroy ourselves by not intervening. So they send messages. But why would they send something we can't understand?"

"Maybe it's like the minimum intrusion. They let us know someone's there, but we have to figure it all out ourselves."

From the mouths of babes!

Lianshen watched them approaching at a leisurely speed, dots on his pinpoint GPS. Time, he thought. The Lees should arrive any minute, too. They were intriguing. He had exchanged greetings with them on the street corner. But Chuanli was their contact. Lianshen had to stay in the background. They moved around most of the time, what with Ms. Lee being in the middle of the election, so Lianshen had three teams on duty for each of them; one active, one backup, one resting. Same for the Rush family. A lot of resources. Sandover was family to someone high up, he knew, but there was more to it than that if they took top priority 24-7. Forty-one lives in his care on this day. Maybe Wen knows why, he thought. I need *not* to know. My life depends on it. But once bitten...

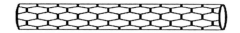

Kat watched Beya as the lights began to dim. She had to be in a fever of doubt and expectation, serious butterflies. Saba looked majestic in her *kangas*, bright-coloured against her ebony skin. They stood at the side with Dylan and Lara as the technical crews finished their set-up and the security teams swarmed through New Madison Square Garden. The floor of the arena was covered by eighty-eight large round tables, eight rows of eleven, each seating sixteen. Fourteen hundred Democrats and powerful friends. Wealthy friends, too, at $25,000 a seat, another thirty-five million for the last days of the campaign. Not that funds were short.

A rainbow of coloured lanterns lit up the wide stage across the west end of the building, soft oranges framing the podium. The massive hexagonal gondola hung from the roof overhead, its six screens ready to relay the proceedings to the guests and the world. After dinner, a bigger audience would be let in to watch Senator Kenzie Moore deliver her speech, the speech Beya had obsessed about for what seemed like a year. Though the ideas were everyone's, Kat knew, Beya felt exposed, responsible. In her own words, "if it bombs, I'll be back in the typing pool."

It would be a friendly audience here in stomach-of-the-whale, but everyone knew this speech was aimed far more at America and the planet than at the assembled faithful. A big gamble, perhaps. The stats team had said it was better to build up the female vote at this stage than cater to increasingly less likely male converts. Saba and the senator nevertheless were doing their best to comfort male insecurity over two female candidates. The GOP had a slight edge there, with a male VP on the ballot. At the same time, Harlan Darling was not as strong as Saba, and Hanna Carnegie had a history of opening her mouth to reveal the quantity of foot therein. A slow tide was washing over the nation: the realization that Moore could possibly win.

"Time, gentlemen." The buzz of conversation faded until silence swallowed the arena. Senator Kenzie Moore let the hush settle for a moment and longer, then still longer. She'd done this before, making everyone nervous. By the time she resumed, there was an almost collective sigh of relief.

"In England, for generations if not eons, barmen in pubs have said 'Time, gentlemen,' when it was time to finish the pint, go home, get some sleep, feed the kids, look after the hearth, village, country, and world as we know it. I want to tell you that there are many things that need urgently to be done in every one of these places. Time, gentlemen.

"Time to take carbon out of the atmosphere and reverse global warming. Time to manage new knowledge and technologies for everyone's benefit, before they destroy us. Time to have near-free energy and communications worldwide. Time for everyone to have the necessities and opportunities that allow for a good life. Time to put to bed a lot of the nonsense that has been driven by greed, envy, and ambition. Time for peace. Time to face the Visitors, whatever they bring.

"Before you call me idealistic and naïve, please let me tell you that I am not. I understand where our species and its civilizations now stand. I do not expect myopia, hate, violence, and war to disappear overnight or disappear completely. What needs to be done by a president and commander-in-chief I will do without hesitation. Security, defence, capability.

"Yet we need to be changing, too — fast, in fact, yesterday. The technologies we command make this easier if we use them well. We may fail because of our history and our fears, but failure today would be disastrous and could be terminal. No one wants to be a part of the generation that *blew* it all when it could have *had* it all with just a little more patience, determination, ingenuity. The generation that was on the brink of wealth, freedom, and exploration, then snatched defeat from the jaws of victory. Is that us? Time, gentlemen.

"The Republicans tell you they will look after domestic security and defence, but they will not make the changes that are vital. They are not capable of it. They have not changed in the past sixteen years. China and India have become powerful and we are no longer dominant. The Republican response is to cling to pre-eminence, back corporate wealth and power, confine new-tech, keep the petroleum economy running for supposed security reasons, fuel conflict, spill carbon, and risk annihilation by nature's retaliation or by our own nanorganic creations.

"This is not set in stone, yet it is too deeply ingrained in the Republicans for them to change. The Christian Right forms almost half of their membership, and with their political and lobbying strength they have much more influence than mere numbers would suggest. The big Energy, Pharma and Finance conglomerates wield critical power in our economies and they are prepared to use violent means to succeed. The GOP should indeed be the *Grand* Old Party, but in fact it is just *Old*, very old, too old to help us all move forward.

"Let me be clear. I am a Christian and I have been a corporate president. The for-profit market economy creates three-quarters of global income and wealth, so it has to be running smoothly for us to prosper. Yet its power and potentates should not also run the other quarter of the show where governments and not-for-profits reside. History tells us this doesn't work. Nor should religions have undue say in the governance of states. History is even less equivocal about that.

"On a personal level, I do not believe that anyone is condemned for having the bad luck not to be Christian. Or Moslem, Hindu, Buddhist, agnostic, or atheist. This is a time when tolerance and cooperation are more important than *all* of our old convictions.

"It takes a lot of courage for us to believe that everyone can live well. But it is true. Every serious analysis in the last decade has said exactly this. Costs of essentials are beginning to fall in the wake of crobies and cheap energy. Costs of food, transport, shelter, and goods in general will follow. Costs of health, education, security, creative expression, and entertainment will fall in tandem, pushed further by advances in bio-health and cognitive technologies.

"It takes a lot of courage for us to go through the transition from a high-cost, high-income world to one that is low cost and low income. In America and the richer countries, we will lose nothing unless we stop the transition from happening or mess it up. We could quite easily mess it up. There will be a lot of winners in the transition, but there will be many losers, too. Your sister loses her job in the shrinking petroleum industry. My son's salary falls faster than housing costs so he can't pay the rent from his own earnings. It takes a lot of courage for a country to make the commitment to look after everyone, to provide a minimum standard for everyone who needs it during the changeover years.

"Poor countries will shift from high-cost, low-income deprivation to a state of low-cost, low-income sufficiency. Some things will be easier for them. Overall, their welfare will be rising faster than ours because it is so low now. They, too, will have many losers along with the winners, and they don't have the safety nets we have. They need them, now. It can be done, must be done. We will assist with finance, time, effort, knowledge, and respect.

"Let me remind you now of the flip side of this coin, the darker side. The same knowledge and technologies that can set us free economically can also destroy us physically. So far, we have been reacting to organisms thrown at us by nature or god, the pandemics. Now we are also making organisms the size of nature's bacteria and giving them simple powers of reproduction and adaptive intelligence. If some get out of control, as tree flu almost did, they may create nandemics that will have to be fought to the death with surveillance, early warning, rapid communication, and real cooperation among countries, religions, Pharmacon, and the nanorg sub-sectors. We will see that this is done in the United States of America. Beyond our own borders, we pledge our full support to improve the containment, combat, and health systems of all countries.

"You can trust the GOP to take us down the road of conflict among countries and religions over new-tech, conflict much too easily lethal for every living being. Why risk this at precisely the moment of time when we can be free from want? The forces of change are at our doors and at our throats. Time, gentlemen."

Kat saw Beya release the breath she'd been holding from the start. Everyone was smiling — good sign. Someone flashed a thumbs-up from the gondola, which meant positive feedback from the online polls. The audience certainly seemed riveted. With anything similar on the home and world stage, things were looking up. Kat watched Beya breathe in as the senator continued.

"*We* will make the changes that are needed in America and in our relations with the world. Here is how, and why you will trust us to get this done.

"First, we need action on removing carbon from the atmosphere. The yearly series of floods, blizzards, earthquakes, hurricanes, tsunamis, and droughts are like the pandemics: catastrophes we have laid upon ourselves by failure of will on global warming. We now know for certain that our own turn surely comes. Soon we will not have enough resources even to save the victims unless we shrink carbon contamination now and fast. My administration will support and abide by the International Carbon Accord. We will finance carbon removal because a home planet that survives is a collective good. We will speed the transition to microbe and hydrogen energies. We will strongly seek international cooperation on these matters.

"Second, we need action on controlling nanorg and artificial intelligence. My administration will work through security, diplomatic, and civilian channels to keep everyone apprised of all dangerous and potentially perilous technology developments. We will cooperate fully with other nations and interests to prevent, contain, and eliminate threats.

"Third, while costs fall, we need safety nets that work for people hit by bad luck or bad timing. My administration will support sufficiency and retraining. We will cooperate with other countries in establishing their safety nets and quadruple our annual aid flows for as long as I am in office to assist in places of greatest need.

"Finally, along with all the governing skills needed to further our prosperity and freedoms, we need tolerance and cooperation. My administration will pursue these with vigour in every part of our work and every part of our world. We will press everyone to share knowledge more openly. Some religious and corporate powers will not respond in kind and may respond negatively, but we will persist. We will confront sworn enemies, but we will always seek new friends.

"Why will you trust us to do this? It is a fair question, and deserves a straight answer. We have the experience; the governors, congressmen and women, senators, corporate and civil leaders, thinkers and achievers. We have the biggest and most active base of support in business, labour, government, and civil society. We represent women more than in any election in our history. This concerns some. It should not. We are a party of men and women whose mission is to serve the people of America and the world.

"We have the right ideas for our time, which is at once so promising and so perilous. If you pause for a moment, you will know this. The old Republican mantra is bankrupt and fatal. Change takes place in steps. It is more important to be going in the right direction than to be getting there fast. At this moment in history, however, we have to do both. In the end, you will trust us because there is no sane alternative, because we will not fail you, and because every day of delay makes time more our enemy. Time, gentlemen."

The crowd erupted. Beya was grinning as Kat turned to look over the audience. A shot rang out and Kat whirled around. A tall kid materialized in front of the podium, then slumped. Hit by a bullet, she saw in a flash. Security hit the stage and the front line of tables as everyone dove for cover.

Lara screamed, and Kat caught a glimpse of Dylan alongside two FSA agents and a Chinese man who looked familiar. Phil had hold of Lara, so she sprinted in Dylan's direction, then ran smack into security. Another shot. It took two minutes for her to reach the square, cursing every step. Sandover found her in the mêlée, under the choppers overhead.

"Dylan's gone."

Somehow she knew. God, help us! Phil was gesticulating at two marines nearby who followed as he set off back to the arena. Sandover shouted in Kat's direction as he turned to join the sprint.

"Dylan went with two FSA men and Lianshen, out another exit or the roof. We'll get them. You're hurt, get help!"

Kat looked in dismay at the growing red stain where she was sure the right side of her body had been just a second ago. She caught a glimpse of fast-approaching medics, felt her shock-survival system boot into action, and passed out.

Desperation

Kat drifted in and out of consciousness. Dreams of Nigel Montgomery flooded the edges of her psyche, memories of lives lost, taken down, exiled in secrecy. Her head cleared an instant before sight resumed. Phil, Sandover, Beya. No one else. The urge to scream died in her throat as an NYPD policewoman brought them warm-looking mugs and some news. Kenzie Moore and Saba Luanzi had been evacuated immediately. No trace of Dylan yet. Lara was hysterical, Phil grim as death. By now they'd talked with everyone they could find, desperate for some kind of lead. The kid who took the first bullet was Chinese. He was rushed to an ambulance that disappeared on the way to the hospital.

"Disappeared?" Kat squeaked.

"Yes, I'm sorry to say that, in the panic, no one got an ID. It might have been part of the medical arrangements for tonight's event, but it could just as easily have been sitting nearby. They're checking all the official ones."

"Kid's name is Michael Ong," Phil added. "Someone recognized him. Works for Saba's campaign office, messages and errands. Was part of the arena set-up team. Clean record, orphan, mother was an immigrant in the Chinese-Korean-Latino garment trade. Father unknown, helped out by an aunt in Midtown, took college classes at night."

Later they learned that Lianshen had been invited to the Madison gala by Arlington Mayfair, his former boss in Shanghai when Mayfair was negotiating the financial services accords. Lianshen was working for a Hong Kong-based company called East Asia Trading. It was not clear whether he had gone with the men who took Dylan or had been taken, too. One lady said from a passing glimpse that he might have gotten in the way.

The shooter was a young man with a cross around his neck and a body full of Redemption, a powerful boutique drug. He used a small plastic gun, almost undetectable. He shot himself in the neck after his first shot missed the woman who would be president. The second bullet went right through his throat and into Kat's abdomen just below the rib cage. Video showed that the assassin's aim at Kenzie Moore was probably good, but Ong had been looking in that direction before he dove into the line of fire.

Kat and Phil went with Lara and a small army of security to the Helmsley to gather their possessions. Sandover and Beya went home with another squadron to pack up Justine and everything they would need for an unknown period of time. They were all brought to an FSA safe house near Princeton, ninety minutes from the city. Kat knew the area from trips with Phil to the Institute for Advanced Study. The Firestone Library tower flashed by and a glimpse of Nassau Inn before they continued out Stockton Street and the Old Post Road. On arrival, Lara accepted a mild sedative and Justine fell asleep, both under medical watch. Kat collapsed against Phil on a sofa muttering "don't let him die" through clenched teeth.

"We won't, Kat. We'll hear something soon. There has to be a reason. We have a lot of people helping us even if their real concern is Moore and Saba. If we don't get word soon, we'll get out of here and track them down. I know there's a way to help. I keep replaying what happened in there, looking for clues."

They turned up the ViD and huddled around. Sandover looked through the quarters for obvious bugs and then activated a small device that Kat made a note to ask him about later, no doubt another gift from Pyramid.

"There was an assassination and a kidnap," Sandover puzzled. "Were they planned together? And why Dylan?"

They were all shattered, but Phil made a show of shrugging it off.

"The assassination attempt looks like the Christian Right. They had everything to gain from the senator's death. At least that part backfired. Little doubt that the shooter planned to kill Kenzie Moore, then himself, like a suicide bombing. He half-succeeded. They haven't identified him yet. If the hardline born-again Bible thumpers did in fact put him up to it, they would know that there would be enough bedlam to pull off a kidnap."

Kat nodded as Sandover took up the thread. Her brain was coming back to life despite the pain. She'd been thinking along the same lines. The failed assassination would probably mean victory for Moore and Saba, but it was going to come at infinitely too high a cost. And it was going to be one hell of a fortnight till the election.

"Someone could have taken advantage of the mêlée to grab Dylan," Phil reasoned.

"To have agents on hand," Kat snapped, "just in case an unknown opportunity arose, seems a bit too accidental. We have to assume they were planned together."

"The only reason for taking Dylan is to get at us," Phil added. "And the obvious partner in crime for the Christian Right is Pharmacon. Abbott and J.C. have been our enemies since Merimbula. I'd be very surprised if we don't hear from them soon."

"They won't try to reach us while we're under a full-court FSA security press," Kat objected.

"We have another reason to get out of its shadow," Sandover added. "Pyramid will have information on what happened to Dylan and Lianshen. They had people watching all of us. They'll be tracking those two. Lianshen must be Pyramid, so he and Dylan both had pinpoint coms with locators. But Pyramid won't contact us here."

"We all push for a change of place," Phil summed up. "You and Beya have the best chance. Saba and the senator are going to need you both again immediately and you'll have plenty of security with them. You'll be able to use your communicators to contact Pyramid."

"We'll ask to be moved to a place near you," Kat pressed. "FSA won't do it unless we agree to surveillance, but they won't follow us into the bathroom. In the end, they'll see that we have to be clear of security some of the time in order to get Dylan back. Right now FSA is our best friend even if Pyramid is our best hope."

They were all running on empty, avoiding the same question. What if the kidnappers demanded information about the Orion transmission. Sandover was the first to broach the subject.

"Dylan has unusual talents, Kat, and Lianshen must be good if he's Pyramid's man in New York. Let's stay mum about the Orion messages until we hear. He's not my son, but no one has any reason to harm him before they demand ransom."

Kat couldn't help pushing back.

"Time is our enemy, Sandover. You're asking me to risk losing Dylan for some vague chance that we're saving humanity. We're being jerked around. I don't think I can do it. Maybe it's time to tell everyone what we know!"

Kat felt a surge of relief at the prospect, but Phil was fidgeting and finally caved in to his angst.

"Maybe, and don't hate me for this, Kat, but we're dealing with someone who tried to kill the next president of the United States. Something tells me not to turn over all our cards quite yet. They must be after what we know. If they learn everything they want, will they give him back? As long as they need something, he may be safe. Could you wait a day to see if they contact us?"

"I think Phil's right, Kat" Beya added. "Dylan's chances are better if we keep both options open. His life may depend on it."

That was not what a mother wanted to hear but it made some kind of distorted sense. Chess pieces on a board.

FSA took them back to New York the next day, to a new location. Nightfall brought their first chance to call out. Sandover had the pinpoint set ready. They had a second to offer a silent prayer as the outgoing signal blinked.

"Sandover?"

"Yes."

"Enlai here. You're at the Carleton on Madison Avenue? Can you talk?"

"Yes, but FSA is outside. Time is short"

"Lianshen went with Dylan. We followed his tracker, lost it in Providence. Watching every route. Van was seen by FSA informer. Full press is on."

"What does 'lost it' mean?"

"Not certain. Not good. Pharmacon active, Jihad, Christian Right, others. Expect demands soon."

Beya and Sandover hit the deck running the next morning, Justine with Beya, the election campaign overheated with accusations of treason. Kat fought desolation. The next chance to meet came a day later at the southeast corner of Madison Square, by the statue of Senator Roy Conkling, who froze to death in the great blizzard of 1888. Security was all around, but FSA silently recognized the elephant in the room. Beya's smile brightened the shadows, a silver lining around the deep abyss.

"We're clear from tomorrow, but I had to swear we'd *liaise* on all our movements."

"About time!" Kat growled. "I don't trust anyone to be what they claim any more. Even if FSA are friends, who says they'll be able to do the job without miscalculation. There's no room for error. My gut tells me it's time to go on offence. Time to plan the attack."

"They've heard from Édouard Moreau," Sandover revealed. "He wants to talk to Phil in Bordeaux. FSA has no evidence he's involved. French SIA wants to stall, but I say Phil has to go. Our friends are also there in number."

Kat was not about to stay home while Phil and Moreau weighed Dylan's life in the balance. Into the mouth of the lion.

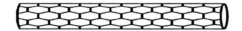

The small convoy rolled along the river, through Margaux toward Pauillac. Lara had looked so forlorn when they left her with Beya and Sandover, before Justine fastened onto her as only a two-year-old can. Kat imagined them all together, crowded but cozy, though in truth Beya and Sandover came and went at all hours as the campaign drew to an end. 'Maybe I should have stayed' was a thought running through her mind. Coming meant she didn't fully trust Phil. He would understand in time, if he didn't already. She was a lot better equipped for this. And she would do anything necessary to get Dylan back. It would be 3:00 am in NYC, ten more jobs for Beya to do before the day even started. It was a blessing for everyone to have Sandover on the inner election team, Saba's doing, mutual advantage. Sandover had brought new com gear for all of them with the message that it would melt down if tampered with.

The road opened onto the great expanse of the Gironde Estuary and the waterfront of Pauillac, bold white buildings and towers against the deep blue channel, tree-lined private roads, and then the massive stone pillars of Chateau Terre.

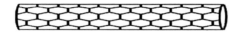

"Philamon Rush, Karyn Macaulay-Rush, it is a pleasure to meet you. May I offer you some refreshment after a long *voyage*? We make some delectable wines."

The accent was pure skunk perfume. The taste of a rare Terre red was tempting, but Kat wanted to smash his smug face too much to think about anything else. Food and drink were too dangerous anyway.

"Thank you Monsieur Moreau. I would like nothing better, but I am taking medicine which forbids alcohol. Please call me Kat."

"Kat, and Édouard *s'il vous plaît*. Let me come to the point. I am sure you do not think well of me. I believe I understand your reasons. Yet I do not wish you harm, nor your family or friends. I was alarmed to hear of your son's kidnapping. I have learned something about this matter which makes it imperative that we talk."

Here it comes. Kat nodded in Phil's direction, an old fencing gesture, *'en garde.'* Their mission was a kind of *prise de fer*, a lunge that pushes the opponent's tip safely off target while yours touches. If Dylan were hurt, her tip was going to more than touch this maggot! She breathed out and rearranged her body language as much as possible to signal *avance*, proceed when ready.

"Jean-Christophe tells me you will remember a colleague in Merimbula," Édouard resumed, "Mathias Abbott. We believe he is the back-office strategist of Golgotha, the Hill of Redemption, the militant wing of the US Christian Right. He is also the CEO of Galilee, as you know, a corporation not to be underestimated. We have worked with Galilee on commercial ventures. We think Golgotha is behind the assassination attempt and the kidnapping."

Good cop.

"I have learned through channels that they want to know about the Orion message. They believe you know more than you have said."

"Do you know if Dylan is safe?"

"I do not have full information, Kat, but I believe so."

"Do you think Golgotha will contact us?"

"I do not know. They are dishevelled after their clumsy failure to end the campaign of Senator Moore. I worry for your son. I could perhaps assist if I knew more about this curious transmission."

Flèche, the quick aggressive fling, in case the opponent is unwary. Said with such concern and sincerity. How she wished they were on the *piste*, tips uncovered! *Parry*, watch for an opening.

"Édouard, I will tell you everything we know. But I am very worried that you are going to be disappointed. I am sure you know more than we do. If we know different things, you are welcome to what we know."

"Who do you think sent this transmission from the direction of Orion?"

Riposte. Phil's glance said 'let me take this one.'

"Let me start one step back, Édouard. I believe the first intelligent patterns we received are not from humans. Why? Because everyone is still stumped by their complexity. I spend what adds up to hours a day talking to the people who are trying to just comprehend their technology, let alone understand what the patterns may mean."

Coupé, cut over. Phil continued the *feint*.

"Almost nothing has been learned yet. That may be unfair to the people who are trying, and it is true that we have to invent new tools before we can even map the Visitors' transmissions. I have to assume that the Visitors intended this. With their capability, they could surely approach lower-technology worlds in an understandable manner if they wanted. My best guess is that the Visitors are far away and unaware of us. They are sending transmissions out in every direction over long periods of time. Any other worlds and beings receiving these will also be propelled onto new paths, probably starting with communications, like us, unless they are too backward."

"Or too advanced," Édouard suggested, "perhaps even more so than the Visitors?"

"Who knows? Attempting to speculate on the risks the Visitors themselves may be taking pushes us into the realm of science fiction. The practical reality is that the Visitors could also be nearby, so we have to prepare. *De facto*, they are nearby. At first, I thought the Orion message was also from the Visitors, a simpler test for humans in a language closer to ours. Because Orion should be much easier to crack, we've worked on its meaning even harder. I keep track of this research, Édouard, but I don't do very much of it myself. As I understand, there are patterns and many repetitions in Orion. Although research has reconstructed one or two fragments, the stuff in between is still gobbledygook. It's as close to random as the world's best decryption methods can tell. If you have any different information, we would be very interested to know."

"You are very convincing, Philamon, but I can see from many angles that you are involved in much more than studying the meaning of these messages. Equally interesting, your wife and friends have powerful connections."

Coupé lancé, a flick of the blade. Phil's body said *second intention*, feinting your opponent into thinking this is your final action while setting up a second. The movements and patterns of combat become instinctive after scores of repetitions.

"You asked who I thought sent the Orion transmission, Édouard. As everyone seems to believe now, there is the likelihood that it is of human origin. I am not convinced. But no one has succeeded in proving or disproving this. So we are back to basics, back to working on the meaning of the message."

"*Pourquoi*? To what end?"

Phil's stance said *retreat*, over to you, Kat.

"You have to remember that the four of us were on the front line for the Orion message, Édouard. Phil and I also experienced the Visitors' patterns first hand. These were defining moments for humanity and even more so for us. We want to know the answers, an addiction that most of the people from the listening stations suffer. I would be surprised if Jean-Christophe were not the same."

Successful *flunge*. Kat killed a smile as a wrinkle crossed Édouard's brow. Jean-Christophe's reputation preceded him everywhere and, better still, he was a thorn in his father's pride.

"He sends his regrets from Jasbhat, detained by operational demands."

Jasbhat was the centre of Terrepharm's growing operations base in the former Turkmenistan, near the meeting point of its southern borders with Afghanistan and Iran. They had braced themselves for encountering J.C. here in Bordeaux. His absence was a relief but a disadvantage. Unlike his son, Édouard revealed few weaknesses, offered little to exploit.

"Again you make a good case, Kat, but again there are many odd parts to this story. Philamon is involved in Pinpoint, nanorg and FreeIP. You are both close to the Lees, whose power has risen remarkably. You are all guarded by friends of Pyramid. You are all wealthy. You communicate with the best hardware and encryption. It is very difficult to see you as amateur scientists and sleuths."

Ballestra, jump and stamp. Phil responded immediately, forestalling the follow up *flèche*.

"I can understand how that looks, Édouard. But please let me continue with the matter of the transmission. *If* Orion came from humans, they have advanced technology. As I understand, the only realistic case is that the message was sent from a satellite. Who could do this? I am trained as a communications specialist, experienced in the deep-space listening program, along with the underlying theory and its technologies. If I weren't interested in these questions, you would be even more suspicious. So, yes, I did get involved. I started devouring everything I could find on the newest advances in communications. I went to a conference at Stanford and met Ben Singer. He was about to launch Pinpoint and asked me to join the board. I was delighted because this gave me a window into the frontiers of a field that might yield some clue about the Orion message and the Visitors."

"Very well," Édouard conceded, "but coming a little closer to home, why does a communications expert get involved in nanorganic technologies and products?"

"I asked myself the same questions that others were asking. Who would send these transmissions? And why? This is where I fear to disappoint. Compared to you, I have little direct access to military or commercial intelligence. And Beya's knowledge is classified way beyond my level of clearance. I'll tell you what I know about Pyramid in a minute. My guess is that the Orion transmission uses some very advanced form of pinpoint technology. If so, there is quite a large range of possibilities in terms of how far the satellite has to be from Earth and how powerfully the transmission must be broadcast. Who could have done this? Anyone around Singer, for example, might have taken the pinpoint idea to new levels. I've looked for clues among his inner circle but I don't see those people often enough. I'm sure the intelligence agencies are watching them closely. I imagine you know more about them than I do."

"Perhaps, but this is still about communications. Why nanorg?"

"Sorry, I was getting there. I don't know who sent Orion so I ask 'why?' And who today could have such motives and capabilities? It is a very elaborate and expensive project. It was probably started not long before Orion was sent, if you had to bet, because the knowledge of pinpoint wasn't around much before then. The project needed concealed satellite launch capability, or an alliance with someone who had it. My candidates are the US, China, Russia, the Islamic Alliance, Christian Right, and Pharmacon."

"You overestimate our reach," Édouard said, "though we will certainly pay more attention to extraterrestrial matters in future."

"Hence your launch facilities in Turkmenistan?"

"*Touché.*"

"I don't mean to accuse or judge, Édouard. I am concerned about the use of space and who controls it. But unlike you, this is beyond my influence. If there are powers-that-be that can use pinpoint to communicate on Earth, why would any of them send messages to the world in some kind of code?"

"Good question, Philamon. What is your conclusion? And how is this related to nanorganics?"

Moreau knew the moves well, a sudden *extend*, used for attacks in distances too close for a lunge. Kat's instinct said *sixte*, cover the fencing arm. Her turn. Perhaps they could outlast him tag-team. But fatal mistakes end skirmishes, seldom lack of endurance. Phil looked her way. If he had an *épée*, it would be tip-to-floor. Kat moved slightly forward.

"It has to be a wakeup call of some kind, Édouard. One or more groups on Earth understand it. So why all the mystery, why not just tell everyone there's a plague coming or whatever? This gets a little clearer when you look at how we have all reacted. We've assumed any number of plots and conspiracies with and without the Visitors in the mix. The result has been to put everyone on high alert. We asked ourselves why anyone would want to do that, and began to read about everything that seemed most dangerous. Global warming, but that was already understood. Artificial intelligence — you remember the Terminator movies — but we are not yet that close to machines that think. Except perhaps for tiny machines — nanorg."

"Ah. So you chose my corner of the world as the subject of the wakeup call?"

"Yes. We couldn't identify any threat greater than the combination of nanorg and AI — the nanorg bots. Phil looked into FreeIP because Claudia Lorca Cortez also had a special interest in keeping nanorg developments open to view. I am sure you disagree with her and us on this, but again, even if we are your opponents, we are not your enemies."

"And Damien Benedykt?"

"I met him last week," Phil responded. "He seems to know as much as anyone about nanorg bot security, at least outside the proprietary boundaries of industry. He is expecting me to visit him again this week."

"You have a curious habit of showing up where big changes are taking place. Let me suggest a different story. One of you understands the Orion message. Perhaps it was a wakeup call, but it was sent to you. It directed you to investigate the pinpoint and nanorg technologies. Someone is using you for their purposes."

Attack, subtlety abandoned. Kat's instincts reacted.

"We've thought about that a lot, of course, Édouard. Pyramid is protecting us. We believe this is on account of Sandover and his father, Eng Kai. Sandover knows more, but not a lot more. He communicates with contacts he has not met. He believes that one of them knew Lianshen, who disappeared with our son. FSA is looking hard for them with no success so far. I would again be surprised if you did not know more about him than I do."

Kat's *riposte* bought time and seemed to puzzle Moreau.

"Lianshen is certainly Pyramid, Kat. His immediate friends are known. But they are a triad and they have very advanced coms, so we cannot discover much about the rest of Pyramid's network. It would be naïve to believe that they are altruistic, not interested in power and control."

"I agree, but to what end? No one seems to know. Pyramid may just be after profit for their shareholders. Isn't that the case with Terrepharm? Some say they have a darker agenda, but Sandover's knowledge and our investigations say they have a clean record so far, a benign history, however brief."

"It is not so brief and not so free of self-interest. You might also wish to reconsider where your friend Sandover fits into their plans."

"If you have information we don't, please tell us, but you have to understand that we trust Sandover. You are going to need him and people like him in public office in the coming years. He is no more your enemy than I am. And it is what you and Pharmacon do with nanorg that will be decisive to a future we hope to see."

"It is not too much to hope, Philamon, but it may be too much to expect. You make a mistake in overlooking one fundamental rule of power in this world. We live and fight in a very imperfect time. You may think of us as the bad guys. In our view we are doing something good. In no one's estimation are we close to being the worst guys. The worst guys will attack first and ask questions later. If they have enough ammunition, they will take you out along with everyone in the vicinity. No doubt you have a sense of the dangers you face, but do not underestimate them. If the bad guys win, there is no second chance."

"I believe you are right, Édouard, and regardless of that, you will pursue your interests as you see them. What I want to say is that we are not serous players in this game. We are involved partly by accident and partly by our own choosing. Sandover has asked Pyramid not to protect us, because it just attracts attention and risk. So far they have not heeded his request."

"They are right, Philamon, and you are lucky. The bad guys would torture you without a moment's pause, just in case you know something of value. Your son would not be alive. I do not think that Golgotha are among the worst, but they are fanatical and they can't decide between paranoia and exaltation at the prospect of the Visitors. They have factions. It does not surprise me that one of them looks to have taken your son. Yet I am merely a messenger. The sender was not precisely identified to me, though the message was simple, to tell you they will give your son back if you tell what you know about Orion."

Kat knew they were running out of rope. If it came down to Dylan's life or what they knew, it was going to be an easy choice, *Disengage*. But Phil's stubborn defences were by now on auto pilot as he re-entered the fray, *parry, remise*, resume the attack without withdrawing.

"I am running out of things to tell you, Édouard. Can I ask you why they did not contact us directly? Surely they would not want to share with you what we are supposed to know, if they could avoid it."

"I cannot answer that. They must have their reasons. Perhaps they do not know how to ask you directly. Having an intermediary may be their only way to keep the big security agencies at arm's length. As we are working closely with Galilee on private ventures these days, they would think of me in this situation."

"Then we are asking you, Édouard, pleading with you, to convey that there is nothing we can add to their knowledge of Orion or nanorg or pinpoint. No parent would risk their child for nothing."

Kat wondered if Édouard would risk Jean-Christophe, but this was definitely not the time to ask. They were on very thin ice here as she plunged on.

"If we knew more about Orion, we would say it to everyone, Édouard. Why not? And if we have to back off on exploring pinpoint and nanorg to get Dylan back, Phil and I will do it immediately. Beya and Sandover would, too, but they can't avoid some parts of it without quitting their jobs with the Democrats and the WEO."

"There is still something about the picture that bothers me, Philamon. Too much coincidence. You get accustomed to looking for it in my business. Like game spotting, it's not the lion that you see first but the bit of the picture that is not quite the landscape. To take an example, there is your wife's relatively brief but dramatic history with British intelligence and her periodic visits to the consulate in New York."

Phil rose to Kat's defence as a diversion rather than an act of chivalry.

"That was before we met, Édouard. I know, of course, about Kat's past in counterterrorism. From what she's told me recently, the British have asked her a lot of the same questions you've just posed, and her response has been what we've just told you."

"Then there is the matter of the communications system you use being beyond decryption, beyond the leading edge."

"The handsets come from Sandover and Pyramid. I don't know how they work. We've been told they will self-destruct if opened."

A pause in the conversation lengthened into a gap as Édouard stared through narrowed eyes. They prayed that Phil's last bit of misdirection might be enough to turn his blade from its main target. Finally he heaved a sigh.

"Well, then let me ponder further and attend to some other pressing matters. Will you stay the night?"

"With regret, Édouard, we had no choice but to promise FSA we would return to their care."

"Understood, Kat. They will know more than I, by the way, about the Golgotha factions. I will send a message concerning our discussion and I pray that when it reaches its ultimate recipient, through channels beyond my knowledge and control, your son will be returned to you."

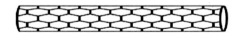

Kat didn't think Édouard bought their story. Back at their *pension* in Bordeaux, Phil agreed. They didn't trust his motives any more than he trusted theirs, 'too much coincidence,' in his own words. If he or Golgotha cranked the pressure up another notch, they would have to spill it all. Right or wrong, they wouldn't go further than this. Life would get really bizarre with inter-place-time communication out of the bag. Even if everyone thought it was nonsense, all four would be under minute scrutiny and intense suspicion, simply because they understood the code and content of Orion. Dylan's release was no more certain in that scenario than if they kept their secrets. Kat knew she wouldn't sleep, but after several hours of debriefing FSA and talking to Phil, she fell into a hard bed on the banks of the Garonne. Raucous birds filled the air in her nightmare, searching for carrion.

Morning brought grey light over the river and the pont de Pierre. They waited with Commander Dale Goswin, who bristled with bottled energy. No news. They made small talk, got a refresher course on FSA counterterrorism, counterintelligence, counternarcotics, covert action, special ops, paramilitary, and '*other*' operations. FSA special staff took pride in their counterterrorist and hostage rescue ops, particularly their ability to 'take down' any type of vehicle, aircraft, ship, building, or other facility when necessary. They weren't taking any chances here. The force at hand was reassuring, but only if it wasn't going to be needed.

Goswin's communicator activated and he set out down the hall. Minutes. He came back looking positive but tense.

"Maurizio Torbido, right hand of Édouard Moreau, was taken captive in Turkmenistan last night or early this morning in the desert. His compound was heavily armed, protected as well by a branch of the old Turkoman army. The raid was carried out by a paramilitary unit with minimum damage to property and life. No indication that your son was there. It could have been done by the Chinese, Russians, Iranians, Pyramid, even by us. If I knew I wouldn't tell you, for everyone's protection. Someone is sending a powerful message."

A recurring pattern, Kat thought.

They called Beya, just to talk, since FSA were also keeping her briefed. Very hard to be confident, but this might be good for Dylan. Especially if Moreau were more than a messenger. Or even if he were only a messenger but held enough power over Galilee and Golgotha. Too many ifs, too little time, and not enough information. While events were unfolding in faraway places, it was humbling to be no more than a half-informed bystander in your own life.

"Your son is back safely."

The room was spinning. Thank the Gods!

"Was he hurt?"

"He's fine. He was dropped off at the police station in Hopkins Hollow, Rhode Island, three hours from New York. Your daughter is on her way there with the Lees and a convoy. Are you all right?"

"Thank you, just a bit stunned."

"Maurizio Torbido was dropped off moments ago at Château Terre. His transit time from Turkmenistan was extremely rapid given the distance. Another convincing demonstration of power, if you want my opinion. Whoever did this has backed down both Pharmacon and Golgotha. Whoever didn't do it will be very wary of that kind of intelligence, mobility, and punch.

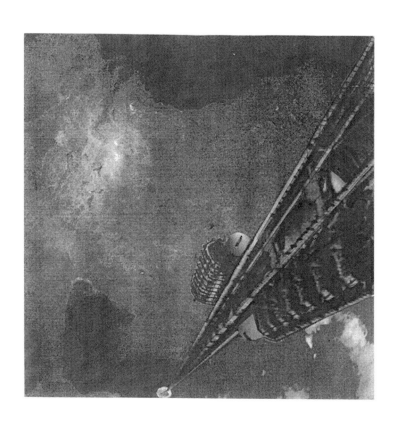

Spacelift

Kat and Phil arrived back in New York the next morning, the first of November, exactly one week before the election. Although security around them remained tight, the tension had eased a notch. Dylan's capture had had an unexpected effect on him, shifting him into a higher gear. He wanted to know everything. The media pursuing him got bored quickly enough when he stuck with the few facts he knew. Privately, he absorbed every shred of intelligence and began to study their implications. More like Sandover than Phil, Kat realized with a shock of recognition. She told Dylan and Lara a little more, but not the whole story.

They learned from Sandover that Lianshen's replacement was none other than Chuanli. When they asked, they were told that Lianshen was gone and not to worry, he knew what he risked. They were dismayed by this sacrifice and depressed by their guilt. Kat and Phil stole a rare hour that night with Beya and Sandover. In a gentle way, Kat asked Sandover what he really knew about Pyramid, recalling Moreau's pointed suspicions.

"Of course, I grew up with the rumours and some bits of fact. Now I can imagine better how they function, though I still don't have any hard knowledge. I didn't see any point in passing on my guesses to you, but I was wrong. We need to have the clearest picture we can put together. Where there's smoke there's fire. Moreau was right about something else: worse guys could have done this. Looking back, from the moment we decided to hide the meaning of the Orion message, something like this was going to happen. I still don't know if we're lucky to have the protection now or stupid not to have told everything then. Ironically, we were also lucky that Moreau was involved."

"Maybe, but Édouard had to be in on it, not just a messenger."

"No doubt, Kat. He's a clever man. He'll just beef up other alliances while Golgotha and Galilee are getting back on their feet. He's not fussy about his friends and he certainly believes in diversifying his portfolio. You can bet he'll push ahead with Terrepharm's spaceport in Turkmenistan."

"Right about that," Phil agreed. "When he speaks in public about orbital habitats, his eyes light up. Torbido's extraction may have been a setback for Terrepharm and Pharmacon, but only a small one and he'll learn from it."

"Did you see his interview on Euroview last week?" Beya asked. "I caught a replay. He scoffed at people who say the big congloms are dinosaurs, boasted that they're still running the world economy and that they'll soon be controlling Earth orbit and outer space. They're looking at manufacturing moon habitats and starting migratory expeditions. When asked if he would join the space elevator conglomerate, he called it open-source fantasy and said he'd be happy to lead a corporate takeover when the daydreamers fouled up construction costs and security."

"I hope he rots in hell."

Everyone looked at Kat. She'd said it like she intended it to happen sometime soon.

"In the interim," Phil reasoned, "he controls most of nanorg one way or another."

"He'll take the nanorg development teams into space as fast as he can."

Kat imagined a day of reckoning, feeling no mercy.

"We have to know his movements," Sandover warned, "his dealings in China, Russia, the Stans, and Iran. We have to get inside his American religious and political affiliates, who he's bought, who owes him. A lot of this can be done with Beya in the White House."

Subliminally, Sandover was organizing the troops. This was timely, Kat's instincts told her, a direction to support.

"Phil and I can concentrate on Crucible, FreeIP, Ellis, Damien Benedykt, and the corridors of science and knowledge," she added. "We'll take the Brits, you concentrate on Pyramid. We'll need secure coms for all the core network."

"Pyramid has a big lead in that field," Sandover agreed, "and Chuanli says they won't lose it any time soon. They've leapfrogged Singer, or they started ahead. If the Imputers and Singer also join our cause, we have a chance to catch Pharmacon and its rogue allies off guard. If you count FSA as well, we'd have the best handle on hardware and security against their lead in nanorg. I'll ask for pinpoint coms for our close friends."

"We're playing a tricky game here," Phil reflected. "Most of our networks function only because they're open to everyone."

Sandover stopped them in their tracks by voicing what they all knew in their own ways.

"Pinpoint and nanorg are the keys to the future. They may be more connected than we thought. If AI gets embedded in nanorg, smart pinpoint will be its trigger and its control. We need Ben Singer and Damien Benedykt if we can persuade them. And it's past time to have a serious chat with Ellis."

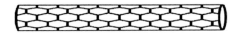

Kat got the ViD feed from Sandover before it hit the evening news. The calming voice of virtual reality's best-known narrator exuded an earnest confidence, flanked onscreen by breath taking photos and mock-ups of the space elevator's construction.

"It is described as 'the greatest open-source project of all time.' Starting at one end on Banks Island off the northern tip of Australia, Spacelift will rise ninety kilometres in a very gradual arc to the outer edge of the atmosphere's mesosphere layer. From there it will continue its arch for just under four thousand kilometres to the asteroid at its far end."

"That's Fuller," Phil interjected.

"While the cable is only about one-ninth the circumference of the Earth at this longitude, the shadow of the lift cable falls along a path through Sumba, Nusa Tenggara, and Timor at the bottom of southern Indonesia — missing the Seychelles before crossing to Africa. From Tanzania, Malawi, Zambia, and Angola the line proceeds across the Atlantic and over the north end of Brazil, Bolivia, and Peru, as foretold by the Incas, just north of Lima and Huancayo. Then it crosses the open Pacific, barely missing the south end of Nake and Tuhuata in the Marquesas and Vostok in Polynesia. The trajectory continues north of the Melanesian Obelisk, Bass, Tumakon and Treasurers Islands, between the Solomon Islands of Nilogo and Pileni, over Papua-New Guinea and on to its point of departure at Banks, northwest of Badu, facing east over a coral sea and what once seemed endless ocean.

"If it came down, the cable would be severed at all points where it met the oceans, and the oceanic portions would sink, dragging along the shallower reefs under them as they domed downward toward the ocean floor. Research on ocean impacts concludes that these risks, while not prohibitive, are serious. The people who would suffer need to be insured. Tsunami warning systems are adequate now, thanks to the serial destructions of the aughts and teens.

"Current design puts the cable's diameter at just four metres, just thirteen metres around it's girth — forty footfalls. It is entirely hollow in the middle, with thin walls of woven nanotubes. Two exterior tracks, and a third small rapid track for service and security, form stripes on the slightly bowed four-thousand-kilometre span.

"The total volume of the cylinder's walls is over two million cubic metres. Each kilometre contains over fifty cubic metres of mass, a very considerable load. Once the cable is made, there is nothing that will corrode it. This prevents leaching of toxic materials into surrounding ecosystems.

"The elevator's construction is nano, not organic. The only smart part is the segment where the cable bridges space and the upper atmosphere. As the carbon cable is spun downwards from the asteroid, a smart collar will be lowered around it, made of materials designed to adjust their properties to fend off the enormous heat and mechanical stresses. Once further down, the cable may be buffeted by atmospheric winds and storms, even hurricanes, but its material is strong enough to withstand any abuse from nature. If these sound like famous last words, the Consortium claims that the cable would survive collision with a megajet, with a wide margin of safety."

The large screen behind simulated the elevator cable's giving way, stretching out but not breaking its arc as a megaliner collided head on. Kat wasn't sure the reminder of 9/11 was the best PR and doubted the cable would be so resistant to attack by explosives, or nanobots programmed to turn a portion of it into spaghetti.

"Once the cable descends well into the atmosphere, the first two-way transportation track is built down, then the carbon extractors lowered and turned on. Gentlemen, start your engines. Energy comes from huge solar nanofilaments placed above and around the asteroid, transmitted through near superconducting filaments woven into the cable between the three tracks on its surface.

"No one expect Spacelift to come down, of course, and the band of destruction would be both narrow and almost entirely in the South Pacific Ocean. Short of the unexpected, the few people in its path could flee in time."

"What's that mean?" Kat snorted.

"Maybe somebody nudges the asteroid into a different path, toward Earth," Phil ventured. "There's always human error, especially with something designed and built by such a large assortment of ventures and people."

"And the asteroid?"

"On its way. It had to be pointed wide of Earth, of course. You remember the Near Earth Asteroid Prospector program about a decade ago? Of the millions of asteroids larger than one kilometre in diameter that circle the Sun, NEAP set out to find a few. They sent out a micro satellite, launched as a secondary payload on a European Ariane 5 expendable launch vehicle. For a mere fifty million, they got good surveys of asteroids picked out by earlier Hubble probes. Spacelift bought the information on the best four asteroids and narrowed in on the two dubbed Fuller and Bucky. At twenty kilometres in diameter, Fuller has an iron-nickel metal core and plenty of accessible carbon throughout its slightly elliptical body."

Phil was in his element now, science fiction come to life.

"As we speak," he continued, "Spacelift is preparing for the mission to nudge Fuller into geosynchronous Earth orbit, four thousand kilometres above Banks. I'm sure you've heard the furor *that's* causing. It's a very big object to ease into orbit safely. Unsafely is unacceptable. This will be an immediate concern for the next US administration — for Moore and Saba, we hope. If it's accomplished, the rest of Spacelift's plans could fall into place quickly. Then they push Bucky in next to Fuller, a five-kilometre sidekick and the place for the more perilous nanorg experiments. But I'm boring you."

"Not at all, I have a feeling about this Bucky."

"I'm not surprised. Once the near end of the cable is close to Earth, they spin down a very slender nanotube tether that will be guided to the ground by a small pack of mammoth dirigibles and their 'tug-plane' guides. 'Point Zero' at Banks Island is already on the road to becoming a busy space port. The aerial transport business is in a pre-boom frenzy, producing bizarre combinations of planes and choppers from high-speed, low-lift 'chanes' to pondering workhorse 'ploppers.'"

"Do you really think the elevator can be protected from terrorism? If the world sees it as a symbol of human achievement and future opportunity in space, won't all the nutbar fundamentalists see it as the grand prize?"

"No doubt, Kat. But it's pretty tough. It will have constant protection from many countries, on the cable and in the air. Only small weapons will be allowed on the elevator for security personnel."

"Trust me, Phil, there's always someone crazier than the last one, and it only takes one."

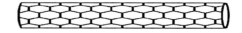

Breathe, Kat told herself. While Phil was home with the kids, she would take their passports to the British embassy along with her own. By way of preparation, FSA had asked State, which had contacted the British ambassador to arrange for Kat's visit to the embassy. A little over the top, she thought, but nice to be ferried around with such dedicated company. She had few illusions about MI8's motives, and the Americans were clearly a little uncomfortable with her periodic visits to the elegant Midtown glass towers of Her Majesty's terrain in Manhattan.

The Americans were also dying to get their hands on the pinpoint communicators, but knew about their anti-intrusion and internal meltdown systems. Lara and Dylan wore theirs soberly on cords around their necks, out of sight, the newest handsets having just arrived. Kat told FSA what she had told Moreau. The tales we spin, she reflected, and the ways we are spun! But having come this far, Phil was right — they needed to keep everyone ignorant of their inner secrets for some time longer.

The shape of the lie was now fairly clear. The blood of her ancestors told her that both kids understood it. They trusted their parents to be telling the truth or to be covering something up for good reason. 'Wronged innocent' was a comfortable role for Dylan, for a while after the kidnapping, a way for him to vent rage against his captors and the terror of helplessness. Underneath, his determination was icy as he devoured every scrap of information about Golgotha, Galilee, Pharmacon, and Pyramid. Beya helped Lara and Dylan to rebuild their balance and confidence.

FSA had got a flat for Kat and Phil in the same building as Beya and Sandover. Very considerate and easier for all. They had a corner suite with the general appearance of the old Chelsea Hotel and a narrow view southeast to the East River as it flows into Upper New York Bay. A nice sliver of a view of Midtown, too. Every place and moment around them seemed imbued with its own grace and history.

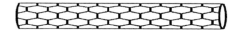

The wedge and tower of the British embassy appeared ahead as Kat pulled into the compound. A rather handsome young man opened the limo door.

"This way, please, Ms. Macaulay."

It was no accident, she knew, that they continued to use her maiden name. It reminded her of earlier years and loyalties. They entered the Empire, passing photos of PM David Mulholland from his recent visit. After corridors, elevators, and keyed-entry rooms, they reached a surprising library with the roof a dome of glass. Clearly, she was not headed for the passport desk. As she entered a glass-walled office, the young man bowed and a familiar figure turned from his view over south Manhattan.

"Kat. A pleasure to see you again."

"Nigel, what a lovely surprise, I didn't know you were posted to New York."

"Not, actually. In the neighbourhood, Assassination attempt and all that. Heard from the Chief you were coming in for passports. We'll look after those, not to worry."

Kat paused to gather her wits as she fished the old passports and application forms out of her all-purpose urban bag. Plausibly in the neighbourhood, she thought, but their meeting would have been planned with the ambassador and the Foreign Office, no doubt MI8 and other 'friends,' too. Too many memories of the Firm, too much of a past with Nigel. Kat saw little flags of caution dancing between them, union jacks nonetheless.

"Thank you, Nigel, that saves an age of standing in line with rosy-cheeked young Britons, feeling my age."

"Not so old, if memory serves."

"It has always served you well, Nigel, and our country. But it seems that a decade of motherhood and life in the colonies, as we like to call ourselves, has brought me to a different place."

"And yet, perhaps in a full circle."

"I doubt it. Tell me where have you been, what are you up to?"

"Ach, well, pretty much the same as ever, except I've been put in charge of strategy on top of ops and it's all got a smidgen more complicated. A knowledge economy, as they say, so for us humble servants much more to do. At the moment, I am concerned with the events in which your family and friends were involved, events with large implications regarding global balances. You were among the best at seeing the minds and motives of the players, my dear, almost too good."

"I know my reputation, Nigel, and I do enjoy flying around at night on the broomstick."

"Quite. So what do you make of all this?"

"I'm sure there's nothing I can tell you about facts, Nigel. If there is, your friends and company have lost some polish. So let's get right to the scenarios, if I recall the drill."

"We speak of scenario building and confirmation these days. A higher demand for accuracy, without enough tools, I might add, in a world of growing opacity. But we try. Please."

"Right. I imagine you are more concerned with the big picture than with the details of Dylan's abduction and return, or Torbido's for that matter. Detail underlies a viable scenario but let's start with the broad brush, some postulates from what we think we know. The Visitors are real, with all that implies. You and I have both been through it all a hundred times in our heads and with 'friends.' We know almost nothing about them, but they have not yet been hostile."

Memories intruded. They had been close. *Back to the future*, Kat admonished herself as she continued.

"Since their presence was first detected, new technologies have appeared. We now strongly believe that one of these was used to send the Orion transmission before emerging as pinpoint comtech. A connection between the Visitors, pinpoint, and the Orion message is a viable scenario. Equally viable, I believe, would be prior discovery of these technologies here on Earth, with no connection between them and the Visitors. Both scenarios raise essentially the same questions about who, when, and why. The *humans-only* theories can be investigated, whereas the Visitors really cannot."

"Indeed. Notwithstanding, we have had partial success at best in confirming specifics of 'humans only.' Pyramid, for example."

"They fit well in either scenario, Nigel. They could be the Visitors' contacts or the technology innovators. But I think neither. Even if they could grab Torbido, it looks like they don't by themselves have the capability for satellite launch. In the words of Édouard Moreau, 'you are lucky to have their

145

protection.' But it comes at a high price. Although Pyramid are a key player, they don't dominate in every dimension."

"Interesting. Brings me to ask about your own apparent prominence in this interlocking array of mysteries."

"Not so prominent, Nigel, and not so pleasant. I was treated very well when I left the service, as you know. I watched out for Her Majesty in Merimbula. Since then I've drifted into a different world, to the extent I'm a player at all. I help Phil with his research and networks. We are suspected of knowledge we don't have. I almost lost my son for that. For nothing."

"Appalling abduction. I need not tell you how delighted we were at Dylan's return. We were surprised at the circumstances."

"That's not reassuring, but good to know."

"We have already spoken about Pyramid my dear, but what about Pinpoint? Ben Singer's company commercialized the technology of the Orion transmission."

"Phil watches Pinpoint, Nigel. He knows Ben Singer well, but he's not there often. No signs of furtive connections, with the Visitors, Pyramid, or anyone else. Pyramid use superior comtech that has to be produced somewhere. I think China."

"Our observation does not rule this out. Yet there is something odd here. You remember the conceptual tests back in training, the one with the diagram that had a part cleverly drawn inside out, once you saw it? It's like that. So I ask you to think about this and let me know if any further scenario building comes to mind."

"I'll do what I can, Nigel. Some things I may believe to be true, but have so little confirmation that I keep them to myself. It's better that way. We should talk when the need arises."

"Now and then. One more thing, Kat, if I may presume. We are working to develop a trustworthy relationship with Pyramid, not at the top, just a working communication channel. I know that your primary loyalties are to your family and to Sandover and Beya, but I can assure you that your safety and theirs are also our first thought. This comes from the top. Dennis, the young man you met on the way in, will stay in touch. I am only an instant away, Kat, a call or a wave of the hand."

What she didn't need just now was Nigel Montgomery watching over her shoulder. Was the connection to Pyramid Nigel's main objective? She thought not. Nigel knew what everyone learned the hard way, that a network is as strong as its weakest link.

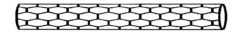

Kat watched a bright scarlet cardinal slip off its branch and swoop low over the snow-dusted grass. The endless renovation of St. Nicholas Park was by all appearances finished. Kids of all varieties played soccer on the once-sketchy grassland of this seventeen-block serpent in the heart of upper Harlem. Above a low line of green and yellow trees rose City College with its main sanctuary and two side-towers, a spitting image of two nights on a chess board, a powerful bishop hovering between. Grey stone and green ivy brought an unwelcome reminder of grey goo and green mush, the twin bogeys of nanotech.

Familiar with the routes and corridors, Phil ushered her through the nanorg labs. Damien Benedykt was sometimes hard to read beneath the folksy public persona. There was definitely something else, but the practised air of informality in his manner spoke of habit and caution. Kat surveyed the well-worn office as Damien prepared herbal tea.

"Take the leather chair, Mrs. Rush, it has the best view of the park. Thank you for coming, I enjoyed our first meeting."

"Kat, please."

"Damien, then. Informality is a luxury in a life scrutinized by the public. Don't win a Nobel Prize."

"I think we can rule that out, Damien," Phil suggested, "in my case, anyway. My intentions are good but my steps always wander from theory to practice. The advice is appreciated, though. I'll remember when those annoying Norwegians are hounding me to accept!"

Damien paused over a long sip of tea.

"I see from the media that you have in fact been a *cause célèbre* of late. My wife and I are very happy for your son's return and sorry for your horror. Our children are younger. I'm afraid I have been rather preoccupied with science. Our marriage surprised us both only a few years ago. We, too, have concerns for our children, because of the public attention around us. But if I am not being inappropriate, Phil, why would your son be a target for kidnappers? I ask because my wife and I are worried about the extra attention and danger that follows you around."

"I understand," Phil responded. "What is an applied scientist like me doing in the middle of a presidential assassination and kidnap?"

"Quite. And in the midst of pinpoint and nanorganic technologies, the latter I assume the reason for your visits."

Nothing ventured, nothing gained. Phil nodded.

"It's a longish story, Damien, and you know the main events.. Visitors' and Orion transmissions, pinpoint comtech and nanorg. Kat and I got involved in Merimbula with the Orion transmission after studying the Visitors' patterns. All remain unsolved."

"Though they have sprouted some new technologies in the attempt, it would seem."

"Yes, I agree with you. Some argue that pinpoint was already coming. Also nanorg, which you know so much better than I. Perhaps the transmissions have pushed things ahead more rapidly than otherwise, but what is the counterfactual? These sciences yield powerful enough tools to give decisive advantage to one or another of the powers that be. They also present a panoply of other promises and risks. Health, safety, equity, environment, survival, development of inner space. Our interest in these opportunities and dangers got us entangled with political and power groups."

"You also have friends in high places, higher next week I would think if the polls are accurate."

"Indeed, and because of Sandover and his family, we apparently have some strong protection. Without going into detail, it looks like they made the kidnappers an offer they couldn't refuse."

"Pyramid?"

"Yes, with Golgotha on the opposite side to the best of our knowledge, which falls far short of complete. FSA has also been generously protective."

"And what did the kidnappers want from you, if I may ask?"

"Information. They believe that we've made some progress with either the Visitors' patterns or the Orion message. They may still believe it, so we don't feel entirely out of danger. I am nevertheless hopeful that Kat and I at least will fade from view because we don't know anything new. And because of our allies."

"Let us hope so. Your allies are quite convincing. But you are in every corner of the picture, Phil, both of you — from an outsider's view, you understand. So you must in some way have a unique perspective."

Kat saw an opportunity.

"I believe someone foresaw great danger in nanorganic developments, Damien. At the same time, they had advanced comtech, or were developing it, or perhaps solved the Visitors' messages enough to obtain it."

"You don't think the Visitors are close at hand?"

"Possibly, but probably not yet. If they are, they're keeping a very low profile. I think the Orion message is a simpler code, aimed by the sender to alert someone who could unscramble the puzzle. While the signal and language of Orion are complex, those of the Visitors are truly alien. If the Visitors sent Orion as well, they are nearby, or they have sensitive enough ears to have learned our ways. Maybe someone Earthside has sent messages back to them. We have all been working very hard to grasp what the Orion message says."

Kat didn't think they had said any outright falsehoods so far, but they were certainly stretching the limits of deliberate misdirection. That wasn't good. Damien looked trustworthy and they needed his trust.

"Damien, I fully appreciate that you excel in nanorganic science and that the rest of this is not your war."

"It is, actually, Kat. More than you might think. Your view is widely held, that the messages are all designed to deliver a nanorganic danger warning. So there are a lot of people interested in what I know or am thinking or may be contemplating. The last two years have toughened me up considerably, after the festivities in Stockholm. Scrutiny has exploded and keeps escalating. It's got to the point where I have to communicate exceedingly carefully even with colleagues I trust. Our R&D output has dropped because of all the precautions. Our ability to stay abreast of the science and its spread is abysmal without a secure communications system."

Bingo!

"That could possibly be arranged," Kat suggested.

"I was hoping you might say that."

"When you wish, Damien, and the sooner the better, please call this number from your office. Spring Air. They can come and change your office environment into one of healthy freshness. The equipment they provide is practically immune to misuse. The usual degree of vigilance is needed, of course, but that should be sufficient. Similar arrangements are available for your immediate colleagues, so please let Spring Air visit the members of your core network. If others are watching you, which must be assumed, they will notice the enhanced security. Yet it is presently impenetrable. I cannot guarantee that no one will bother you or your family, after the recent events in which we've been involved. At the same time, Pyramid are very family oriented. They would be keeping a close eye on everyone around you as well. I hope you do not think me too forward, Damien, but we came prepared for this possibility. The decision may not be so easy for you and it certainly remains yours to take."

"Perhaps not so difficult given the alternatives. Like you, I could disengage, but that wouldn't guarantee any safety. Better to have proven friends than none."

Election night was creeping into history, a wash of blue. What a night! Some moments in life you have to absorb, bathe in the aromas, savour, dissolve within. Flags and banners lay in statuesque heaps around the floor of the convention centre. While the thunderous joy of the crowd was gone, its echo still filled the halls. The media had called it a substantial majority, with control of both houses and the executive. President Moore's speech was gracious and inspiring, delivered to a thousand of her close friends and allies. Saba was magnificent in a no-nonsense way. She had perfect pitch in several dimensions, like Sandover, and it was easy to trust her. Time to get home to Lara and Dylan, Kat worried. Beya looked like she was having similar thoughts about Justine as she stifled a yawn and smiled.

"Rest of the night off, comrades, till 07:00."

"Now it all starts," Sandover added.

Kat felt the exhaustion then, that leaden weariness in your bones. If almost losing a son was what happened before the starting line, she failed to see how they could finish. There was a lot of darkness in the future. But they had survived. For the first time in a long time she could see a little hope. The skeleton of a coalition that might defy the growing axis of greed and anarchy had begun to take shape.

"Doesn't this ever make your bones weary?" Phil asked, mirroring her thoughts as he often did.

"Now and then. Now we have a chance, but then again, it's a long way from won. Still the needle in the haystack, still too much to do. Now and again."

Two days later, she and Phil were planted before a large monitor. With Ellis, it was different. There was only one way to talk and that was online. It took some time to set up all the protocols. They had agreed on Kat's doing most of the talking.

"Hello, Kat. That's quite a com system you've got there, Phil, a new technology, but I've seen it enough times now to be getting the knack."

"Hi, Ellis, good to see you, too. The comtech is from Sandover."

"Well, we know what that means. The good news is that pinpoint technologies won't be able to be used for hacking themselves. So everyone with money can have perfectly private conversations whenever they want. When we don't want, we have the luxury of sharing the relatively open and easily watched Nets with the rest of the world. The bad news, of course, is pinpoint's big advantage for terrorists. No leaks."

"Pinpoint will certainly spread quickly in this country, Ellis. There's really no stopping it. Government agencies will be acquiring it from Ben Singer and others by now. You, too, by the sound of it."

"It's a work in progress."

"The president will push hard for rapid rollout. Pinpoint may also play a key role in the management of nanorg."

"Meaning survival?"

"Well, yes, but we should aim a little higher. And I'm thinking of everyone surviving, not just the powerful and the wealthy."

"Of course. And why me?"

"You have the best com surveillance in the world, Ellis. I appreciate that pinpoint changes the game. I'm also sure you're being modest when you say 'getting the knack.' Our objective in seeking your help is to be able to watch nanorg development."

"And I should work with you because you represent the good guys?"

"No, we've known you long enough to be sure you'll always work independently and with your team. On our side, we're involved in many of the civilian networks in nanorg. Beya and Sandover are in the middle of the political arena. It could be important if we talked when we wished."

"Let me concentrate on adding pinpoint to my security arsenal. After that, the hardest part of monitoring targeted communications is choosing the targets. We know some of them, so we have a start. *Au revoir*, Phil and Kat. I will be in touch. Net speed!"

Ellis disappeared like a nineteenth-century magician. Phil raised an eyebrow. Neither a disaster nor a triumph. Likely, they were not at the top of Ellis's list of friends and clients.

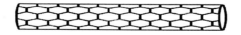

Ellis stewed as he moved the pieces of obfuscation that kept his prints off the Net, studying the movements of the opposition. *There's something they're not saying. Why so*

bent about nanorg? Sure, everyone's worried about nanorg, but there's a lot of other things to be worried about, maybe even worse. They know something. From the transmissions, from Pyramid? Something about nanorg.

The shape of the lie.

NOA

Beya watched the sun sink slowly into the hills across the wide mouth of Msasani Bay. Dar es Salaam, harbour of peace, a world soft as silk. Yet life remained hard for the *wananchi*, her people. To stand here again brought back an explosion of memories: the Dar of her childhood, the islands on the horizon, Oyster Bay Beach and the old hotel with the roof that rolled back under the stars by the ocean, palm trees decorated in December, an old cassette player belting out *White Christmas*, the aromas at night after the long Asian walk along the beach, Arlechino's where they went for real Italian gelato with Uma and Baba when they came to Dar for the government consultations, the Shish Mahal for brilliant chicken biryani and a bad stomach the next day.

One year they had driven right up the coast to Tanga and Lamu, sailed on a dhow into the Indian Ocean. In those days they called it the African Ocean, as it was theirs as much as anyone's and their coastline doubled the length of west India's. One evening they walked out on a sandbar for more than a mile, wading back ashore as the tide came in and the sun set over the ridge behind the village. Baba got them their first video camera and they made a movie, *All's Well That Ends*. Further north, Lamu was mysterious, a little sinister, alien, though the soft Swahili and enigmatic Arab cultures mixed well there, like the scents in the villages at night. Another time they drove to Dar with country and western music from Iringa on the radio and a sonorous elephant trumpeting their passage as they went by the game park at Mikumi.

Later that trip, they went up a mountain to Bunduki, an old fly-fishing lodge built by the Brits, bathed in the low falls and swirling currents. *Baridi sana*, very cold! From Iringa to Dar it was all big horizons, what she missed most in the madness of Washington. One summer, she had lived with her cousins on Lake Naivasha and worked at the carnation plantation. They filled a 747 every Sunday with cut flowers bound for Frankfurt. In the evenings, the flamingos skimmed over the flats in reedy bays and landed in eruptions of pink.

It had changed so much over the years, some for the better, too much for the worse. Bahari beach resort was long gone, Kunduchi too — the white Arab complex brought alive by brilliant purple curtains and multicoloured cushions on broad low benches. In their place were Sunrise Villa and the breathtaking light mauve of Bougainvillea Lodge. To be here again with Justine in the dwindling sunlight! If only they had time to drive up into the Paré mountains on the way to Arusha, to Lushoto and the old lodge with the huge slate pool table that only German engineering could have delivered up the mountains of Tanganyika. To stay at the base of Mount Meru in a stone manor house that had once been the plantation's bustling centre, gurgles of water constantly in the background as sluices and pipes pushed the mountain stream through the orchards on down to the valley and the growing town. To drive to Ngorongoro Crater and the Serengeti, so much beauty but so few people, the lodges abandoned by all but the hardiest tourists, the Scandinavian aid workers, and a few rich enthusiasts in their exclusive bubbles.

It was good to be back. As always, their hosts had been effusive in their hospitality. Where there is poverty there is generosity. As the sun disappeared, Beya watched the children on the beach as they mimicked the few foreigners enjoying the strand, imitating their walk and mannerisms, reverting to innocent play with bursts of giggles when someone turned to catch them at it. It took her back again to earlier years, imitating the adults as they watched the early morning sun cast long shadows on the slopes of Kitulo, back across the savannah. Dew bent the long grass over, glistening in the first light. The sounds of life would begin in their endless harmony, water running over pebbles and sand. Baba had said this land is yours, but it will be here in a thousand years and you will not. Covet the land and it will possess you, abuse it and be soon forgotten, cultivate it and world will be reborn. She was right. It was the judgment of Beya's generation, they who forgot, drove the land to its limits, threatened the earth to its living roots and its physical core, to burn or die. Time now to renew, a chance, a mandate and a means. Three more years in the White House. Being here made her remember why she was there. For the smallest sparrow on a twig by the river. For Uma's land.

Justine sat on the bench beside her with an all-grown-up sort of look on her face, three going on twenty, watching the shore birds, daydreaming like her mother. Beya had come to show her a place she should know, and they had needed a break. Time flies. December, snow on the ground in DC, and never so much as a hint of a pause in the countless detail of daily arrangements and all-night traumas over crises at home and abroad. Beya was getting hardened by a constant diet of calamity, the seemingly inevitable contingent of failures and downright disasters. They were still winning the war, but it felt like they were losing too many battles. New adversaries popped up to replace old ones in an ever-growing crescendo. The mid-term elections were starting to gather like an unwelcome blot on the horizon.

Tomorrow would bring more meetings, of course, never *really* a rest, a private visit with Tanzania's president. They had met once before when Baba had been appointed to the provincial government in Arusha and Mosi Nkaidi was a young minister of local government. On to Arusha on Wednesday, where the ESA Parliament was debating the Nanorg-AI Treaty. Then the memorial ceremony for Kilifi on Sunday, an annual gathering before the long haul back through Heathrow to Dulles and home.

"*Karibu sana*, Beatrice Wanyika."

"Beya, please, Mr. President, I am so accustomed to it by now."

"Then you must call me Charles, Mosi if you wish"

"First born."

"Yes, and the 'father' of my family at age twelve. So many of us lost our parents and grandparents in the elder epidemic. And you are all grown up, forgive me, I remember you as a school girl. Now you are the left hand of power, as my father once called me in our small homeland. Please sit. To what do I owe this visit, so far from the corridors of command?"

They both knew, but it was the gracious concern of a nation that sparkled in his grey eyes.

"Let us trade stories, Mosi."

"Excellent. Will you start?"

"Thank you. You know most of mine so I can cut grass. Things go well, but tensions are high. We campaigned on global cooling, nanorg and AI control, safety nets while costs of living fall, and cooperation instead of conflict. On the first, good progress. Carbon fuel is getting rarer, extractors are working, and the space cable is giving it another boost. Living costs are still declining worldwide, stabilizing now that the impacts of cheap energy are getting played out. Most countries are coping, or better, some much better. A dozen at the bottom end of the barrel need a lot of help. International cooperation in the global cooling and economic adjustment ordeals started well but stalled under self-serving governments in Washington, Europe, and Asia."

"I understand there is bad news in nanorg and AI?"

"It's not all bad news, but dangers wax while negotiations stumble."

"Factions and nations still don't trust each other, Beya. Global warming taught us a lesson, that our sins fall eventually on ourselves. The poor were hardest hit and the rich to blame, but in the end nature's retribution has been even-handed. Your floods and droughts hurt as much as ours. Mutual destruction, but who would pay the price of salvation? When Obama arrived, scientists were saying that the safe level of carbon emissions was 2.7 tons per person per year. The US and Canada were at 20, Europe at 10, China and the fast-growing countries around five, and everyone else insignificant. When your Democrats have been in power, the world has cobbled together some real teamwork in spite of the posturing. In the end, the rich pay most of the cost because they have the most to lose. On this account, you and Saba have done much in the past year."

"Thank you, Mosi, this is good to hear from you."

"I fear that nanorg is different, Beya. When it comes to powers and weapons like this, we don't yet see that it's mutual destruction. No one has been hit by the storm that is surely coming. But this is my story, and I am interrupting yours. Please continue."

"Mine is almost done, Mosi. You have said it. We need your help. Tanzania is hosting the new ESA Parliament, all the countries of East and Southern Africa. Everyone listens to you, poor *wananchi*, rich *wabenzi*, and foreign *wazungu*. The Nanorg-AI treaty is simple: you monitor and report. In exchange, you share in all the information from all the treaty countries. If we don't do this, the congloms will impose their way in all parts of the world. It does take resources, and it has to be done with high care and consistency or its value is lost."

"Then I think it is time for my story, Beya, so that my answer may appear to have some reason. Things have not been easy here. Yes, we are richer because the cost of energy has fallen, and so too the things that energy makes. The rich *wabenzi* buy their ethanol and their hydrogen-powered Mercedes for less and less, their fuel for pennies. Some of them lost their companies in the economic restructuring, but most had land or family wealth as a cushion. Because they still hold the balance of power, our politics teeters on with too many jealousies, roadblocks, and poor compromises. Still, we are surviving and making some headway. The best politician we have is Ameena, your friend from school days. Almost everyone thinks she will be the next president. I am sure you have heard most of my story from her."

"Not enough, Mosi, I am happy to listen."

"The *wananchi* have had a tough row to hoe. As the economy changed, so many people had instant disasters. You can imagine. Drivers had to convert their vans to ethanol or hydrogen with their families just getting by, no money to spend. If they could borrow enough, they went for ethanol because the conversion is cheaper, but then they lost fares to drivers who had enough to go for hydrogen. Multiply this story by hundreds and thousands. No bank credit to convert farm machinery or move from a shrinking industry to one with a future. No working capital to save a small business or build a new one in the growth sectors, to employ the displaced. Everyone has family and friends who are struggling. In a perfect world, the gains from restructuring would easily cover the costs, with a good return to boot. But our financial markets and micro credit systems are stretched to the limit and they are still failing to help half the people who need money to tide them over, to get started again. Safety nets and credit. Right now, for a while, we need more cash in the system, even if it is used imperfectly."

"Like the 09 stimulus packages."

"Exactly. Throw all you have at it because it can all come apart, all you have made. It is the fundamental asymmetry of human life that everything we build so gradually, so tortuously, so lovingly can be extinguished in a moment by conflict or greed or even accident. The rich saw this instantly in '08, even Americans, but they couldn't swallow their fear and hatred of *Government*. The poor who faced extinction on a daily basis simply nodded at the new sea of calamities and said 'welcome to the world'."

"Just like 9/11, Mosi. I remember at that moment there was armed insurrection and violence in one-third of the districts in India. Most of the world was not very shocked by the attacks on America. The number of deaths was very small in the picture of global carnage at the turn of the millennium. This, too, was a 'welcome to the world' for America."

"If we had been strong going into this, Beya, it would have been much easier. But there was AIDS and then rounds of animal and fowl flu before the elder losses. I spent a whole year disabled by tree flu residue. All this on top of two decades of ruinous global warming and ravenous corporate avarice over the gains of globalization, backed by your charming Republicans. We watched and argued while our land was in flood and drought. It is not the same, Beya — your eyes have told you the truth. We need to save it, to bring it back. We need the nanorg, to recover the land, but we need to be sure it is safe first. We have no margin for error in the downward direction. We are not even keeping everything and everyone afloat. Our neighbours and our ESA Union partners are in the same boat, surviving and sometimes hopeful, but drained."

"I understand."

"Abiding by the treaty has a cost to us, yet it is right, so please allow me to be precise. We want to be free of this nano-organic-AI matter, this NOA. We are very eager to keep informed of research around the world. We are happy to share any knowledge we have. But we want to prohibit active development of products, including these nanorg bots, until the technologies are shown to be safe and beneficial elsewhere. I am afraid that you are going to have to experiment on yourselves this time. We know it's not that simple, that we won't avoid the dangers simply by declaring ourselves NOA free. With the world so closely connected, a crisis anywhere could easily wipe us out too.

"In the end, Beya, we will have to enforce a ban on NOA, so the treaty doesn't add much to that burden. Once again, however, it is the actions of the rich nations that are imposing this burden on us. We desperately need help with enforcement and training. More development finance would work wonders with peoples' lives. That's all. The treaty should recognize the right of countries to be free of NOA technologies, to decide at their own pace. We will join and respect the treaty as we do with nuclear. We will work with the International NOA Treaty Agency, 'INTO the future,' as the media like to say. In this effort, your American corporations will be forced to obey the rules."

"Even so, Mosi. I have always liked stories with happy endings. I share your mistrust of NOA, I can feel it in my bones. In the moments of reckless bravado that our species seems doomed to repeat, we could injure ourselves and the planet too deeply. It's all we have. NOA must go ahead carefully. Pharmacon and their friends will have to accept inspection in treaty countries, whether or not they are NOA free."

"I know we have no choice, Beya, but I wonder if we have made progress from the days when our futures depended on ourselves, before 'ourselves' changed from family and community to 'everyone' in the blink of an eye."

"The globalization of I. The battle is taking shape, Mosi. We have had a year of calm while the forces were organizing in the boardrooms. To be NOA free is a good story to my ears, the way you have told it, for a time and with our help. Development finance we can do, with other costs falling. We'll get some people redrafting the INTO articles. We could have something this week, before the ESA debate. I'll ask Saba and the president to send a message of support to the delegates."

"I haven't heard these kinds of words for a long time, Beya. They give us heart. If we are very lucky, they may even give us a lifeline."

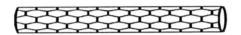

The rest of the week went by in minutes, conference calls with treaty lawyers, a long talk with Saba after her meeting with the president, sessions with Ameena and her staff, Arusha and back too quick to stop and be thankful for the piercing beauty of the plains and foothills.

Mosi was brilliant. They needn't have worked so meticulously on the crafting of words as he moulded their offering with ease into the eloquent tradition of Mwalimu and teachers of the past. The opposition was vocal and debate impassioned. The vote was postponed to allow for further consultations.

Back in Dar, Ameena's family had been looking after Justine. She was speaking a lot more Swahili than Beya had taught her, with the slightly annoying ease of a three-year-old brain. Beya tried to explain to her about Kilifi, the pain and anger, but how can you tell a child that you don't know if her uncle suffered a senseless random ending, caught in a crossfire, or if he died bravely trying to help someone, save lives, save the world. That would be Kilifi. She hoped in the last moments he knew how much he was loved, the rock, the one they all leaned on, the one who took your burden with a smile. It was sometimes so hard without him. Thank the Lord that Uma and Baba had already gone.

The memorial was on the beach, with so many friends and so little time to catch up with everyone. Erasto found Beya staring at pastel colours forming over the long ocean horizon. A late afternoon breeze stirred the palms and the little white spider crabs darted out to find food in the retreating tide.

"The sea makes me feel born again, Beya. I wish it could bring Kilifi back."

"You suffered the most, Ras, you were closest to him. But you look better somehow."

"Life goes on. I teach and paint. It's enough, I'm thankful for it. My born-again friends feel strongly that I would be better off with my faith re-awakened. This could happen, I suppose. I was certainly born the first time without being consulted or fully briefed on the matter. What I want to tell you is that there have been men asking questions about you. They say they are Christian but they're not nice people, not my kind. They asked about your family and friends. Be careful, Beya, these ones do not wish you well."

Beya called Sandover straight away on pinpoint. When they met at Dulles, she learned that Erasto had two new friends assigned to his security. She had forewarned him to watch for *his* kind of people, Sandover's family.

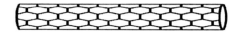

Beya promised herself that she'd be home for Justine from eight to midnight and made it most of the time. Sandover's life was a bit more flexible than hers, though his promotion to deputy managing director had shot him straight into the politics of the WEO Council.

Whenever a moment materialized out of all the bedlam, they gathered on the balcony looking over Olive Street and Rock Creek. Georgetown was a pampered puppy heaven but easy to love, tucked in behind the sprawling array of George Washington University's Foggy Bottom campus and the twin buttresses of the IMF and WEO, a hop-skip from the White House and the Capitol. They had the illusion of normal lives for a few hours a day, enough to save a handful of sanity. Beya's second home was the VP's Office in the *Casa Blanca* where Saba and the president conspired. Last night the frost had covered the nation's capital. Snow danced in the streets.

Mosi carried the day in Arusha. The idea of NOA-free countries was growing into a movement. The other members of INTO agreed to develop NOA carefully and cooperatively. Opposing INTO was a growing Freedom And Faith movement that rejected all international obligations. For the most part, FAF were the right-wing political and religious regimes, drawn together by a common hatred of international controls. The INTO countries were gathering slowly toward a Prosperity and Development coalition, with. FAF and PAD squaring off for a war of attrition, if not open conflict.

Pharmacon remained at the top of the list of FAF outlaws. Although PAD was slowly winning the war of NOA control, that unfortunately wasn't anywhere nearly good enough. With NOA, losing one crucial battle could mean extinction. They had to fight every encounter as if it would be the last.

Beya let out a long breath of dull exhaustion as Sandover began to massage the fused muscles in the back of her neck.

"It's mostly good news from Phil and Kat. My God, Beya, your neck is like a tree trunk. Where was I?"

"You said Ellis is on board."

"Right. Ellis is tracking NOA and talking to us. He's got software that learns the com patterns of companies known to be active in NOA, then looks for similar ones everywhere on the Nets and in the more secure channels that the Imputers are able to access. Phil and Damien's group distil information coming from scientists and give the leads to Ellis. A lot of the best leads come from Crucible."

"But is it a fine enough sieve to catch the plague in its infancy? And don't stop that, my neck is starting to feel human again."

Two of Sandover's most endearing features were his hands, strong and subtle like those of the best masseurs. This was only going to end one way.

"We can only try. FAF companies will learn to mask their coms better. There are limits to how much information we can count on from independent scientists and Ellis, and how fast it gets to us. On top of that, the 'software' Ellis is using could be very dangerous in itself. It falls short of having a consciousness, but not that far short. In one sense, it's like a version of NOA that's pure AI, loose on the Nets, the first of its kind but certainly not the last. Ellis calls his first Netbot *Seeker*. It's actually a descendent of the ware we used in Merimbula to analyze the incoming patterns."

"Very scary, no?"

"Hard to believe it could do us harm, as it's programmed only to identify, communicate, and learn. But it's also easy to imagine more sinister Net persona. With the US leading the INTO charge, we'll have to go public with the Netbot technology and the secrets it uncovers. Ellis agrees."

"Kat isn't going to like this, love. The battlefront is expanding faster than we can populate it. A little lower."

"Ellis is working hard on ways to handle hostile Netbots. It's exactly parallel to what Damien and his teams are doing with NOA. In Damien's case, the bots have bodies, nano and organic with only a trace of AI, while these Netbots are pure artificial intelligence, bytes on the Nets, nano but not organic. Though they are very simple persona, it's hard to predict where their learning capability could take them, so they are potentially very dangerous. Similar laws of robotics are needed — don't harm humans, obey humans, protect human environments, protect yourself. The problem is to ensure that the creators of Netbots embed these laws in their creations, together with the means of enforcement. Unfortunately, it's by no means clear what '*means*' actually means, in concrete terms."

"What do you mean?" Beya couldn't resist.

"Take *Seeker*, for example. Ellis programmed *Seeker* to detect patterns. This conveys no direct threat to humans. *Seeker* obeys, protects the Net environment, and protects itself.

But if you look more closely, the problem is with the first law. *Seeker* is much too simple to know if its actions have anything more than direct immediate impact on humans, positive or negative. So humans have to decide for Netbots if they are threats because of unintended consequences. In the end, humans have to be willing and able to destroy any hostile Netbot creations without fail, the same as for NOAbots. "

"They are intelligent, these Netbots?"

"Yes. I mean, not yet but soon, so destroying them becomes a murder of the mind. These minds can be re-created, having been created in the first place. Humans have to be able and willing to kill destructive Netbots and then keep them dead. That doesn't seem likely."

As it happened, 'dead' was not where their nonverbal conversation had arrived.

"Mmm, do that again," Beya purred.

Her mind conjured a Netbot gentle in its understanding. Could Netbots love? Why not? There is love without body. Then again, there was this love, bodies lifting, losing the mind, gentle rhythm softly building, extending, unfolding, yielding, bursting, disappearing. When they came up for air, all thoughts had left her head. Sandover reverted to massaging her neck as he picked up their former train of thought.

"Whoever gets ahead in the technology can use their Netbots to find and destroy the ones they don't like. Bottom line, this is another battlefront we have to contest and secure, as if we needed another! The good news is that with Ellis, Pyramid, Damien, and pinpoint, we have a chance, whether it's against smart Netbots or minuscule corporeal NOAbots. *Seeker* and his successors are tracking down suspicious activity on the Nets, and Damien's cabal has developed some potent weapons to destroy outbreaks of destructive NOAbots."

"How on earth can you do that?"

"Getting the destroyers to infected areas fast enough is the key, should the need arise. We're all watching for the flashpoints. We'll have the weapons to fight back if we get the chance."

"I'll get Saba up to speed on the Netbots right away, love. At least the INTO disclosure and inspection protocols are up and running, so technically it won't take long to add in the Netbot technologies."

"If the politics were only so easy! But we can also help at the WEO."

Beya didn't need rocket science to know this was going to cause more endless hours and headaches, digesting the incoming intelligence and keeping the president briefed. Time she didn't have. Sandover traced fingers gently over her temples as if to ease the coming pains. This could get out of hand again. Mmm, quite easily. This time she dreamt without robots. Do robots dream? Awoke again to Sandover's voice.

"Some news from Chuanli on the people Erasto warned you about. Whoever it was, they vanished very quickly, professionally. This smacks of J.C. but I'd bet on Golgotha. Abbott has to be our most devoted enemy. Golgotha is almost back to strength."

"So we're back in jail."

"Afraid so. You already are, in the White House, but Justine and I have to be more careful, no slip-ups."

"God help us. Is that all?"

"Well, given everything else that's going on, we tend to forget that there's still the chance of inter-place-time communication."

"But this gets too hard for my brain to process. I can't shake the belief that time and causality are linear, that they can't be everywhere the same."

"You get used to it — give yourself a little time."

"Funny, but is Phil ready to try it?"

"No, not that close. He's been going to conferences in cosmology and fundamental physics, making contacts, finding out about the leading labs. Like everything else, we might need this soon, so he has to trust someone."

"Who?"

"Ben Singer for one, and a controversial scientist he just met in London."

Nuclear

Beya stopped, distracted, forgetting where she was. One of those mysterious spring mists had slipped into the valley while they talked, Justine asleep. Outside, the evening haze thickened until they felt they were floating on the balcony, disembodied, with specks of light and colour in the uncertain distance, the Capitol down there somewhere. Bound to be there tomorrow, she thought with an unwanted shiver.

Sandover's latest news was bad. J.C. was coming to the INTO meetings to represent his country, possibly to take France out of the treaty, certainly to denounce the INTO accords and propose something closer to anarchy. In two days they would meet at the National Lab complex in Maryland. Might be worth it to break his neck, she imagined with delight, a creative use for the Shequan training Kilifi saved so hard to give her way back when. Fantasy. She had bigger worries.

"Not to change the subject," she began, fully intending to change the subject, "but we're getting pounded by the right-wing lunatic fringe on the economy. Problem is, the fringe can sway about forty percent of US voters and that can swell to a majority at the drop of a job. The president is getting a lot of conflicting advice, even from inside her Economic Council."

"Don't quote me on this, Beya, if you want me to stay employed. I can't say these kinds of things at the WEO unless they're vastly more nuanced. The right-wing extremists are perfectly willing to use disinformation, lies, misdirection, and eventually violence, whereas you're not. The left-wing extremists are willing let government seep into every cranny of the nation, whereas you are not. Aristotle pointed to the golden mean between the extremes. To get there, you can't just duck when the crap comes from both sides. You have to fight back, stake your ground."

"Meaning?"

"There is no economy in modern history that has succeeded without a first-rate private sector and a high-quality government. Those who say government isn't needed, or government can do it all, are both so full of diarrhoea that it's coming out their mouths. There is no economic theory or evidence to justify either bag of rubbish. While the rednecks and pinkos have fought over bogus ideologies in the US, the smart countries have moved way ahead."

"Then what are governments supposed to do?"

"Efficiency, equity, stability. They make sure goods and services are provided efficiently where markets fail to do so."

"The market fundamentalists don't believe markets fail."

"More ideological twaddle, Beya. They fail for public goods, things we use together — defence, justice, and security. Also health and education to a degree."

"I don't understand. If I get an education, I get the higher salary and the perks."

"Yes, but I benefit as your husband, Justine as your daughter. The private sector can't get money from us, so there would be too little investment in education. That's why countries fund part of their education and health systems collectively through taxes and governments."

"If you say 'collectively,' the rednecks will call you a commie."

"More ignorant hogwash, Beya. Markets also fail where there's too little competition. Consumers get ripped off. Governments use regulation and competition policy to break up the monopolies. Markets fail to protect the environment where no one has to pay for the damage. Left to itself, the private sector would let the planet burn to a cinder."

"It can't be that easy, San."

"It is, really, cutting through the ifs and buts and fancy theories. The same goes for equity and stability. Markets don't redistribute income or opportunity. Space yachts don't trickle down. If societies want redistribution, they have to tackle it through governments. And markets go haywire, evidence the Big Short of '08. Stability requires governments to regulate before the fact and stabilize after, preventive and curative medicine."

"I still don't get it. If it's that clear, why so much distrust of governments?"

"Because they earn it, Beya. Unlike private enterprises, they have no bottom line, little incentive to be efficient or innovate, and no consequences if they screw up. The answer is forcing them to do better, not getting rid of them. The golden mean. People have to do this by electing good leaders and keeping them under the microscope. That's where you come in."

"What about the poor countries?"

"The price of energy is in free fall. It's a perfect opportunity to enrich the poor and defuse conflict — tilt the gains more to them than us. The cynics say we'll gobble our share of this fast-growing pie with cherries dripping from our jam-packed jaws. Yet history says never miss a chance to play Robin Hood when it costs you little or nothing. One thing you should definitely do is straighten out the WEO, quickly. Your man Crockett is the behemoth in the china shop, so to speak. He gets too much direction from Golgotha, not enough from Congress. He is a flashback, a *déjà vu* stuck in the Washington Consensus of the last century."

This was as good an entry as Beya was going to get, so she took the plunge.

"The president wants to replace Crockett. She's thinking about you. Sorry, I should have waited till you finished that sip. Looks like it went right up both nostrils."

"But that's crazy. I've only been an American citizen for six years. It's unheard of."

"Well, it's about to be heard of unless you say no. They trust you. You have impeccable credentials and interesting connections. First and foremost, they think you know what has to be done."

"When would I start?"

"After breakfast tomorrow, if you want some time off between jobs."

"Very funny. Would it mean I'd have to behave impeccably?"

"Hopefully not. They'd have to demote you again if you did. But there *is* a lot of formality, a lot of meaning attached to your words, a lot to do in a short time."

"It worries me, Beya. We may be the first humans to be truly pinioned between the understanding of past barbarity and the awareness of future promise. A fork in time."

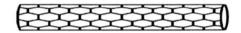

Saba called Beya early the next morning to draft the economic policy statement for an afternoon meeting with the president and put the finishing touches on the emir's visit. She stiffened as Sandover's raised voice jumped from the pincom. Sandover never raised his voice.

"Houston, we have a problem."

This was their code for kiss your nether regions goodbye. Every brain cell snapped to attention. A shiver jolted her entire body.

"We're told there's a bomb in DC, armed or ready to be armed. We may have minutes or hours to do what can be done."

"How can this happen without any warning? Where's Justine?"

"Headed home, go there now, Beya. FSA says the bogey is a paramilitary unit, Islamic, rogue Russian, maybe both."

Beya gave a passing thought to the imminent arrival of Emir Ahmed Mohammad to renew talks between the US and the moderate majority in the Islamic Alliance. An eternity of preparation down the drain, a peaceful path blown right out of the water, maybe along with everyone else on the Potomac. Her brain raced, balked, halted. Ten million people at risk. The moment of silence stretched. Saba's stern face appeared on her com.

"Bail, Beya. Martial law is being declared as we speak. Everyone from police to FSA will be on the streets to evacuate as many as they can. All the media are under orders, but there'll be panic. We need you and Sandover to live. That is your job and a direct order from the president. I have to stay here. Don't argue, go home, get Justine, go straight to the bunker at Camp David. Your transport is picking up Justine from school. A chopper will be at your flat by the time you get there. I'll be safe here in the deep foxhole. Go, Godspeed!"

Sandover was still connected.

"Go, Beya."

"See you at home!"

"Um."

"Oh no!"

"I'm the link, president to Pyramid. They both asked. Remember, we wondered what price we'd pay for friends? This may be it. The bunker under the Pentagon will survive anything but a direct hit."

"You have to live."

"OK, just this once."

I'm expendable, Beya thought as the floater shot her toward Georgetown. He's the one who has to live, with a lot more than Washington at stake. She wasn't so sure that bunker would survive a nuke, either. Someone protect him, please! I'll be good, work harder, do anything, just let him live. It hit her with a slight jolt that this was not the first time she'd offered this prayer. Time is a backdrop. Sandover had a habit of being at the centre of trouble.

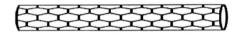

"Sandover?"
"Yes."
"Chuanli."
"Shequan, snake fist."
"Wife, daughter, exit confirmed."
"Nothing here you don't know."
"Think clearly, my brother."
"If we have one chance, we will be lucky."

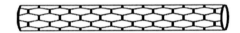

An hour later, Washington was still whole and Beya was safe. Justine knew there was trouble but soldiered on, didn't ask, lovely child. Better for a child to have one parent than none, Beya knew. But she couldn't hide the anguish. Beya had lost him before, under the water, and not survived entirely whole. Do you only get so many strokes before the curtain falls?

Saba authorized Beya's presence in the Camp David command centre. She fixed her attention on watching and helping where she could. Justine cheered up the troops outside the cavernous command bunker under the watchful and competent eye of Sergeant Ester Mahone.

The paramilitary unit had a name, they were told, information conveyed from Russian intelligence chief Valery Mikhailovich tersely to President Moore. Emir Ahmed Mohammad was reached on his flight and diverted to

Bethesda after a brief exchange. Warcom did the com links in minutes as voices crackled into life.

"I had no idea, President Moore. Is it the Wrath of Allah?"

"We believe so. The leak came from a ghost in rogue Russia. Russian agents are closest, working with us."

"You may not trust me, Mme. President, but if it is the Wrath or others who work with them, we can help you find them. Ismael is our best in the capital and the world. He is near your bunker, talk to him and decide. I will join you as soon as you allow, to help and to show the world that the Islamic Alliance is not part of this."

Terrified would not even begin to cover it. In two hours, a quarter of Washington was emptied. The terrorists would have to act soon to have anything like full impact. The seconds ticked by loudly on the old mechanical clock in the southeast corner of the briefing room, above banks of servers and screens, reminding Beya eerily of the big hall at Merimbula.

Her com vibrated. Sandover!

"I'm leaving, Beya, time to go. Saba spoke with the president. We've just climbed through the uplifts and airlocks to the surface. Listen in."

"You understand, sir, that no one is permitted to move through our defences, air, land, or sea?"

"I understand, Commander Haley."

Sandover's com transmitted video. He headed for a hanger where Chuanli waited with a team. Only on a closer look did Beya see the sleek airship, camouflage imitating its surroundings. Haley looked at Sandover with a frown.

"If the president hadn't OK'd this, I'd be arresting you for treason or the like. Aside from that, how did they do it, get the bomb in?"

"Not my specialty, Commander, but I am told that true stealth first requires doing an accurate impression of nothing and then of your surroundings. That's the easy part. The hard part is doing it irrespective of who is watching and what instruments they are using to detect you. Among other things, this takes speed. We must go, God be with you!"

"Live another day!"

"Beya?"

"I'm here, watching on com."

"We're up and away. I have one thing to do on the way home."

The floor she was standing on disappeared again, suddenly bottomless. If someone didn't kill this man, she might have to do it herself.

"What?"

"Help find the bomb, but not in the line of fire."

"Still the link?"

"Still in the linkage."

"Pick me up a loaf of bread."

"Don't worry."

"That's a good one!"

Beya watched her screen as a sleek craft landed way above, half-snake half-dragon. Phil appeared with a guard. She headed upward to meet him half-way.

"Was that FSA?"

"I don't know, Beya. Didn't ask, but likely Shandong or a sister enterprise. Kat stayed in New York. Sandover?"

"En route, one detour."

"That sounds ominous. And now for the bad news. The president has asked us to represent her at the INTO Council reception and dinner here tonight. I know, it's unimaginable that this is going ahead, but that's life. The world doesn't stop just because Washington may go up in a mushroom cloud.

We're far enough away to be safe and it's all been planned for months. Our *friends* will be here; J.C., Édouard, Torbido, Abbott, Sokolov, and the whole charade. I wish I believed in assassination."

By the time they reached the entrance hall two hours later, the grand congress was full, many faces looking their way, lit by a galaxy of chandeliers, a pause in the whispered news and rumours. About the bomb, of course.

True to form, Abbott stepped forward and broke the silence.

"Our prayers are with the president and the people of Washington."

J.C. came into focus over Mathias's shoulder, unable to hide a smirk. Beya fought to keep her composure, sure she had murder in her eyes.

"I see we are both out of danger, Mathias. I suppose we are not important enough to remain at the centre of power."

That got a reaction from J.C.

"Power is fickle. Ask Mathias. It would be a tragedy if the president and half her team evaporated in this inexcusable, unspeakable attack."

"A tragedy of the highest order," Mathias echoed, "unthinkable."

Too many unmentionables for Beya's taste.

"Accidents do happen, J.C. It would be just as unfortunate if Pharmacon and Golgotha were to experience unanticipated misfortune. So many terrorists these days."

By now they had a crowd. Dinner was called in the nick of time. Beya and Phil joined the head table beside Moore's appointees, headed by INTO's secretary and CEO Miriam Caine. The Brits were back in the fore. J.C.'s crowd was thankfully in a group on the other side of Caine and her two deputies, one a scientist and the other a manager, a striking woman who leaned their way after all were seated.

"Mr. Rush, pleasure to meet you. Beya, we have a problem. It is customary to welcome new representatives after the meal. If we do, J.C. will speak first, the newest. If we don't, he will protest."

"You may as well follow tradition. I can't see any way to avoid a confrontation with that pack of cutthroats."

"Thanks. I'm Adalene Saebo, Director of Operations. Treaty intelligence, inspection and enforcement."

They listened. She knew a lot about them, somewhat unnerving, but Beya had heard she was a strong supporter of Moore's views, another friend in the haystack adventure. Inexorably the time came for toasts and welcoming remarks. Miriam Caine introduced Monsieur Jean-Christophe Moreau with a gracious but steely manner and asked if he wished to say a few words.

"*Merci*, Madame Caine. It is a pleasure to be here, to represent France at this moment, however briefly. It is my pleasure to inform you that my country has made a decision to support the Freedom And Faith axis in all matters concerning NOA."

Dead silence. Not unexpected, but what can you say?

"The rest of you who crawl at a snail's pace have the time to debate and discuss until the cows come in. We do not have that kind of time. Governments do not have the skills to manage NOA. Pharmacon and its allies do. We will proceed with NOA in the FAF nations and in space. We do this not to defy you but to protect you from yourselves. France is with Pharmacon and FAF. We therefore withdraw from the NOA Treaty. I would wish you well, were you not bent on suffocating the drive and ingenuity of our species. Humans are too important to trust to humanity. I weep for you and the prison you lock yourselves INTO. *Au revoir*, we will meet again."

Caine looked toward Beya as she spoke to the gathering. "We also have two envoys from President Moore with us tonight. As her representatives, I welcome them to our gathering and ask if either would care to speak as we watch and pray for Washington."

Phil looked at Beya. She knew he would do it, but in for a nickel. She walked slowly to the podium.

"Secretary Caine, INTO colleagues, guests, friends, and others."

This got another hostile reaction from J.C. Clearly, he hated Beya, but she knew it was more about Sandover. Women are possessions to him, she thought, in my case despicable for not being his. She shuddered visibly, to her discredit, but what can you do?

"Let me first report on the situation in Washington and then reply on behalf of President Moore to the antics of France. I have received the following information as we dined. The bomb is not yet found. It was smuggled into Washington by the Wrath of God, an organization based near Zahedan at the point where Iran, Afghanistan, and Pakistan meet. All three countries deny involvement or knowledge. The leader of the Wrath is Selim Ibadi, as he names himself, already known to most of you."

Silence. Saebo's briefing and a call from Sandover had put Beya well ahead of what J.C. assumed they would know.

"Selim Ibadi is unstable. He started life as a cleric. His heart turned to vengeance when his wife and children were murdered by a drone. The Iranian Faction has provided him space and resources. We have leads but time grows short."

J.C. had his com on. Beya would have given a lot to listen in on that conversation. The Iranian Faction was one crucial piece of FAF and there was something too coincidental about J.C.'s denunciation here and the Wrath of God next door in the capital.

"As to Pharmacon, France, and the FAF, it is no surprise to anyone that they look after themselves and put the rest of us in grave danger. FAF detests the will of good people to advance together. They are outlaws who buy friends and murder enemies. Their vision is crooked and their morals bankrupt. Live by the sword, die by the sword. The line is drawn and we fear it not. We say this not to defy you but to protect ourselves from you, whatever it takes."

"We will see, Béatrice," J.C. chimed in from the floor. "It is too bad your clever husband is not here to back your bluff. I think you are running out of time."

Maggot! He had to be involved with the Wrath. He knew too much. If Washington disappeared, the Moore administration would be quite literally toast. Beya had no idea how many senators, congressmen and women, and civil servants were left in the city. Whatever the number, it would be a catastrophe, their hopes would go down the drain. But anger trumps fear and tactics trump anger. She was stifling a hot reply as the ViD wall flashed on to a familiar smile.

"Good evening, J.C. Clever husband here. Don't count your chickens. Miles to go before we sleep."

Sandover disappeared and Miriam Caine jumped in, bringing the evening smoothly to a close. Adalene Saebo said good night with a smile that none of them felt.

"Leave the INTO meetings to us. Without the FAF thugs around disrupting us, the rest will be easy. Get back to helping the president and Saba. You have a lot of work to do. If you get a chance to skin that murdering psychopath and hang him in an acid drip, permission granted."

Oddly, Beya felt they'd won a skirmish. France and the FAF were fools to withdraw from INTO. They'd lost a good source of intelligence even if they still had a friend or two inside. They'd lost a platform for disrupting the progress of PAD. But the converse was also true. Beya and her friends had lost one good way to keep an eye on the enemy.

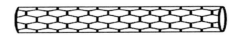

Selim Ibadi looked beyond the glass walls of the elegant boardroom toward the city, alone, feeling the detonator in one hand and the pistol in the other. Voices spoke within his head.

"They look for us in dimly lit crannies while we wait in the heavens for the moment of truth. Go away voices, let me be."

"Is it time, Selim?"

"Yes, it is time, my friend and child of my friend. But which comes first, creation or destruction?"

"Destruction, I can see it in your eyes!"

"Then it follows that you die."

"One shot, Allah take your soul."

"And yours."

"We could let them go."

"Or not."

"Bring down the butchers of Abidah."

"With the twitch of a finger."

"God is great."

"Which hand?"

"The right!"

"You would martyr them?"

"They are heathens."

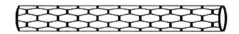

Beya fought panic as the night and the bunker pressed down like a gigantic screw. Then came that astonished feeling when you wake up and you're still alive. Play it again, Uncle Sam, how did that happen? Washington still there. The moments ticked by, Justine still asleep. Then a beep, Sandover's com.

"We're almost there, Beya. Picked up their trail on Fishers Island, a thousand agents combing the hundreds of miles of coast east of Washington. By chance, an island resident was watching the sea traffic with high-res video gear. The trail led to shore south of Annapolis, through Largo to Coral Hills. Then it went cold."

"How far are you?"

"Not too close. I'm not the general, but there are many teams to coordinate. I can help."

"As long as you stay alive."

"Good point, I'll mention that to the folks here."

A detonation of static ended the connection. Beya's heart skipped. Then her com re-activated. It was Saba, thank God still alive.

"We've found it, Sandover. If this is the end, may God forgive and receive us. A man called in a tip from a building a mile away. He saw light and motion at the top of the Yaseen Center in a penthouse under renovation. An FSA nuke team is on the way, another watching through a telescope. Selim Ibadi is alone beside the bomb with a detonator in one hand and a gun in the other. Two dead bodies lie in the foyer. They don't know if the detonator is a dead-man's switch. Patching you in and will record. If this goes wrong, the world should see it."

Sweet Jesus. No feed. There, coming back. Beya and Sandover stopped breathing as one, though miles apart, as the screen displayed a man who looked dazed. He turned to the glass wall and began firing the pistol as if trying to shoot something out in the night sky. The frame zoomed in. He was firing at his reflection in the glass, then stopped, turned the gun on himself and pulled the trigger. It was a moment you remember in slow motion. FSA charged as he collapsed, the detonator spilling onto the floor. Beya's virtual hand dug into Sandover's virtual shoulder. Two heartbeats, no explosion. A voice joined the picture.

"Detonator is countdown, Sir. Manual override not activated. Sixteen minutes, forty-three seconds."

"Up to the chopper pad, carefully, fast."

The image wheeled as the nuke team moved. President Moore's voice interrupted the silence.

"Fly the bomb as far as you can into the Atlantic and ditch it."

"Due respect, Ma'am, there's nowhere safe to put it down in the next fifteen minutes. We'll be far enough from Washington, but preventing tsunami and nuclear fallout are worth risking my team. Request permission to disarm it at the end."

"Bless you, Commander, and your team."

"Thank you, Ma'am, we are doubly blessed to have found it in time."

The minutes ticked by like thieves, silence interrupted by the chatter of the team as the detonator was examined and prepared. Beya didn't dare ask Sandover if his distance was enough. Surely.

"One minute, go!"

"Opening."

"Nano encrypted, Sir, one electron at a time."

"We need a code. Ideas!"

Silence, then a new voice joined the conversation.

"Ismael, Madam President, Intelops with Counsellor Mohammad."

"You're on-line."

"Seven-oh-one-oh-seven."

Seconds, silence, the image disappeared with a shudder. Sandover bowed his head and closed his eyes. He could feel everyone on the link doing the same, a very long silence.

"Do you read?"

An image came back, dust, debris, and figures moving."

"We read," Moore's voice replied." Status!"

"Stopped, Ma'am, thirteen seconds. Detonator self-destructed when the countdown was terminated, bit of a mess but our heli's still aloft. Looks like we'll make it."

Beya leapt up as the world seemed to come back to life, a surge of hope, relief, gratitude only to be cut short by President Moore.

"I want to know how the Wrath got into Washington and who helped them. We were a madman's impulse from annihilation. This is not something we can live with. Commander Ismael, we owe you millions of lives and more. How did you know?"

"I am sorry to say it was a guess, Madam President, among a half-dozen alternatives that came to mind. The one I chose represents an order of symbols that translate as *God is great*."

"God is indeed great and we are truly fortunate."

"We will leave no stone unturned, Madam President, to help you find what you need to know."

Sandover arrived at Camp David in what seemed like seconds. Nothing in the world like that first embrace, all was lost and all is found. Justine made the most of her father's reappearance and wailed when he said he had to go upstairs. In the end he convinced her he'd be safe atop and back in a flash. Bad choice of word. More howls. Minutes later, at dawn's first light, Beya and Sandover were patched into a link with the president and Ahmad Mohammad.

"It has been a hard day for you, President Moore."

"It has been a hard three decades for you, too, Emir Ahmad, going on four since 9/11. I wouldn't bet that the worst is over yet. I pray and I also wish."

"It has indeed been feast or famine for the doctrinaire, up and down like the price of oil. Neither of us is naïve enough to think it will be easy now, but everything is possible. If we have the chance, we will not waste it. Do not underestimate the Iranian Faction. Now that they have cast their fate with FAF, the Moslem world is irretrievably divided. FAF will show even less mercy for us than they planned for your country and its capital. In all but declaration, we are at war."

"A sad day, Ahmad. A long way from the vision of you and I have served."

"You remember the Peace Prize, Madame President. Our hotheads denounced it just as yours did. They were afraid. Peace was hope and possibilities, smashed and mutilated by decades of unbridled greed, then once again trying to open a window at the top."

"Kenzie, please. We've known each other long enough. The promise couldn't be delivered to all?"

"The expectations were too high and the hand they were dealt was too weak. The fascists were still out there lying and bludgeoning, disowning their attempted murder of the economy. They turned on the soothsayers, an old story."

"It was our fault, Ahmad, we were the majority. We let them get away with it, then and now, cowed by their methods. No more. We will rejoin the battle on offence. With your help, we have hope."

Rhetoric

Beya thanked heaven a millionth time for the moments of joy, watching Justine skip along the path with Sandover. Time crept like a spider into the first days of November 2038, a week to go until the mid-term elections. They had narrowly avoided global disasters and survived the ones that couldn't be missed. The nuclear attempt on Washington had gained them support. Renewed cooperation with the Islamic Alliance had improved the sense of security among *populus americanus* and *globalus*. At the same time, everyone knew how close a call this had been, a near fatal blow for the capital and the party in power.

Though the Republicans were gathering for a blow, underneath they were still stuttering. The fall from power of Hanna Carnegie and Harlan Darling had thrown the party into a prolonged introversion. The wounds sustained by Golgotha had healed, but the belief that they were invincible had been shattered. Once again, in the face of no progress and no more news, the shock of the Visitors' and Orion receptions had faded into the shadowy land of make-believe. Christian unity dissolved, independents multiplied, and the reach of Golgotha and the GOP dallied below the majority line. Then came the explosive convention, where the surprise ticket of Rupert Brandon and Salma Mendoza, governor and congresswoman, had caught the dormant imagination of the GOP, repackaging the old promise of greater security through strong military and corporate alliances. Against them were arrayed the wounds of everyone on the right who had trusted the successive Coalitions of the Willing and the Able and the Blessed to deliver any hint of safety, let alone inspiration. With luck, Brandon and Mendoza were too little too late.

The Summer Olympics in Delhi had been a showcase of moderates and humanists. Underneath, as greater prosperity dawned, hope was slowly waxing, fear on the wane. Given one more week without calamity, Beya prayed, they would have two years more. Funny how you get to like the halls of power. Granted there was still fear in America, the instinct to use force when the rubber hits the road. But what force do you use if the rubber is the bots and the road is the entire highway of life? Brandon's dire warnings on NOA were well crafted and even better marketed, but his solution was empty. Neither the threat nor the act of nuking the Freedom And Faith alliance carried any water. Voters knew by now that it was mostly about NOA.

Far above them, after two years of frantic activity, the asteroid Fuller and its moon Bucky were in place, the carbon mining and spinning equipment on site at Fuller, and the elevator cable starting down. Banks Island was a crowded space port and supply centre, with the tug planes beginning to test the lifting of the bottom-end tether. Spacelift was proclaiming that the first cars going from top to bottom and bottom to top would salute each other at mid-course within eighteen months. This would be the most vulnerable time for terrorism.

Sandover's inauguration speech as managing director of the WEO approached. He covered his inner fidgeting with outward calm. Though he had done well as deputy director, thirty-seven was still young for the top job. An old apprehension slipped in behind the blessings Beya was counting. Despite all their efforts and alliances, they had made no certain progress in predicting the source of an NOA outbreak. Nor in reaching any certainty about the source of the Orion message. 'Glass half full' said there was still time left. 'Glass half empty' said there might not be much. 'Glass might spill' said they would hear again soon from J.C. or Abbott.

As they approached, Justine looked wide eyed while Sandover expanded on some apparently momentous secret between them.

"You look like you swallowed a cookie and a lemon at the same time," Justine giggled.

No secrets from a curious six-year-old. Beya abandoned her fruitless worries and gave her daughter a supersized hug.

"Me, too," Sandover appealed. Well, he was rather appealing.

"Time to get home and get ready, you two vagabonds."

"Nomads. I have the prettiest dress."

"Perfect for your best behaviour, Tina."

As they left. Beya could almost forget about the two FSA agents by the park entrance, devoting their Sunday to her family instead of theirs.

Beya said a little prayer as Sandover bowed to the dignitaries and guests in the grand marble arches of the WEO concourse.

"Heads of government, leaders of global and local societies, ministers, CEOs, people of the world, people who are poor and oppressed.

"There is still a long way to go.

"There has been enormous human and economic development over the past decade. We near the point of lowering atmospheric carbon fast enough to reverse global warming, to end the cascading destruction of natural and unnatural disasters. A decade ago, this was imagined by many but believed by few. We have avoided annihilation at the hands of our NOA creations and we have some grounds to hope for continued survival.

"You are not accustomed to straight talk from the WEO, yet I intend to be blunt. We still have a billion people who are poor and victimized. Not as many as before, but still too many. In the thirty-nine years of this century, the rate of poverty has fallen by half, from a third of all people to 16 percent. This took constant struggle. In the same thirty-nine years, the world's population has risen from six to over eight billion, despite the devastation from pandemics and climatic disasters. There were two billion poor people in 2000 and still over a billion today. There is still a long way to go.

"You want peace. The poorest and most horrible lives continue to be lived in war zones. Conflicts set societies back by generations and cost hundreds of billions of dollars every year. Having every twentieth human being make devices that destroy other humans is not a vision of economic performance the WEO sees in any way but barbaric. All these people should be producing vaccines or food. There is still a long way to go.

"The risks associated with NOA are enormous, easily large enough for reasonable peoples to agree on shared knowledge as the goal, and the NOA Treaty as the means. We are on a precipice here, balanced between affluence and oblivion. Everything that reduces the chances and impacts of a catastrophe is a bargain at a thousand times its actual cost. We need to be very careful. There is still a long way to go.

"If there is one thing we have learned over the past fifty years, it is that each society creates a unique recipe for progress. There is nevertheless a common set of basic ingredients. Peace and security, education, smart economic policies, impartial laws, open media, good infrastructure, public engagement, and growing connections with regional and global economies and societies.

"Beyond that, we have focused our attention for a century on fast growth. When I ask poor villagers what they want, they do not say 'fast growth.' They say school for their children, freedom from violence and repression, enough food and medicine, some of the luxuries of life. Fast growth has diverted our attention from political, social, and cultural development, and from values we need to survive and prosper.

"In the race for wealth, we have caused instability, distrust, violence, and destruction of the planet. Beware of what you ask. If balance is not restored, apocalypse is at hand. The WEO can no longer dither. Poverty can be ended. Peace and safety must override the infantile fight between FAF and PAD. It is time to grow up. To this we dedicate our lives. There is still a long way to go."

Beya was anticipating some instant feedback from the pollsters, but of course the WEO doesn't operate like the White House. She would have to wait for the media pundits to make their pronouncements. Sandover's reach and rating mattered a lot to the Democrats with the election so close. Unless the public reaction was horrendous, it looked like he'd given a boost to the their re-election chances.

A cool November breeze caressed the Lees as they wandered along the embankment. Justine ran ahead of Rambo, their new beagle-hound bundle of puppy. In a short break before the ViD interviews began in earnest, Sandover looked as though he was running all the likely questions through his positronic brain. A moment of peace for Beya. A pinnacle of anxiety for him. A fragment of an old song crossed her mind.

> If I could save time in a bottle,
> The very first thing I would do
> Is to save every day till eternity passes
> Away, just to spend them with you.

'There never seemed to be enough time.' Foreboding never wandered far away.

So far, so good. The ViD interviews usually loved Sandover. Moore had to work at it, and Beya was uncomfortable in any kind of limelight, but he was a natural, full of clarity and commitment, pulling off the bluff that he knew much more than he was saying.

"And a final question, Dr. Lee. In the boy is seen the man. What was the most important thing you learned in your economics education?"

Sandover looked at the interviewer and then straight at the camera.

"There's a simple truth in economics. If an economy is working well, the value of each person's contribution is equal to the wage each person is paid. I've always taken that personally. It's often very hard to assess the value of what you do in a day or in a year, but if it's always in the back of your mind to compare it with what you earn, you get a sense over time of whether you're paying your way. The rich scoff at such a notion, knowing their contribution could not positively be worth the billions they earn. That just tells you there are excess profits, created and skimmed off happily by the rich."

Back on the balcony under clear skies and the vigilant indifference of the stars, Beya and Sandover watched the early newsmeisters on the wall ViD. Earlier and lesser commentaries were mixed. Sandover watched transfixed as first Logan and then Dunst gave him the thumbs up. Such relief spread over his face that Beya giggled. It was as though he'd been given a reprieve from execution. Which he had, he reminded her, even if it was only a temporary pardon.

Some of the reviews were negative, but they were the expected ones, newsfeeds controlled by Allcorp, Pharmacon, and FAF. The majority ranged from strongly supportive to 'might be convinced.' He looked so guileless, but she sensed something illusive in his candour.

"You look very relieved!"

"Pathetic, aren't we?"

"You mean just us, or the species?"

"Definitely. Truth is, we're not doing so well, not even OK, really, but we're not dead yet. If Orion was sent in 2041 as claimed, we're getting close to the time."

"So far, so good."

"That's what the guy who fell off the top of the skyscraper shouted as he fell."

Sandover eyed his daughter with mock severity.

"Bed, Justine. Sleep, dream, school tomorrow."

"Tell me a story, daddy. Like the ones Lara tells me."

"And what kind of story would that be?"

"About adventures in space and stuff."

"Right. Well, Lara knows a lot more about space and stuff than I do, but here's one that came from my father, at least the idea. Once upon a time, there were fifteen planets near a star that's far away in space. Five planets had people but each of these was different. On Alfazar, the desert people grew rich from the metals and minerals that ran in streams below the sand, and they were the first to send signals to the others and go into space. On Durn, a poor and hungry population survived on the meagre soil and water that supported life. On Lesarge, robber barons lived in luxury while the middle class supervised the plants and the workers slaved to produce the goods."

"That's not fair."

"That's a good point. Fairness was something people thought about really only on Prufrock, where they had everything they needed, so they spent all their time on music and dancing. They were the third to visit another planet, after Alfazar and Lesarge. The last planet was the home of the Kazeen. They were watchers and loners. They had the best tech and they listened to the other planets. They were the first to know all the languages and peoples on all the inhabited spheres. But they didn't want to visit the others. There had been wars in their own history, a long time ago, until they stopped making weapons.

"When the kingpins of Lesarge had built enough space ships, they attacked the Kazeen. They wanted to take over their planet and turn the Kazeen into slaves, to make their luxuries and their space ships. They took the planet without resistance. The Kazeen had foreseen the attack and did not want to fight, so they'd left."

"Where did they go?"

"They sent themselves by transponder beam to Jasmine, a planet in a nearby galaxy that they had discovered and explored. They kept an eye on their old home after that, but their enemies were a long way away, and watching brought back bad memories. So in the end they turned their eyes toward other parts of the universe."

"Are they the Visitors?"

"I don't know. I mean, I don't think so, but who knows? Whom could we ask? Who was there, once upon a time long ago?"

"Night, dad."

"Sleep tight, dewdrop."

House in order, tomorrow's schedules planned and synchronized, Beya snuggled in under Sandover's robe and rested her head on his shoulder, a moment of calm before the storm. A dash of starlight lit the rainstar as their lips touched. Time out of mind.

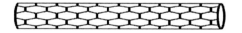

A friendly sun peeked over the sill, heralding the morning of election eve. The ViD switched on as the smell of coffee crept into the room. The president of Iran stepped to the podium half a world away, nine time zones ahead. Not in our future, Beya reminded herself groggily, but in our face with startling clarity.

"*Assalamu alaikum*, friends in all countries. By decision of the people and Supreme Assembly of the Allied Iranian Nations, we move today to join with Freedom And Faith. To this we commit our lives. To this we commit our weapons. We do not intend to use them. We understand the rules of deterrence, which now work in our favour. If you attack us, you will be deeply wounded by the allies of the Iranian Faction."

"We ask Emir Ahmed Mohammad and the people of the Islamic Alliance, once our brothers and sisters, to reconsider their servitude to the arrogant PAD confederacy. You covet their wealth but you will rot in your riches, lose your way, and fail to act. Theirs is not the true vision. We will be strong unto ourselves. We will live in freedom. We will move to the stars. We will take all our knowledge and technology with us. It is our will and our destiny. It is our time."

The lean, angry face of Édouard Moreau snapped into view before Beya could react to this onslaught. Not that the Iranian move into FAF was unexpected, but the message was chilling nonetheless. Moreau's voice interrupted her nascent deliberations with its superior and slightly sneering *accent français*.

"People of the world. We have made an historic agreement today with Spacelift to deliver to Fuller the means to harvest raw materials from the asteroid belt, to manufacture giant habitats, and shape whole asteroids for human occupation and travel. We will supply the Earth with manufactures, materials, and energy in free competition with any who dare."

"Will you take NOA technologies and labs into space, Monsieur Moreau?"

"We will not take NOA up or down the Lift unless that is sanctioned. But, yes, we will make use of NOA in space, in safety, and in the interests of our customers and friends. It is the moment for mankind to go beyond timid steps, to take our venture bravely to the stars. We seize our freedom and faith, our future. It is our time."

The big news hounds pounded on relentlessly. It looked like all the announcements had been well planned and timed. Pharmacon joined the Christian Right in pledging their solidarity with FAF. Beya knew it was a strong enough alliance to give them too much room to manoeuvre, especially if the big non-treaty countries sat on the fence and let their corporations play. Moscow stayed firm with PAD but had its hands full up to its eyeballs with the rogue enclaves in Russia.

If they could just win this never-ending election and get back to work. On top of that, they had a civil war to face right here in America. It wasn't the South against the North — the South now too ravaged by global warming. But the hard-core Golgotha membership in the South stirred old resentments into the fears of their born-again brothers in the North, enough to mobilize the Republican dread machine and back the FAF. The vote was going to be tight. It was sobering that the ineptitude of their opponents might be their only salvation.

Ahmad Mohammad and the Islamic Alliance held with PAD, thank the stars and the emir for doing the gruelling job of gathering and holding his flock in Malaysia, Turkey, Indonesia, Egypt, Morocco, Pakistan, the Gulf principalities, and other moderate forces in North Africa. By the end of the afternoon, when the president gave her last public address, their fate hung over the void.

"Don't be fooled," Kenzie Moore said to Americans and the world. "If you join FAF you will receive the scraps they offer. But there will be conflict and danger, because they are the self-chosen elite. They will exploit you, give you a taste of what you want and nothing more. If you join us, we will reach the same places that they promise — affluence, freedom, space, and human destiny. It will be a journey that we all take together. It will be slower. It will regenerate the Earth and its people as it unfolds instead of leaving them dead in its wake. Don't be fooled. You need a Democratic government to serve your interests and support our allies in PAD. Elites rule FAF, not the majority. Minorities suffer and die. Don't be fooled. Vote for the only real freedom. Join a better path to human progress. There is much to be done by everyone. It will take time."

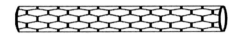

Ellis Holland chuckled, then let out a belly laugh, the sounds lost to the thrum of the dory's fuel-injected ethanol two-stroke.

Though he could never give up New York or Boston, this exquisite, cool Canadian November was still warm enough for Danielle to lower the old dory into the bay and motor up the coast to meet him, now rolling through long waves and a slight chop, an osprey drifting over the pine-spotted shoreline, the brilliant colours of October gone, a chill in the wind, and a shiver of expectation in the fading fall hues.

Count your blessings, he reminded himself. Danielle looks fabulous, all *québécoise* in layers of wool. We should have married years ago. Maybe I'm too weird, too private, too afraid to trust. Too late now.

They both knew that a showdown was building on the Nets, a war of Netbots, the victor to possess unprecedented power over global communications, power only rivalled by the masters of Pinpoint.

"You're worried about our safety," Danielle teased. "The invincible Ellis, master of global comtech."

"I'm more worried about control of the Net, but yes, we should think more about our own cover. We make a lovely target out here on the water. We could have bugs on us regardless of the precautions we take. You can't count on privacy any more, but we have to talk."

"Sandover's friends are never far away, in case of emergency."

"The fishing trawler?"

"Good eye, mon Ellis. It turned up on the horizon just before you arrived."

"So, we have protection. But we're going to need a small army working together on the Nets. We have to be ready to link up in an instant. Better if we're physically together when we need to be."

"You can stay whenever you want. The kids can go to my sister's when the crunch hits. I've got everything we need, and backups. You've checked it all out."

"You're right, Dani, I should be here. We'll activate the ghost net tomorrow with Kat, Beya, Damien, and Ben."

"And Pyramid?"

"They'll be in the loop through Sandover. Better let him handle that end. Truth is, I don't trust Pyramid. Nonetheless, we have to trust someone. They've been the best of the lot so far."

"Can't live without 'em?"

"Probably not. We'll see about living with 'em if we manage to live. Time is short, a midget and a fugitive at that!"

Beya gave way to the repose that follows exhaustion and success. The election results almost seemed anticlimactic amid the furor of global posturing, FAF versus PAD, nations dividing. Victory with a majority in Congress but not the Senate. The Republicans and FAF held a majority of governors, too, not to mention the mega-corps among USTEK and the Christian Right. The ideological rift in America mirrored the world's. But one can do a lot with the balance of power, no matter how thin.

Celebrations followed the election, good hope and cheer, congratulations, commitments from liberals and others willing to try for wider prosperity and democracy. Many in the political centre were holding their cards close. A time to catch their breath before the battles resumed. Together in Georgetown with Phil and Kat, Beya and Sandover watched the late ViDs with some desultory interest.

"The world is turning into a security nightmare," Phil reflected. "Not that it hasn't been that way for quite some time. But this has to be a new level of hell for the agencies and the armed forces, an autonomous band of nations that might do anything to get what they want. Several are nuclear, many NOA. Using force against them is an empty threat."

"Control of the Nets is coming to a crunch," Sandover added, "and it's going to be fought out by bands of Netbot soldiers! We can't destroy them all for fear of taking down the Nets and throwing the world economy into total disorder. We might not know *how* to take them all out even if we wanted to. Although these are intelligences of a very limited order, they have genius within them to learn, designed by a few hundred of humanity's most creative people."

A wee-hours-of-the-morning pause descended over them as they nibbled at the last remains of the food on hand.

"Does this mean we put inter-place-time communication on the back burner?" Kat levelled a no-nonsense glower at Phil.

"I would love to," Phil sighed. "But unfortunately I am convinced that inter-place-time may in the end prove feasible. Or at least we can't dismiss it. That doesn't mean it will work, just that we have to be ready to try, whether we believe Orion was from the future or the present or even the Visitors."

"We don't hear much from the Visitors these days."

"Perhaps they're just biding their time."

Ensemble

Phil waited in the lobby of the Ritz, snug in his soft leather jacket, late May blossoming all around. London never ceased to amaze. He had learned to love the rhythms of the city despite the sore spots. Societies once divided by class, now by race, religion, wealth, and culture somehow still functioned as a whole, a potpourri and a caldron.

He needed to focus on the here-and-now, to trust the where and when to the there and then. This wasn't his nature, of course, much more at home with the dynamic progression of events. Yet the near annihilation of Washington had certainly driven home the here and now, what you have, what you can make of it, what matters most, what matters now, the very small nuances that determine outcomes.

A car and driver pulled up in front of the flower-strewn lobby. The hour had come. As they passed familiar places and memories, his chauffeur caught him up on the heartbeat of London and the Empire. The old limousine rolled in leisurely fashion along the bottom of High Park and pulled in to the Westbury Mayfair on Bond Street.

Dr. Rana Myagdi arrived at 18:30 on the dot. They camped in the atrium bar in front of stylish photos of the Westbury's most illustrious guests, beginning with Lord Nelson.

"It's good to meet you, Dr. Rush," she said, "after so many frustrations on the electronic corridors."

"Phil, please. I have to admit to being responsible for some of the frustrations. I have constant concerns about the privacy of my conversations and do not wish to inconvenience you in any way by my troubles."

"Then Rana, please; more formality is wasted breath. We have much to discuss. You must visit the university tomorrow, but it is less private there and I wanted to meet in a comfortable setting."

This was not the Rana Myagdi Phil had been expecting, not the rather stern academic that the world knew from the media.

"The thing is, Phil, there could be a third explanation. One, there are the Visitors, or other aliens. Two, there are advanced humans who have sent out satellites to send back messages."

A jolt of alarm ran through Phil's spine, but she paused long enough to compel him to ask the obvious question.

"A third explanation? What could that be?"

"Good question, Phil, but we have to talk about other things before we get to that. For example, you suspect me of keeping connections with the Iranian Faction."

"I worry about the nature of the connections more than their existence. Are they also aware of your third explanation?"

"I appreciate your candour. No, not yet and I think not ever. At this time, it is between two scientists. It should remain so until further notice."

"And you are telling me because?"

"One good turn deserves another. Because you are the other scientist who knows."

Phil thought very briefly about fleeing, but, of course, reality is not so kind. He wasn't about to open his mouth, though. This could be pure bluff. He held on fiercely to his unfeigned speechlessness. As if reading his expression exactly, she continued.

"I would do likewise, Phil. Silence is golden. Simple logic says, three, communication from a different time."

Crappers.

"Cat got your tongue? Let me elaborate. Using pinpoint and black holes, it may be possible to send a message to some point in the future or past. From the past doesn't make much sense. You could warn the future about something, but how would you know, and what could they do about it? But if someone sent a message from future to past, they would know what to say and who should hear it. That might change some strands in the fabric of the present. Not only that, the recipients could keep their future selves posted, up to a point, simply using the media of their time."

Phil tried to look thoughtful, appraising her words, but in truth thinking frantically for a rebuttal or at least a diversion.

"That's a very interesting theory, Rana. But if it were true, who do you think would send such a message, from the future?"

"Who would not, if they could? The equations would look something like this."

She opened a smart screen and placed the equations carefully in his view, out of general sight. Very much like the equations they had received in the Orion message. Had she developed a virtually identical theory, or did she have some channel into Sandover's cipher and the meaning of Orion?

"You would do well in poker, Phil. I produced these equations from studying the Orion message. This was one of three parts with enough resemblance to scientific notation to catch my attention. I made one lucky guess. There are vanishingly few people alive who would see the relevance to cosmology and advanced physics. You may think me immodest, but cosmology *is* my field and I have always had a flair for pattern recognition."

One of the top three cosmologists in the world, he knew, but decided to throw in his last improbable stall.

"And why would you assume that I also know of this third explanation?"

"Logic and empiricism. What would I do if I knew of this possibility, say, six years ago when Orion arrived? Who is acting in such a way?"

Sometimes you meet people who are just plain smarter than you. Quicker. He needed to find out her intentions.

"This strikes me as a technology that could be very dangerous in the wrong hands."

"A good reason to avoid anyone else getting the same idea."

"But what would you do, Rana, if you learned how to send a message to someone in the past?"

"I would prefer to collaborate on that matter, Phil, specifically with you."

No turning back now, but some instinct kept him from the whole truth.

"My wife is also very good at pattern recognition, Rana. You must meet her. Some sparks might fly but fires would also start. She made a lucky guess, too, which led us to interpret the equations. Though we don't know who sent Orion, I think that inter-place-time communication can't be ruled out. I have been learning as much as I can about the science."

"I know a lot of theory, Phil, and it might yield the right ideas. I haven't done the research to find that exact confluence of ingredients that could bridge place-time. I have a sense of what is missing and a feel for the ingredients, just no clear picture of the recipe as yet."

"Then we must indeed work together."

She had taken risks. Now the onus turned to Phil to provide some tangible reason he could be helpful to her. Although it was still early days, he had come a long way on inter-place-time since Merimbula.

"What strikes me as missing is an idea of the *form* of the communication between two place-times that are very close together in space and not too far apart in time. It has to be something akin to pairs, one in each place-time, providing a reverse image like a mirror to their mate and anyone watching. If Dr. Schrödinger would allow anyone to watch. It would be a tall order, of course. You would have to find or create the right pairs to start with."

"That is an interesting thought, Phil, frightening. At that level, theoretically there might be multiple place-times, at least briefly — identical except for the expanding influence of the intervention. Chain reactions are very unwelcome news in nature and science unless you know how to stop them. With inter-place-time inter-connection, we might have no idea whatsoever."

She might be able to do it. That was his sense. The next day at the University of London gave them more time to talk science and test a fragile first instinct of trust. In a quiet moment, walking down the well-worn halls, he gave her a phone number for advice on communications security. She understood instantly the real offer and its value. He asked her to meet Kat and Damien.

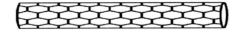

Next morning, he was on a plane to Russia. No time to lose. The Finnair flight touched down at St. Petersburg in a heat haze. The long nights of June were approaching like a promise, darkness at midnight and dawn at three. He had dreamt of coming here in this season. Kat's dream, too; she'd arrived in late afternoon direct from New York. The trim Mercedes felt like an oasis in the heat of the evening sun.

Dimitri Petrov, well accustomed to transporting foreign visitors, chatted as he drove past the long columns of massive housing blocks and parks into the grandest of cities, by rivers and canals, over a dozen of the city's thousand bridges. They passed the candied onion domes of the Church of the Spilled Blood, where Alexander II was murdered by a bomb blast in 1881, twenty years after he had freed the serfs. Dimitri's comment seemed to sum up a history of tragedy, passion, and endurance.

"Good guys finish last. Let's face it, lots of people weren't happy about the serfs being free."

They passed the Hermitage, the wondrous collection of buildings and treasures so much the child of Catherine the Great.

"Imagine buying a million pieces of art from Europe in the glory days of the Romanov Empire!" Dimitri exclaimed. "When it came time for our Revolution, the churches were desecrated, used to store potatoes. One became a swimming pool."

Dimitri's thumbnail sketches of history continued as they coasted by the Admiralty Park and pulled in to the Astoria Hotel. Two hours later, they were at the Grand Hotel on Nevsky Prospekt, the private guests of Dr. Yefgheny Valderov, Minister of Foreign Affairs and Deputy Prime Minister. Saint Petersburgeois to his boots, Valderov knew the city's history from the day it was founded by Peter the Great in 1703, stamping Russian sovereignty once again upon lands lost in wars with the marauding Swedes.

"The Revolution and the days of communism are now far in our past, Dr. Rush, but it took decades to recover. Times change."

An image of two times changing places with each other flashed through Phil's mind, past and future, a foreboding, a familiar shift.

"We become more liberal in Russia, Dr. Rush. All the arts are flourishing, the ideas are brewing and percolating, we are changing again. There is pride in what we have done, however tragic and flawed."

"And would I be right in thinking," Kat enquired, "that your invitation to us has its roots in some tortured Russian drama of today?"

"Ah, Mrs. Rush, now you raise a matter that is indeed full of thorns. In its simplest guise, we have a handful of powerful rogue industries. They are in league with FAF. They have plunged into pinpoint technology like bears into honey. They will soon be capable of space-launch and retrieval, even near-space exploration."

"Could you force them to retreat if it came to the crunch?"

"It would be close, Mrs. Rush. They are both employer and government in hundreds of villages and dozens of cities, all fiercely loyal. In a stroke of Russian irony and tastelessness, they have taken the corporate name the People's Technology Company. It is an awkward standoff between Moscow and P-TEK."

"How do they find enough scientists?"

"Many fear to work with them, so they pay top rouble. And once on board, no one leaves. A few have disappeared, which underlines the point for the rest. We inspect, of course, but the inspectors are either working for P-TEK or they are soon found missing. It is said that the entire Russian infantry could be hidden in the blind spots of our inspection system."

"I begin to appreciate the nature of the problem, Dr. Valderov," Kat responded. "More difficult but less tortuous than I feared."

"Yes. Well, we haven't quite finished, and nothing goes exactly according to plan, a lesson the early communists learned as it proceeded to kill them. P-TEK has at least three factions within one organization. Gregor Sokolov is the brains and the founder, still young by my standards, quite fearless. Boris Tselikova is the financier who could possibly wrest control, but he is more likely to wind up not so alive and knows it. Viktor Smolenskii has backed an open alliance with Beijing and favours the building of space habitats to preserve deserving individuals, as the rest of us destroy one other and the planet."

"They sound a lovely lot."

"Our best hope is they shoot it out for top dog."

"Very risky for all of us, if they don't."

"Precisely, Mrs. Rush, I am happy you see it in this light. It is much more than a Russian problem. If P-TEK holds together, FAF can do anything they want with NOA, here and in space. They've restarted the experiments that were banned in the aughts."

"Human trials?"

"Volunteers are not hard to find, I am told. If they produce a race of Russian super humans, you can expect no mercy."

Their flight to Warsaw and on through Munich to Washington was delayed by the fierce spring typhoons that came year after year now, levelling whole towns in Europe. Phil's mind wandered as they waited. Damage control. Another flank unguarded.

Two days later, Phil was feeling like a fly on the wall. The elegant suit jackets of Édouard Moreau had been equipped with a new technology, a small fabric added to the inside lining that was programmed to listen and transmit by smart pinpoint bursts. The deed had been done one night, without the knowledge of the tailor whose shop was breached.

An intimate group had been invited by President Moore. The White House held the other key to catch the transmissions by using their paired pinpoint particles. The voice of Édouard Moreau filled the room as if he were speaking to them.

"Fools, Maurizio. The rich will inherit the Earth and the stars. There is no God. No God would create so many fools.

Take what is yours and leave the leftovers from this ball of dirt to the weak and the lazy. Fools need not apply. If it comes down to me or you, will you not fight me? Fools to believe we can share the Earth or the stars!"

"I would not fight you *capo*, Maurizio avowed. I would find a way to serve us both. But you are right. Politicos and bureaucrats lay a suffocating blanket over the face of the Earth."

"We have to move faster. Humour an old man, believe you can fail. Time stands still for no one."

Silence. A smile froze on Phil's face. They'd been found out. Then some rustling sounds. Silence again. Sandover's eyes widened.

"He's changing jackets."

Saba flipped a switch, complaining.

"Should be automatic."

Édouard's Teflon voice returned.

"They will be here soon. In this chamber of barons, discussing what the barons discussed, managing production, collecting taxes, defeating enemies. What has changed? The serfs are unruly. They have been allowed too much freedom. We forced them to unite against us."

"Life continues, *capo*. Not all is lost"

"Yet FAF grows tedious, a federation of friction and fracas. PAD comes to our rescue, disorganized, without focus. It is easier to act in the name of God or money than in the name of some half-baked vision of humanity. Their fatal inefficiency is why we will succeed, why we will control them or leave them behind."

"They believe a standoff is possible."

"That is the greatest deceit of the PAD leaders. This is centre court. The players do not shake hands and agree to call it a draw. It is not the way of the world, Maurizio. Not the way my world has ever worked."

A half-hour of greetings and exchanges followed. Listening intently, Phil and Kat recognized some voices. Mostly Pharmacon, but also a quorum of FAF's top leaders.

"*Mes amis.*" Édouard's voice boomed through the nano transmitter, startling the listeners assembled in the president's office. "*Bienvenu*, welcome. I am grateful to you for your company. We are close to victory if we make no mistakes. Let us commence with situation reports. Our custom is one minute or less."

A parade of intelligence followed, like the playbook of the opposing team.

"Space ops are on target. The second asteroid, Bucky, will be in place and prepped by the time the elevator is operating commercially. Our first thousand runs have been booked with Spacelift and covered by deposits. The first round of big-ticket items for sale to Earth will be churning out cash inside a year. Our habitat program starts as soon as the factories on Fuller and Bucky are minting the cash. The major risks are a terrorist attack on the Lift, difficulties with Bucky's insertion, wrong choice of big-ticket products, unexpected events."

"PAD cannot do much to stop us but they could slow us down. The two main problems are Spacelift and Pyramid. Spacelift is legally a collective and the masses who own it could possibly unite to oppose our plans. Pyramid may be ahead of us in both organization and technology. We hear from reliable sources that cell members who have been tortured simply do not know anything. They have forgotten. This makes it almost impossible to penetrate their cells."

"Some in the Iranian Faction are against the Lift, but we will not attack it. In return, you give us freedom in space, no opposition as we move to the moon and beyond."

"You have the numbers in front of you. If we get three years clear, with a constant share of Lift bookings, we're off and flying. Ten habitats, one asteroid, fifty thousand people. If we lose the Lift before that, we would have to trim the vision. The Lift is our best friend."

"We have to get it right on the choice of the first NOA industries to start up on Bucky. Prospects in energy are quite limited, since crobies and nano-hydrogen have already taken the big gains. Demand for precision products and equipment is growing. But we need NOA sales to Earth in order to be unstoppable."

"Our first habitat, *Freedom Force*, will be devoted mostly to NOA. This is a great stride ahead of the vulnerable land labs and space stations we are using now. In time this will give us the high ground for the journey into space."

"We recommend four NOA sub sectors to begin with. Human cell regenerators are the mainstay. Environmental regenerators and their terraforming offspring are the second-biggest money makers. Closely allied are the tailored all-condition food producers. Finally are the narrow niche products and many-purpose agents: adaptable friction reducers, molecular extractors, and conductivity enhancers."

"Most of our opponents, including the civil society alliances, appear to be connected with Pyramid. Their comtech remains superior to ours. Ellis and the Imputers are a random element we can't ignore. And then there is the Fantastic Four, as the paparazzi have named them: the wizard, the witch, the huntress, and the mirage. They are pathetic, but where there is smoke, there is fire. We will probe these enemies until they talk. No option is ruled out."

Silence stretched among the group in the Oval Office as they listened. Torbido had given approval to use any method against them. Phil looked around the circle. Each face showed a different kind of rage. Kenzie Moore had murder in her eyes as she turned to Phil.

"Dr. Rush, it is time for me to depart for Banks. I would like you to come with me and to say a few words at Spacelift's opening ceremony."

Phil knew what 'say a few words' meant — a speech heard by billions.

"Of course, Madam President. But I do not have the skills of a politician."

"That's the point. And your wife does. I hope you will join us, Kat."

From the suite on top of the Banks Hilton, Phil watched the unending bustle of the streets below and the movements of the tug planes above. Sixty floors up, the bulk of the buzz was still far above him, where a very long cord hanging down from space ended ten kilometres from his head. A thin tether hung down, closer each day, almost to the ground, guided by a fleet doing justice to Coruscant, the centre of Azimov's Galactic Empire. A tug passed close overhead, a motley coloured East European joint venture by the looks and logo. Tipped a wing as he saw the lone figure on the balcony. Phil savoured the moment. This is where he was meant to be, at the crossroads, the pathway to the stars.

Next morning they were ushered aboard the more than comfortable Airforce One passenger tug for the ride up to Vantage. On arrival, a landing pad and a diamond-forged auditorium hung on opposite sides of the cable's bottom end, where it changed to tether. A diamond hallway connected the two halves, crystal clear but thankfully with an opaque bottom. The view out the sides and ceiling was spectacular. An unexpected clear section in the floor tripped Phil's vertigo switch momentarily until he looked up and away.

It was good to feel needed. It would be fun if not for the speech. Heads of state and their alter egos were all here. By the time they'd reached Vantage, hanging in the sky at twice the height of Everest, the president had received an invitation to meet Édouard Moreau right after the ceremony. With other fish to fry, she designated Saba, with Kat and Phil to ride shotgun.

The crowd was more PAD than FAF. Many of the FAF assembly were reportedly too nervous about their personal security to gather in a liberal stronghold. The proceedings began in a self-congratulatory extravaganza, annoying, but a small price for the view. Then the room hushed and the Convenor of the United Societies of Earth walked to the podium. As she introduced one speaker after another, the fragments of the speeches drifted by the edge of Phil's consciousness, no match for the marvels of the clear walls and floor panels, hung on the end of a thread from the sky. Scalloped clouds parted below to reveal Banks and the azure ocean.

The oily voice of Édouard Moreau brought him back to the moment.

"Ladies and gentlemen. I am honoured to be here, at this point in time when our link with the universe changes. We move on from an expensive dotted line made up of a few dozen rockets and their tiny payloads, to a highway that will grow and flourish. We go now to Fuller and Bucky, by ship to the moon and planets, to more distant stars, wherever the ingenuity and enterprise of humanity may take us."

"As history said to Vladimir Ilyich Lenin, democracy has its limits. The stars will be reached by free enterprise. The bureaucrats could do it if they had a millennium or two to spare, but time is short. Freedom And Faith is proud to be the largest customer of the Lift. We will send up equipment and knowledge, send back life- and Earth-saving products."

"We will abide by Spacelift's laws on NOA. We are pleased to take on the risks of beneficial NOA development for mankind, to take the steps but to keep them from endangering humanity. I hope to see you all atop the Lift in the nearest of futures."

Phil was the next to be called to the podium. The last words of his short address brought approbation from friends amid rude remarks from the FAF contingent.

"Ladies and gentlemen. I am a scientist. What I see is that humanity's march to prosperity is accelerating. Fighting over shares of the pie has always been standard human behaviour. If we don't change this standard, we may all die. NOA is deadly. In space there will have to be rules agreed. PAD countries will maintain a presence in space sufficient to deal with all eventualities. A council is needed to resolve the differences with FAF."

The convenor wrapped it up, and parties drifted into discussion in other rooms. Phil and Kat found Édouard in a small chamber he had rented.

"We meet again in better circumstances. A toast to the future!"

"Health and prosperity," Kat replied.

"Are you satisfied with our NOA commitments?"

"The president is satisfied with your own intentions, Édouard, but worried about some of your associates. The world will need to know the details of NOA development. There will need to be inspection. You implied that you would consult with PAD and INTO."

"'Inform' is all I can promise. But we will inform enough in advance so that concerns can be addressed among nations."

"What about rogue groups?"

"I cannot say for certain, Kat, but since you have asked, FAF will help to police them. We will need a treaty that stipulates obligations and rights in near-orbit. While I detest such obligations, and the Iranian Faction will resist them, we are not foolish enough to believe that we will enjoy unfettered action in near-space."

"Yet something is unnerving me about your conceding so readily to PAD's wishes."

"We simply want freedom to move. We are ahead of PAD in many ways. The Iranians will be among the first to seek a new home world. Even they realize that some rules are needed. From our side, we are unclear about the intentions of Pyramid."

"Welcome to the club, Édouard."

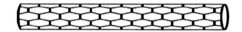

Ellis's thoughts drifted for a moment before Danielle reappeared with wine,. The look on her face was a quick antidote for his reverie.

"*J'ai peur*, Ellis."

"I'm afraid too, Dani. You have to be insane to be fearless. But we're as ready as we're ever going to be. Time to link up with the big team. FAF are clever, you have to give them that. Can't see their intentions on NOA being anything good. But Old Man Moreau agreed to everything PAD demanded, made solemn vows. They've got him exactly where he wants them."

"Before that we have to fight a war for the Nets, a war we cannot at any cost afford to lose."

"The list of enemies is long. The line between incremental and excremental has a nasty habit of vanishing. Tell me about the Netbots, Dani. Where are they right now in virtual space?"

"Top-left of your screen, that's *Kalima*, 'the Creed,' a most dangerous Netbot created in Iran."

"The imagery is breath-taking."

"We owe that to an ancestor of *Hunter*, your first creation, Ellis, still the best finder on the Nets. All the warrior bots are based on the same premise, that the continuous surveillance of enemies provides the only chance of survival. Who sees best wins. Of course, you also need the firepower to destroy the enemy bots you find."

"They are learning?"

"All the time. That's the part that no one controls."

Netwar

Phil drew a chair up to Kat's left hand, watching the monitor as shapes changed slowly, then too rapidly to follow. Around them, equally chained to visual arrays, were the best technicians of the US intelligence agencies, flanked by Saba Luanzi, Beya, and Sandover. Linked to capitals around the world and to Ellis and Danielle in their northern electronic stronghold, they watched and plotted, ready to attack or defend. Ellis took the lead at the outset, for reasons no one questioned.

"Here are the patterns *Hunter* is seeing. The clusters are Netbots, built on the patterns of life, the architectures of DNA, brain cells, proteins, nucleotides. But unlike live forms, these are entirely virtual. They can hide themselves beautifully against the background of the other living and inert molecules of cyberspace."

On-screen they saw concentrations of colour and light, pictured by their AI-enhanced analysis systems like comic book heroes.

"If you set your screens right down to nanometres," Ellis continued, "you can see all the complex structures that make up the Netbots. Then zoom out again and you see the complexity of a whole persona. They are nano and AI, learning and reproducing, controllable so far. They exist only on the Nets. The entire picture can change in a millionth of a second, like DNA unfolding. Beautiful and terrifying.

"Here are the main contestants. Each has its own character on your screen. This is the best view until something starts to happen in any one sector, an attack or a move. Then we've all got our assignments. Danielle has been tracking these warriors minute by minute. The war is starting. *Kalima* has been moving, so we've initiated our first set of responses.

We watch, we move. The more we stay ahead, the better our chances."

The characters were reconfiguring in cyberspace. In the background, Ellis's band of Imputers chattered, the front line of PAD's technical backbone and strike force. Ellis resumed his analysis in a sombre tone.

"I don't need to remind anyone of the stakes. This war may take minutes or days. Whenever possible, Danielle, Kat, and I should be on-line. You know the warrior bots from your briefings. Here they are in real time. That's *Murrow*, with its driving intensity to unravel tangled images — a creation of Pyramid that kills by confounding its adversary, generating the equivalent of bot insanity and dysfunction."

Ellis was in full swing now, the voice of the boxing announcer with a cynical edge.

"Beside *Murrow*, in the northwest corner, ladies and gentlemen, is one we call *Mitty*. It makes deals, betrays any bot to any other when advantageous. Pharmacon, probably Torbido's design and J.C. Moreau in control, instinctive seeker, ruthless attacker.

"Next to the right is *Harrod*, from Golgotha, cuts a swath and asks questions later. Makes up in aggression what it lacks in finesse.

"In the left quadrant is *Samson*, courtesy of Israeli intelligence and Giza Weiss at the helm. Behind is FSA's *Crockett*, which floods the Net with its own version of reality and kills by exposure. Beside is *Lionheart*, sleuth of MI8 and Kat's old chums.

"Then *Noora*, from Emir Ahmad and the Islamic Alliance, sees truth, the mirror opposite of *Kalima*, a highly adept seeker but short on firepower.

"Below on your screen, *Zhukov*, created by P-TEK, cunning and ruthless. Then Japan's *Satoshi*, solitary and lethal in its pursuit of all but the self.

"Beside is *Ea*, the European Union's keen strategist and effective eradicator. Finally *Ti*, son of heaven, China's fierce and cunning fighter, overwhelming opponents by its massive presence and pattern bombardment, independent of both PAD and FAF clusters but interacting with both."

Phil's brain was full, trying to watch them all and anticipate their movements. Danielle was initiating interventions with Kat, as Ellis zoomed in and renewed his colour commentary.

"There are more. FAF's *Confessor*, built and run by dissident opposition within the Vatican. Not powerful in mass of force, yet most intuitive in finding bots and killing them by disassembly. There's *Enterprise*, the champion of the liberal USCORP coalition, a principal target of *Mitty* and *Harrod*.

"Finally, the small armies of minor PAD and FAF bots that you can see if you zoom in further. Remember that there's no way to picture the whole Net accurately. What we're seeing is a composite sketch drawn by massive amounts of computation. Here's a final zoom out where you can see concentrations of bots in different sectors of the Net.

"Every bot and every master will be getting data from sensors within or left hidden on the Nets. We believe we have a better picture than FAF does, from *Hunter* and the other PAD bots. Most of the soldier bots are fodder, but even these are dangerous as distractions. Don't be tempted to fight campaigns solo, unlinked. Winning a battle, if it's a feint, could cost us the war. "

Danielle's chill voice interrupted.

"Game's on! *Mitty*'s moving on the routers, all of them. Countering."

PAD's fighters chased, but the FAF alliance had a lead. Danielle spoke as she acted.

"They're going after the software switches that control the flow of information on the Net. They can't mean to break the Net into segments unless they're sure of superiority in every sector. *Lionheart* says no, they can't hold them all. Must be trying to take control of the routers. Then they could attack where they want without any fear of enemy reinforcements. We have to stop them!"

The armies sent by *Mitty* and *Kalima* were suddenly bombarded by striating patterns, copied from their own image by PAD's advancing force, but subtly different. *Kalima's* minions warded them off with shields, like the force fields of the starship *Enterprise*. Then the shields started to flicker at the edges, to falter. Just as abruptly, they crumbled and faded into black background. There was enough time to take back control of the routers. Kat redeployed guards and destroyers to all the key junctions while looking for the next enemy move.

"Be happy," Danielle whispered, "every non-defeat is a victory. We didn't give enough thought to wetware. We should have seen that coming."

"We now have clear termination intention from *Mitty, Kalima,* and FAF," Ellis barked. Let's step up the volume, lads. Uploading our next strikes."

Silence. A moment in time. Phil sensed another fork in the road of the species. Temporarily, PAD controlled the commanding intersections of the Net, the meeting points of the dominant channels. Danielle used their router control to close some Net sectors, minimizing the movement of FAF reinforcements. With just a glance from Danielle or Kat, the Imputers executed orders with a deceiving ease bred of bottomless experience.

"Thank you, ladies and gentlemen," Danielle voiced. "Now attacking in force in every sector."

Chaos. Each battle was going to be run by the field commanders now, but Ellis and Kat had to keep the game plan ahead of FAF's as they advanced across the board. Ellis' icy voice cut through the mêlée.

"Imputers, drop everything. We're going to need Netbots that can penetrate the Net's hardware and remake the wetware of the routers. Soon, if not sooner. And then start on how to rebuild the entire Net softecture if it all goes down. Put *Hunter* on it, too, priority one!"

If it was possible to cringe virtually, Phil was doing it. What was coming? How much more weight could Danielle take? A pause as they watched in anguish.

"*Ti*'s army is making new routers," Ellis snapped, "with the hardware captured from the carpet bombing of the old ones. Look there! We don't have enough guards for everywhere and *Ti*'s pace is astonishing. FAF warriors are escaping. Back to square one everyone. Gareth, what've you got on router makers?"

"Thought you'd never ask, boss. Ten *Constructors* pilot tested. Best is *Mole*."

"You're a life saver! Release them, we'll make an alter-Net. The Net is being damaged and we can't withstand isolation in any sector for very long. Danielle, Kat?"

"Go," they signalled together.

Success. Now *Ti* was trapped and had to escape. Kat cut their jubilation short.

"Net damage is causing widespread disruption and panic in the real world. Communications are going down sporadically across the planet."

The ViDs showed shock or silence in stock exchanges and corporate headquarters as people watched the big screens for signs of life or explanation. Word was out that the Net was being destroyed from within. A virus. Not that far wrong.

"Danielle here. We're rebuilding the router protocols, courtesy Imputers — the Constructor bots and some new ones they've just come up with called Replicators. *Hunter* is protecting their flanks, so don't expect any help from that source for a while. We're way too slow, but we're working on that too."

"Standoff," Ellis pronounced. "We've done damage to FAF. Now we're looking at three Nets, all on the same hardware but with different roadmaps and interchanges. You can see the original Internet, then the architecture of *Ti*, and now our own alter-Net. What now? Do we wait until FAF comes up with some new bot weapons system? Surely neither China nor FAF would take down the original Net after the damage we've seen outside."

The screens were filling with colour, like a ViD of a star going supernova.

"Kat here. They're reproducing at explosive rates. *Kalima, Mitty, Zhukov, Harrod*. Jamming everything. Suicide run. We've no way to stop it. Why would they take down the Net. They lose everything if the world tilts into chaos, even their hopes for the stars. They must be able to rebuild. We need to look for their Remainders in the carnage. Fast! Maybe they have a deal with China. They must think they'll end up in control. If we can't stop them, we'll have to rebuild and repair much faster to stay on top."

Phil watched helplessly as the screens went into a blaze of colour, then opaque, a flatlining of the Net and its inhabitants. ViDs were sporadically showing panic and rioting outside, using the old cable and wireless networks. Heads of countries appeared, imploring people to restore calm, promising the Net's return in no time.

No time. Danielle appeared on-screen with a weak smile aimed at Ellis. Her face looked grey. It couldn't be long before the Imputer team cracked. Ellis broke the silence.

"Kat, you're in charge, I'm going into cyberspace with Danielle. Disturb us if you must. Best if you don't."

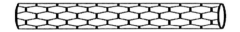

"Kat to Ellis. Situations please. How much longer do we have?"

"We're rebuilding, Kat, but it's too slow. The main intersections are badly damaged. We have an architecture in place. Linking it to the outside is extremely delicate as we can fix only one major junction at a time, sometimes a few if they're identical. It will take hours or days. Dani can't keep the team linked together that much longer. Without that, we're cyber-toast."

They were going to lose the race. The outside world was still deteriorating. Stampedes were starting for food and water, medicines. They needed some calming force.

"Ellis, can you get one message to most of the ViD screens of the world?"

"Might be possible, Kat. We'd have to make a million lightning strikes through our alter-Net but the peripherals are all on the same protocols. Gareth?"

"On it."

They cheered as the ViDs lit up across the globe.
HOLD ON, FULL NET FUNCTION IMINENT

"We hit about a hundred million screens. Five thousand languages."

"Nice work, lads," Ellis applauded. "I'm going back into the loop with Dani. We have two big problems on the inside. If *Mitty* and the others are still there, or there Remainders, they won't let us send out another message like that. We don't have the numbers to force the issue. Second, there is no way we can have the Net up soon. We've won only a small pardon. We'd better use it well!"

Outside was calm except for a few places already too far gone into violence. President Moore was pleading for patience. Kat's soft rebuke cut through the network.

"We should have been better prepared, should have thought less about war on the Nets and more about war on the streets."

"Ellis here. Danielle's down and out. May be a coma. We need help quick. Send meds by seaplane to Manitou. Phil has the coordinates."

"Talking to Camp Borden," Kat interjected. "Meds and medics there in twenty minutes, hang on."

The Imputer link was broken. Phil's hope sank. Suddenly their screens darkened. The panels went to black. They watched, horrified and fascinated. The Netbots were gone but it looked like the Net was up. Impossible! Some ViDs flickered back into life. On their screens, the Net looked clear and the switches that hadn't been rebuilt were clicking back into operation on their own accord. Some fancy repair programming! A timidly smiling face appeared in one corner of the screens.

"Greetings. I am sorry to interrupt. I am Zhi, communications technology student at the Open World University. My apologies for intruding upon your war. I waited until I thought there was no other hope of stopping the violence.

"My friends and I have created a bot we call *Zhaolin*. It studies, copies, and befriends others. We have studied your bots. All have the very human weakness of failing to recognize flattery, extensions of themselves that they assume they must have created.

"*Zhaolin* befriended every bot on the Net and came to live without distrust or alarm in the same neighbourhoods. These extensions became Trojan horses, armed with well-hidden firepower. In the end, as you saw, we destroyed all the Netbots together in the same instant of time. Net mop-up was slower but infinitely easier once the big guns were not roaming and reproducing.

"You may be able to copy *Zhaolin* in time, or produce others like it. You may even overcome the bots' fatal flaw of self-deception, to some degree. But if bots create other bots, and these adapt, none can ever be sure of the identity of its neighbours. This certainty of successful deception, no matter how small the odds, is what will keep the Net open. No one can gain control while others have the option to destroy all bots. Although terrorists might provoke this destruction for pure malice, the bots are easily replaced. With or without bots, the Net stays open. *Zaijian, see you again.*"

That was that. Kat leaned on Phil's shoulder in the wake of the battle, as drained as he was.

"Jesus, Phil, we were headed for the cliff edge without a chute and those FAF swine were ready to toss the world into hell. For what? What kind of madmen do that?"

"Aside from J.C.?"

"Point."

"I hate to say this because it's probably racist, but it's the same kind of madmen who send their daughters out attached to suicide bombs. It's FAF, that's all. Determined not to lose, which was where they were headed, they saw no alternative but to blow up the whole pop stand. Ugly testosterone. When you think about it, they may have thought they risked less than us. Maybe they were right. They'd have no compunction about putting down riots in the streets. They'd get food and coms working faster than us. They don't give a crap about the peons. They have enough pinpoint to get by. They'd do better than us in a world plunged in chaos."

"OK, but we'd all be incredibly worse off. They had it made, a deal to go into space with NOA, with only limited policing and controls."

"Maybe when the fighting began, they thought we'd use our control over the Net to put them more under our thumb."

"Maybe they just panicked at losing too much of their puerile 'touch me and I'll blow your head off' freedom. If so, they'd do it again. There's absolutely no level of rationality or sanity on their part that we can take for granted."

Phil and Kat caught up with Beya and Sandover shortly after. Kat pointed an accusatory finger at Sandover.

"Is it remotely possible that a tech student at the Open World University could have bettered us all? That easily?"

"It could be possible but it's a lot more likely if he had help."

"You mean Pyramid?"

"Probably, Kat. *Murrow*'s absence was striking but it was the first bot back on the Net by a mile. Everyone will draw the same conclusion."

"That *Murrow* was busy making sure *Zhaolin* was spread throughout the Net, undetected even by *Hunter*. Again they demonstrate technology in advance of the leading edge. Getting to be a habit."

"They'll call it the Imputer War," Sandover conceded, "and that's right — without them, we wouldn't have got to the battlefield. For those watching more closely, however, it's another victory for Pyramid."

"Is Zhi right about the Nets staying up, about no one being able to control them?"

Phil and Beya watched like spectators at a tennis match.

"I don't see any fly in the ointment," Sandover shrugged.

Kat looked hesitant but determined.

"If you were captured, could you 'forget' all knowledge of Pyramid?"

"It isn't much knowledge really, the identity of my triad. But, yes, I could do that. I had the training, in China, before Singapore."

Kat's com sounded softly.

"Guess what? There is no one named Zhi at the Open University."

Phil made a secure link with Damien in New York and Rana in London.

"It's going well on pre-production of the universal boticides," Damien began, "the killer bots. The bad news is that we need enough punch to find and destroy *every single* NOAbot on the Earth's surface, above it, and below it, too. It's a tall order and we're not even close. Our best chance would be a dusting from the upper atmosphere. We need to have a very large stock on the ready, which means Spacelift."

"From what I know," Rana added, "the Iranian Faction will develop releasable NOA cocktails - and molecides to destroy the plagues of others. It will be just as easy for Pharmacon, and it is impossible to believe that P-TEK and Golgotha aren't working on it, too."

"Could any of this work in our favour?"

"If their molecides are all-NOA killers like ours, they should do the same job in a global outbreak. What worries me most is that any party could start experimenting with the adaptive capabilities of their bots. Not all would be careful. This could be the source of an unstoppable plague."

"Unstoppable?"

"We'd have to be able to extinguish all NOA bots everywhere instantaneously, in competition with growing and not fully predictable enemy bots and exterminators."

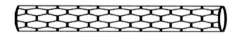

Jean-Christophe pulled the fur blanket more tightly around his shoulders.

"Gregor, it is good to see you in your natural habitat for a change."

"J.C., a pleasure in any circumstance. How do you like the Russian autumn — is it not magnificent?"

"The climax before the death and tragedy of winter, the rebirth in the next cycle of life."

"I think you share our penchant for long suffering, my friend, the long suffering of your enemies. Some champagne for the occasion? French, of course."

"*Merci*, Gregor. To our success!"

"To the ultimate deterrent!"

"You have found a way?"

"There is always a way, Jean-Christophe — this is the lesson of the people. No matter how much you trample the obvious solution into oblivion, or simply lose it against the backdrop of political and bureaucratic incompetence, it comes back to bite your rear end. If you are looking in that direction, you can claim it as your brainchild before your adversary wakes up. Such was our luck. Are you ready to put your soul into it?"

"With more than pleasure, Gregor, but it must absolutely stay between us. I will take care of the old man when the time comes, so to speak, but this is not the time. And PAD must not suspect."

"To our secret!"

"What secret is that?"

"*Touché*!"

"And what of the habitats, Gregor?"

"A little ahead of schedule despite delays and annoyances. It is illuminating how energetically the people respond to a lit torch up their unmentionables. We start building the first six habitats by year-end, three months at most. Two are labs, one NOA."

"The old man doesn't want to let go, even a little, as though the labs and the tech are his children."

"I heard he wanted to head out on an exploration habitat, lured by the chance of greater longevity."

"He's a fool. In the end he's too tied to that ancient monstrosity in Bordeaux. He won't go out on a lab ship or even a lavish social cruise. You won't catch me straying past inner space, either. I would not care to live in such provincial isolation."

"Will he cause trouble, the old man?"

"He can be pig-headed and wrong, but I persuaded him to endorse the new FAF Council, where we hold sway among the eight founding members. It will be my particular pleasure to prevent their inanity from crushing our dreams. It falls on us, my friend of the people. A time will come when we must act in unison. Destiny has never been decided by the faint. When the time comes, will you waver?"

"I will not put humanity at risk of extinction, if that is what you are asking. Even a crotchety old bear has that much sense. Short of that, I am with you to the end of time."

Cameo

Beya savoured a quiet moment at home with Sandover. Another election year was coming to the boil, probably the last before their potential rendezvous with whoever sent Orion. Life seemed an endless series of elections interspersed with crises, not a good recipe for an obsessive nature. Time had flown like the great grey heron since the mid-term ballots for the House and Senate. Here they were on the same balcony in Georgetown, the muggy July night settling in like a silent host around them. This was the big one, Saba for president. The capital was bristling with excitement under sudden fierce storms that attacked before the meteorologists could see them coming. Sandover had a quizzical expression on his somewhat more wrinkled but still strikingly distinguished face.

"So, you never really told me why you didn't go for VP. You say 'it's not me,' but what does that mean? You have all the skills and instincts, everyone agrees. And everyone falls under your spell."

"Mmmm, a reasonable question, where to start. Unlike Saba, I wasn't born in America. That's a factor. Bottom line, though, I'm not a politician by desire or instinct, better as an advisor or confidant, the perfect sidekick. There are others who really want the job; why not let them? Why rock the boat and our chances? Besides, the country isn't quite ready for two black women. Trust me."

"That's almost convincing but there's something else?"

"No. Maybe. I don't know. When I was fifteen, my mother and father went to the African Union, as it was called then, in Addis Ababa. He talked to senior officials while she chatted with the receptionists and secretaries. By the time they left, Uma was so shocked that she couldn't speak. She told me that to keep jobs and get promotions, women had to give sexual favours more as the rule than as the exception. So the female employees, like the female traders who travelled Africa, were branded as whores by the very men who took advantage of them, shunned or punished by husbands, often given HIV/AIDS for their last reward. You never had that in your childhood. It was a moment in time in Africa when the level of depravity of men became obvious to everyone. It was a pause and a look in the mirror, a recognition that many leaders were by any reasonable standards far from completely sane. For a teenager, it was terrifying."

"Yet you recovered."

"On the surface. I learned to rise above it in the eyes of others. But the awful thing about growing up in that sub-human depravity is that the shock never really goes away. It fills you with fear and hatred, not good assets for a politician. So I take the back seat. It fits my profile, fits my faith, fits the fear of putting your head up too high, getting noticed by the butchers."

"We're all so deeply formed by our childhoods. We can change, but then we are uneasy in our skins. In my youth, it was the spread of nuclear weapons in Asia that struck the most fear. China, India and Pakistan, Iran, North Korea, and the next wave; the near certainty that a shooting war inevitably would be set off by some deranged splinter group, and goodbye everything! Even more than that, what moulded me was the superficiality all around. I went to high school in Washington when Eng Kai was posted there. Television became the Church of Ultimate Shallowness, centred on *reality,* which was of course one hundred percent contrived, like most of the fight shows, in sum an offensive load of nonsense. The tabloids ruled with sagas of divas and paparazzi who happily manipulated each other in a lotus-strewn bliss of publicity."

"A different kind of insanity."

"Idiots became celebrities. Quality, truth, and integrity flew out the window. Soon it spilled over into politics."

"You opposed it?"

"I was ashamed."

"So you stepped aside and watched?."

"Yes, abstained. Then I went to Pakistan — Islamabad for a year. Eng Kai was doing something that I might now guess was forging connections. I was instantly struck by the contrast between the grace of their culture and the one-dimensionality of the fundamentalist vision that fought to throttle an intelligent modernizing society. Most of the madrassa children were raised to follow dogma with a loyalty bred of constant indoctrination. While they were worlds apart, the madrassa graduates shared one thing with the American diva-heiress trollops. Their view of the world was shallow to the core."

Beya caught a shaft of sunlight as she and Sandover passed the French doors in the long hallway of the Rush's home on the Potomac. The wealth that followed Orion had allowed them to afford some luxury. They hadn't wanted their kids drawn into the isolated lifestyle of private limos and gated communities, so they had found a large old townhouse with a roof garden and an iron staircase that spiralled down through the two-storey living-room facing the garden. A friendly row of cherry trees beckoned from the bottom of the hill. Below that, the distant skyline of the capital slipped in and out of view with the sun's daily cycle. In the living-room, Kat moved a photo of Lara to clear a space for the tea, sighing as she looked at the picture.

"How could her teens go by that fast? Twelve yesterday, twenty-three next month. Where did those years go?"

"We've been pretty occupied with other things," Phil half joked. "But take cheer, you spent a lot of time with them while they were growing up. Lara is beginning to think of us as human again and Dylan seems to be in a gear I don't have."

"We were right to tell them most of the truth about Orion. Dylan had already figured out a lot of it anyway. It seems he followed the trails and made the deductions from what we and the ViDs have said. He sees how things connect way faster than I do."

"I know, Kat. In a real battle of wits, I'd last about two minutes. It's an interesting time in life when your kids whiz past you."

Sandover was listening intently to these exchanges as Kat continued.

"He's maybe a little too much his own person for my taste. It would be good for him to learn more about relying on others, needing others. I also worry about him getting too involved in what we're doing. I don't want him in the line of fire. You can say 'oh, no, of course not,' but I know how fine is the line between the thought and the deed. I know what happens when the line is crossed."

"Here comes the interview."

The SmartSuite dimmed the lights and edged up the volume on the ViD. Balthazar Kumanecki of Gloview, the most widely respected journalist in the Western media, introduced Emir Ahmad Mohammad and wasted no time in asking about the prospects for reconciliation between the Islamic Alliance and the Iranian Faction. The cameras zoomed in on the thoughtful features of the emir, craggier after two long terms of moderating the Islamic Alliance.

"Changes of this nature take a long time. The Americans and the West never really understood what it's like to live in a dog-eat-dog world controlled by their armies and corporations. On the other hand, they cannot deal with people whose primary aim is to wipe them off the face of the Earth. If Moslems speak through the mouths of the fundamentalists among us, our intolerance will ensure war. I believe that this realization has been the major force behind our reform. And behind the split with the Iranian Faction."

"Why Iran?"

"This was ironic to me because Iran has always had large numbers who were peaceful, thoughtful, and highly aware of international affairs. They were among the most advanced and the most proud in the Arab world. After the inevitable end of the opulence and waste of the shahs, they suffered for decades under autocratic ayatollahs, increasingly angry with the Americans. Every time Iranians stood up for progress, the Revolutionary Guard bared its teeth."

"There is too much spilled blood for conciliation?"

"The fanatics will never reconcile. The Iranian Faction leaders will not relinquish power unless they are overthrown from within. They will never be happy until they have their own world. This is as true of your extremists as ours. The return to power of the Christian fundamentalists in America would be most dangerous."

As the ViD faded, the image of a coral reef appeared around them. The SmartSuite added a refreshing breeze and the sound of waves lapping gently on a sandy shore. Kat had a faraway look in her eyes as she reminisced.

"In the early aughts, I was about the same age as Ahmed, nearby at the London School of Economics. As I graduated, an invitation came for discussion with what was then MI6. They studied my test results and put me in strategy, then special ops support. It was their practice at that time to involve us in a few field ops so we'd understand the realities on the ground. Eventually, everyone ended up through error or accident on the front line, faced with a 'them or me' situation. Those who pulled the trigger stayed in ops. Those who didn't went into strategy, logistics, communications, weapons. In my case, it was clear they would have put me in strategy anyway."

Sandover voiced their thoughts.

"You didn't pull the trigger?"

"I did, but unfortunately I went a little further. With a lot of luck, a little quick thinking, and a degree of relish, I annihilated the opposition. I'd probably do it again. Turned out I had some dark instincts. That's what put me in strategy. That's what took me right out of the game later. Aside, of course, from meeting the man of my dreams."

Phil responded with a mock-humble smile.

"I guess I've always known you were capable of dropping the guillotine."

"I didn't think in any depth about the world until later. My loyalties and duties were clear enough. I watched what the politicos and the military brass did. I had a view or two of my own, but it isn't a healthy place to be if your allegiance is in any way uncertain."

Phil looked rueful.

"I was twenty-two then, about to head to Princeton to master the world of science. An exciting time, but the war in Iraq was notching up and the hate mongers were working overtime to spread the war. The world was going amok. 'But no,' I thought, maybe this was just the customary way of the world, that it was *my* vision that was off. Maybe it would clear. Naiveté would be cast out."

"Don't despair," Kat laughed, "it could still happen!"

"I was doomed to live at a moment of planetary brinksmanship where human capability reached the stars while our brutality was stuck in the mud. The hawks believed a fourth world war was coming, against the Islamic fascists, as they labelled their counterparts in ironic miscomprehension. A self-fulfilling prophesy if there ever was one. They would have no problem bombing Iran if that's what it took to destroy their nuclear ambitions."

"Would we today?" Kat asked, looking at Beya.

"Only as a last resort."

"It was hard to find any ethics," Phil continued. "Bush and Chavez were being called the two clowns in Latin America. It was species folly of the highest level, flirting with ultimate extinction for no reason but power. The ideologues were going to wreck humanity and the planet out of ignorance and stupidity."

"You opposed."

"Mostly I watched, ever the scientist. I wanted to keep reason alive, to know the history of thought that represents the civilization of mankind. I wanted to know the truth about something, anything, what to value regardless of the blindness of ideologies. A couple of years later, America started to change."

"It's been a long haul," Kat muttered."

"If Saba wins next month," Sandover countered, "and takes both houses with her, it could mark the end of power for the extremists. At least for a long while, and they know it. What can they do that we don't already expect?"

"We're part-blind with Ellis and Danielle off-line," Phil admitted. "Though she's recovering, they've gone private, bitter with everyone."

Back in Georgetown, Beya tucked Justine in and tiptoed down the stairs. Sandover looked sheepish, which often meant more, so she gave him a quizzical look.

"I've done a bad thing. I got Phil to slip a nano pinpoint transmitter into Damien's kit. He's in London as we speak, with Rana Myagdi. Chuanli gave me the receiver and codes. I know it's wrong but we've put a lot of faith in Rana's loyalty to PAD."

"Park your principles, let's listen."

"There is no bone in my body, Rana, that does not want to stay here in London. But my work is piled up to the ceiling and New York calls me back. I'll go to New Haven on the way to speak at my twenty-fifth reunion, something that makes me feel old at a mere forty-seven. I was lucky at Yale, not knowing in advance how good the Keck Facility really was. I studied, taught, stayed on for a cascade of years. In the end, the Nobel came from the early work on nanorg. Not long after that, I met Philamon Rush and my life changed again completely."

"I can imagine, Damien. Though Phil comes from science, he lives in very different circles."

"That was almost four years ago. In the interim, my wife has left me and taken our children. I see them, of course, I wasn't a bad husband, but once this circus started I was never there. At the end of the day, I suppose I was a bad husband. Life has been full to bursting, but lonely."

"I have a small bottle of champagne if you would care for a nightcap."

Sandover raised his eyebrows as he turned the volume up a pinch.

"The moon lights our way, Damien, a crescent come to bless or haunt us through the old gothic windows of London."

"A toast to the future."

"To freedom."

They lost the signal — separation of subject from transmitter in all probability. Nothing incriminating, but a close relationship growing closer, something to beware. Sandover's *comme ci, comme ça* gesture spoke his agreement.

Jean-Christophe clenched his fists in a peak of silent rapture.

"Ever closer, Gregor, circling in on the prey like the wild dogs on the savannah."

"Or the Russian bear. It is good to be on the hunt again, J.C. Time to lock and load, to rediscover the courage to kill. The ultimate bluff requires the ultimate commitment. What are you made of?"

"People who have stood in my way have found ways to be parted from their annoying habits. I pity my father. I revel in a thousand versions of the fall of the fabulous effing four. Count me in, Gregor. Time is wasting."

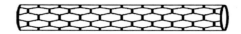

Wajid paused to take in the twilight apparition. A promising wind brushed the face of Rajasthan. Dry gusts moved sand and saris as the small procession leaned slowly into the dunes and the fading sun. Red cloths hung across the entrance of the tents, where curry stewed and saffron rice bloomed from black pots.

After dinner, he walked to the festival. The last day. The bathers were back from the ghats and the Brahma temple, the fairground quiet on this eve of departure. Shadows sprung and retreated as gossiping knots of friends passed before the soft light among the tents and animals. There was a magic in the swirling breezes, a magic with a sinister edge, patient, watching, not interfering in the passages of this night. The figure he faced as Amal drew him into the rich darkness of flickering candles was beyond his wildest imagination.

"Be you welcome, Wajid."

"*Diwan.*" Wajid could only bow before this voice from the veils of the Langas.

"Be not afraid, my son. This is the land of God. And God has asked you to follow a path, to serve a purpose, fulfill a destiny."

"I am not worthy."

"It is your karma, your future."

"Where does it lead, father?"

"You will go into the heavens. We have commenced the building of a citadel in space, to be ready by next dry season. You have nine months to assemble the scientists and prepare their families. A return to Earth is not anticipated. You will take charge of the NOA lab, separated forever from the other passengers on the voyage. Your ship will be a blessed vessel of discovery and renewal."

"Where is the voyage, father?"

"You are going to Moksha, Wajid, a new planet, one of six in its system, abundantly favoured by red deserts, a new Rajasthan. The voyage will take your lifetime. You will write the next chapter of the Mahabharata. You will take with you all of the yogas, Bhakti, Raja, Karma, and Jnana. You are blessed beyond others, chosen to experience God and the ātman."

"I am deeply honoured."

"Choose carefully and work quickly, Wajid. You are the best scientist, our best hope. Do not concern yourself with the rest of the habitat in space unless it has direct impact on what you are doing. This is Pratik, I believe you know each other."

The tall and slightly emaciated figure of the Indian president advanced into the light, smiling, yet with a determined set to his eyes.

"Of course, father, and my deepest respect to you, President."

"You two may talk with ease at the Society or where you wish. Pratik will keep you informed of the grand design. In return, he must know everything about the lab. I will smooth your way should the need arise. Go with God, Wajid."

The breeze caressed the back of his neck as he walked through the quiet of the night toward Pushkar. All the hairs stood straight up, stretching toward the stars, tingling with dread and joy.

WMD

Beya screamed in denial. Saba's voice hung in the air like an abyss between the phone receiver and her ear.

"You heard. A nuclear blast in Tampa Bay. Three million souls. St. Petersburg, Clearwater, Brandon, Lakeland, Winter Haven, Sarasota, gone. Meet me here as soon as possible — sooner! Tell Sandover. We've sent a bird for him."

The world was changing gears again. Beya could feel it right down to her genes as she scrambled into clothes and opened the ViD. The president was declaring a nationwide state of emergency. Her com bleeped; FSA transport downstairs. On the way down, she called Sandover in New York.

"I'm watching."

"Chopper's coming, FSA."

"See you in two. We have to avoid a shooting war."

One deep breath and into the chasm.

Kenzie Moore scowled from the chair. Beya knew from long experience that her expression was not hostile, just the accumulation of stress. One week left in two terms of office and it all hits the fan.

"Most of you will be surprised by what you are about to hear. For the first part, General Arnold will provide the briefing. Jim?"

"Madame President, colleagues. The components of the nuclear device were delivered in a pleasure yacht named *Marvel*, owned by Taylor McDermott, a respected business leader not associated with FAF. The yacht went out with the McDermotts and some guests on board and returned two days later. It was checked by the Coast Guard on its way in and allowed to proceed. We have a brief report from the inspecting officer, who admitted on further questioning that there was some unidentified equipment in the gym that looked like high-end exercise apparatus. He is a young man who will have nightmares for the rest of his life. Everyone else directly concerned was obliterated in the blast."

The general paused momentarily as they absorbed the news.

"We looked through all of the satellite imagery from the past two days and found nothing at first. The blast occurred at 19:00, twilight. At 19:20, we received an unsigned message on one of our most secure channels, giving longitude and latitude that proved to be far from *Marvel*'s home marina. Satellite imagery revealed that a light-class submarine, identified by its energy signature as *Incursion*, had stopped and boarded *Marvel* before departing twenty-seven minutes later."

They could sense what was coming.

"*Incursion* is FAF, based in P-TEK Russia. The sub stopped in Bushehr in the Persian Gulf nineteen days ago. Satellite images show the loading of large metal boxes covered by tarps. Intelligence confirms prior shipments from a nuclear facility in the former Turkmenistan, through Iran to the Gulf. There is further incontrovertible evidence that this device comes from P-TEK and the Iranian Faction, with the possible complicity of Golgotha and Pharmacon. The vice president has been kept informed but we are otherwise protecting our sources at this time."

"Thank you, Jim. And now my own update. Because of the evidence, I have launched two strikes, which will be taking place at 20:00, as we speak. The strikes are not nuclear, but they are severe. They are aimed at the largest military and strategic industrial sites in PTEK Russia and the Faction states. They will wreak much more damage to those economies than was done to ours, with less than a tenth of the loss of human life. I ordered these strikes in consultation with Saba, Meg, and Jim."

The defence secretary and the top general looked as worn out as the president, though their expressions gave away little.

"I believe that FAF has done this to destabilize America long enough to get their Republican cronies elected next week. I believe they have a good chance of success. Besides taking care of the survivors in Florida and beyond, we must prevent a collapse of civil order and political will. I have ordered the strikes for this reason, as either a gift or a curse to you. I have only a week left. For my part, I wanted to leave Saba free to play her own hand. But as president and commander-in-chief, I had to deliver two messages to our enemies. First, that we will not accept attack without inflicting greater damage. It is not enough for them to pretend ignorance. Second, that we do not kill for hate or for pleasure, as they apparently do. We target strategic objectives and minimize the loss of life."

By morning, the death toll in Florida had reached four million. Another million had radiation sickness or serious injury. Although the damage to P-TEK and Faction territories was ferocious, fewer than sixty thousand died, even by FAF's inflated figures. There was a stand-off whose silence was deafening, with everyone on red alert .

Beya and Sandover left Justine with Kat on the way to the White House. The streets of Washington were eerily quiet. Again in the Oval Office, they waited for more details. The wait lingered on. There was some talk of members of the yacht's crew being involved, but none had escaped the blast area. *Incursion* had disappeared, likely into an undersea bunker. The identity of the party that had sent the coordinates of the sub's meeting with the yacht remained unresolved. They assumed Pyramid — Occam's razor — but they had no evidence. Sandover said once again that he couldn't get any inside information. All the FAF leaders denied involvement, pointing to extremists acting in stealth in their midst. While no one was fooled, further retribution was forestalled. Whatever the evidence shared only among Saba, the president, and Jim Moore, their reasons for protecting it must have been humungous. Without it, no link to Golgotha or Americans existed in the public domain.

Daryl Blanton and Eleanor Coughlin launched furious media attacks on Kenzie Moore, almost too quickly to have been caught by surprise. They were backed by Harbison, the whole GOP machine and the Christian Right. They hauled the president over the coals for suicidally inadequate home security and no plan for the future. Righteous destruction would rain down upon the terrorists and the godless liberals when the faithful united to take power. Between the lines of their rhetoric, however, it was becoming clear that their thunder had been stolen by the steely response of the president, ironically a liberal and a woman. 'Only as a last resort,' Beya recalled with a shiver.

Until the other shoe fell or until the election, the Democrats' future hung again on a thread. Beya watched in fascination and terror as perceptions shifted and settled across the country and the world. Saba went on camera in the evening.

"Four years ago, a nuclear detonation in Washington was very narrowly averted. When the Republicans attacked us with the same hate they are trying to sell you now, my president said 'Don't be fooled.' I say the same today. The GOP cares about power, not about you. Their allies in FAF have done this to get them elected. Don't be fooled."

Hawksley Everett was already travelling the swing states in his neck of the country. 'Don't be fooled' became a rallying cry for liberals and centrists on whose final decisions Saba's fate increasingly depended. The curfew was lifted during daylight but strictly enforced at night. Beya and Sandover worked day and night on speeches for Saba, analyzing the polls and counterpunching the more and more vicious attacks from the GOP.

The morning of Election Eve finally came. As the first suspicion of light stole into the bedroom, Beya and Sandover held a long embrace. An incoming pinpoint burst from Phil caught Beya's eye as it appeared on the wall screen unencrypted.

Beya, Sandover, Kat

Sorry to be missing the action. If you have to be stuck somewhere, Pinpoint HQ comes highly recommended, across the Foothills Expressway from Stanford's graceful towers in a high valley by the Russian Ridge. The mountains protect the rugged Pacific coast south to Santa Cruz from the relentless advance of the Bay area to the north and San Jose to the south.

Evening finds me in the VIP guest house, tucked up behind a redwood-topped ridge, halfway drunk, the other half sick with worry about you. We may be safe for the moment, but peace is not the fate of the wicked. I watch the ViD recordings over and over as Tampa is obliterated, the circle of death creeping outward.

Here there is nowhere to go, too much time to think. I'll speak with Ben tonight. It's time to stir his interest in inter-place-time communication. If Tampa can happen, time may be speeding up. Most people out here are scared to death, three thousand miles from Florida. San Francisco must be a prime target for FAF.

Ben is building the new Pinpoint labs near Seaside on the northern Oregon coast. Today's disaster will speed the move. They'll be near enough to the space port but far enough for comfort. Here and in space, we'll push the pinpoint power-distance parameters to their limits. If we survive this round of global brinksmanship, Kat and I should be at Seaside. Dylan will be commuting from Stanford to Banks in his work with Spacelift. We'll be a rather mobile team with nodes at Seaside, Banks, and up top on Fuller. We've bought lab space in the main facility, four acres of surface, and I've got my eye on a spot on Bucky. We'll have everything we need to attempt an inter-place-time transmission if we can find the last piece of the puzzle, something still missing in the physics.

We've been focused on NOA for a long time. I still think that's what's most likely to bring the future crashing down. At the same time, inter-place-time may be the critical safety valve. If you can reconfigure the past, right up to the point of a terminal disaster, there's a second chance.

Talked with Ben. He raised the issue quite by chance. Perhaps. He started the conversation by saying he'd like to send a note to the future, if there is one, ask them to come back and rescue us. A joke, but too good an opening, so I suggested a message to the past, to warn them. That certainly caught his attention, so I said it was worth thinking about, that there might be a way to speed communications to relativistic levels, in some sense engulf all 'present' time across all places. He argued that transcending time must be different, that the times would have be 'adjacent' in ways that could be pierced. That made him think of black holes so I proposed exploring this at Seaside

He brought up the risks involved in communicating across time, the potential power it could give its masters? He also asked what we would say to the past, so I suggested a warning about NOA, to give them some information to help them come out better. In the end, we agreed we'd work together on the science and he'd leave the rest to me. Deniability. But if the time comes to experiment, he wants to be there, whether it's down here or up there.

I'll will fly to Washington tomorrow to join you for the election results. Over and out, I'm praying for you.

Beya stretched as Sandover rubbed her back. This was always a dangerous practice,. Something about living under threat of extermination had put both of their bodies on an even higher level of alert. The alarm clock sounded, 04:00, time dissolving the wee hours of the morning.

"A penny for your thoughts."

"Economists! Always the low-price offer."

"OK, a zillion dollars for your thoughts, payable in small unmarked notes."

"That's better, don't stop that."

"And your thoughts?"

"Nothing and everything. The undecided are still at a record high. It will come down to four states for control of Congress and three for the Senate. Two of these are the same, Florida and Texas."

"Any last-minute ammo?"

"Saba has evidence that the top echelon of FAF in America knew about the Tampa strike. Letting it out would clinch victory. It would also drive home the wedge that's dividing the country. Blanton is talking openly of civil war. God help us, that ended almost two centuries ago. That's the brakes on spilling the evidence. It smacks of expediency and could cause war."

"It might. But your options are very limited. If you wait and you shouldn't have, you lose the whole farm. With what's at stake, you can't afford to lose power. It will be disastrous if America is not a leading force in PAD. So you have to go public and start to heal the schism in the same breath. Heal it enough to keep the lid on and plant the seeds of reconciliation."

Sandover had that Asian way of dissolving complex issues. Beya reset the alarm to alert her at 04:30 and disappeared into the beat of a dance that joined the mystery of the Orient with the ageless rhythm of the land. The future could find its own way for a moment or two.

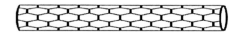

"Ladies and gentlemen, the next president of the United States. Saba Luanzi!"

Saba looked calm. She had reached some inner place where choices are made. She arrived at the podium with purposeful grace, the ultimate political catwalk.

"Fellow Americans, whatever divides us, we are Americans. I have undeniable evidence that the Central Committee of the FAF knew about the nuclear attack on Florida and did nothing to interfere with the actions of the perpetrators, extremist groups living within FAF borders.

"Our strikes on FAF targets were made with this knowledge. We have waited as long as possible to release the evidence, while removing the sources of that information from danger. They have served you very well and deserve at least that much of your gratitude.

"Some of the conspirators are Americans. They are also prominent figures in the Republican Party and the Christian Right. They have allowed millions of Americans to die. That amounts to the highest treason. They have been arrested. Their trials and sentences will be the responsibility of the courts to decide and of the government to oversee. If I am elected, any who are innocent will be released and compensated as the courts decide. Those found guilty will be sentenced accordingly. I am informed that one of the accused has already fled to P-TEK Russia.

"If the FAF Coalition within America takes power, I think you know what you can expect. Traitors will not see justice. Those of you who believe in this country and our people will stand by powerless as America gives the FAF a monopoly in NOA and in space.

"You will then have war, the second global gunfight of this century, much worse this time because America will not only be guilty, but also in direct military conflict with our allies, the states of PAD. They will not accept that FAF be gifted monopoly over science and space. The war that FAF will bring to you will be fought against our friends, the most advanced nations and societies on the planet. It will be fought on Earth and in space.

"I believe that a substantial majority of Americans do not want this to happen. If you elect Hawksley Everett and me, if you give us majorities to work with in Congress and the Senate, here is what you can expect.

"We will give the accused a fair trial. We will keep space open, for FAF as well as for PAD.

"We will cooperate in the drafting and negotiation of inner space law. We will commission and equip our near-space navy together with our friends and allies.

"FAF may also promise freedom. They will deliver it only to their elites. It is time for all Americans to decide which future they choose. You must vote tomorrow if you want peace, democracy, and justice instead of corporate feudalism. You must vote tomorrow if you want reconciliation. Our enemies have been severely punished. Let us again seek friends."

So far, so good, Beya thought. It would be hard for the undecided to vote for traitors and the spectre of civil and global war. Hawksley Everett was still part-mystery; she held her breath as he stepped before the cameras.

"Fellow Americans. I would like to say one more thing about reconciliation. I am from the South and my roots are deep Christian roots. I think it is time for the South to rise again. This time we should unite with the North and PAD, to take our true place in the world, in the service of God and humankind."

Beya held her breath a little longer.

"The Republicans and their FAF cronies paint a picture of victory, dominance, and glory. It is a false path. It is not the Christian way. The true path is the human quest laid down by God to attain the glory of creation, not to destroy the divinity and diversity of life.

"All creation now calls you forth to render your own judgment. You will in turn be judged by what you do and what that brings. Do not bring division. Do not bring war. It is the time for the South to truly rise, to take our place in the divine mission and the true search.

"You know me. You know I tell you the truth. The path of conflict and violence is the way of the past, full of betrayal and blood. Look ahead. Join together in finding the path of the truly faithful, the concourse of tolerance, and the way of peace."

A moment of silence, cameras off. Saba joined Beya and her campaign team in the Lodge, their euphemistic name for the logistics room. Hawksley went straight on to Oklahoma City. The first reactions came in slightly positive in the swing states and better everywhere else. Still in the game! Then again, fate is a fickle companion.

Daryl Blanton countered late that morning in the strong reassuring voice that Beya had heard so often issuing sleaze that she couldn't hear it any other way. She caught the feed at the Lodge, now mostly empty, staff out with candidates or organizing final events.

"Friends, Americans. I am here to say to you 'Do not be fooled.' You have heard the incompetent administration mouth these words while they lie to you. What have they brought you? Security? No. Massive death and disorder? Yes. Would this have happened if I had been president? No. Why not? We are friends with FAF. We would not be a target for any of them.

"Our FAF partners and friends here in America, now accused of treason, are innocent. Why did they not speak?

They did not know. They have been accused. Where is the evidence claimed by the president? I call upon Americans to honour the foundation of our justice system, innocent until proven guilty. I ask Americans to repay the dishonesty of the Democrats with their dismissal from government!

"Do not believe the lie that we will be at war with Europe and the West. We will not. We support our allies in PAD by the same logic that we support our allies in FAF. Our first duty is always to America. Saba Luanzi forgets this or pretends it isn't true. In a world divided into two camps, a division created over the last eight years of Moore and the Democrats, Americans must again have the power to advance our own interests first, in balance with the interests of our allies in both camps.

"All their lies are a last-ditch ploy to cover their childish naiveté and their genocidal blundering. Do not be fooled. If you allow them to continue the carnage they have wrought, you will be at war with FAF. You will spend billions fighting them and policing space. If you give us the mandate, you will be at war with no one. Americans will take our rightful place on the Earth and in all of God's creation."

Regrettably, not bad at all. Saba held up one hand, fingers spread. Beya had five minutes to send ideas for her riposte. Four minutes later, she touched *send*.

He didn't counter the treason charges – hammer on the evidence and its verification by everyone in the military and the government.

Here are latest quotes from PAD leaders on imminent conflict with PAD if the Republicans win. Use these to reverse their claim of who will bring peace and who will bring war.

Call their bluff. They've abandoned their first duty to their countrymen and women – four million DEAD, and for what? To toady favour with a band of mass murderers. Who trusts the Iranian Faction and P-TEK?

Hawksley struck a strong chord in all the swing states, and Blanton didn't alter that. Remind America to listen to the voices of the new South, to believe in the true Christian prophecy, the divinity of ALL that God has created.

Beya had a moment of déjà-vu as the last polls closed and the final results started to come in. Gathered in the Cabinet Room beside the Oval Office were Saba and Hawksley, Jim Arnold and Meg Matheson, Phil, Kat, and Beya. Sandover arrived with Justine. The president came in with her family for her last moments of real power, though her term would leave her in office until January. The company was easily as good as it gets. They were comfortably running out of things to say as the trends solidified and the whole kit and caboodle came down to a few handfuls of undecided congressional districts and senatorial constituencies in the five swing states.

There was less than 1 percent difference in the presidential vote. The Electoral College outcome, the count that mattered, was up in the air. Beya was feeling too old for this. On the other hand, if they lost tonight, she's have the rest of her life to recuperate.

"Look, that one's ours!"

The president's uncharacteristically boisterous whoop brought Beya out of her reverie.

"They've declared it ours. That means Congress. Is it close enough for Blanton to demand a recount? We don't know yet? I think we've got it!"

With Congress they could block any violent moves by a Republican Executive and Senate. A smile gave the lie to Beya's outward calm. The returning beams from around the room showed her more starkly than she cared to admit how much pressure they'd been under. Nothing was impossible now.

"Here comes Florida!" Kat hollered.

With two Democratic senators in Florida, there would be a tie in the Senate, with one, a Republican majority. Beya's mind raced. If they got the Senate tie and won the presidency, the VP's deciding vote in the Senate would give the Democrats control of both houses — one of the bizarre minutiae of American political law. It was going to take another couple of hours to decide the presidency. Saba was now ahead in the popular vote by a hair, in the Electoral College by less than that.

No further news, time for a break. Justine strolled off with Saba, quite a nice relationship developing between a six-year-old girl and her fifty-year-old idol. Justine loved to tell stories, and Saba had a few of her own. Beya and Sandover found themselves momentarily alone with Phil and Kat.

"What now?"

Nothing to say. They laughed.

"Still depends too much on the next few hours," Beya sighed. "We have to talk as soon as it's all decided. Let's stay here. The Lodge is my second home. The others will drift off once we know the final tallies and the verdict."

Ascent

Beya saw red numbers flashing on the ViD screen.

"Look!" Saba was shouting. "Something on the Electoral College votes. And something on Florida. Hold onto your seats!"

One minute to midnight. They'd been waiting a lifetime for this moment. Florida was coming in first. The Gloview cameras focused in on Balthazar Kumanecki and the scroll board behind him. Two large check marks appeared in blue and they let out a yell. Although central Florida trashed them completely for the Tampa disaster, north and south Florida had held. It was a victory with a vast hollow place at the centre. They all felt it together like a blow as the ViD went remorselessly on. It all came down to Saba versus Blanton now. And further, to the VP candidates Hawksley Everett and Elaine Coughlin. Beya's old political science classes came back with riveting import.

Each State's allotment of electors is equal to the number of House members to which it is entitled plus two Senators. A majority of 270 electoral votes is required to elect the President and Vice President. No Constitutional provision or Federal law requires electors to vote in accordance with the popular vote in their State. If no presidential candidate wins a majority of electoral votes, the presidential election is decided by the House of Representatives by majority vote from the top three candidates. If no Vice Presidential candidate wins a majority of electoral votes, the Senate selects the Vice President by majority vote from the top two candidates.

Two states were still undecided in the Electoral College: Florida and Texas. Somewhat fitting, the old GOP heartland still half-lost in a bygone era and the old Republican stronghold bankrolled by retired tycoons. Though these states had changed in revolutionary ways since the millennium, blood runs deep. The old libertarian strains were never far beneath the freshly painted surface.

"In a breaking development, Gloview now projects the Texas vote to go to Luanzi and Everett." Balthazar Kumanecki smiled as he continued. "If Florida follows suit, the Democrats take all three Houses; Congress, Senate, and White. If Florida goes to the GOP, the Electoral College will be in a dead draw on both the president and the VP. Saba Luanzi will get the presidency by vote of Congress. But the Senate, without the deciding vote of the vice president, will be unable to elect the vice president. Catch 22. I have with me Dr. Paula Giacometti, professor of constitutional law at Columbia University, to explain what would then happen."

"Apparently this was never anticipated, Mr. Kumanecki. The procedure for replacing the vice president, should there be a vacancy, is nomination by the president and confirmation by both houses.."

"Also catch 22, no? Saba would nominate Hawksley, but his election in the Senate would be a draw without the VP's vote."

"I believe that the next determining factor would be the total popular vote for each candidate, and that would give Everett the victory. But the Supreme Court could decide on other grounds. Although precedent is missing, prior rulings indicate that the Court would decide as quickly as possible to avoid a long impasse. After two terms of Democratic appointments, the balance of opinion in the Court would tend toward liberal."

"Thank you, Paula. There you have it. While the Democrats are poised on the edge of total victory, they may have problems taking that last step *over* the edge. Hold on a moment. This coming in from our central desk. Gloview now predicts the popular vote in Florida will go to Blanton and Coughlin."

Lord love a duck!

"But wait a moment. In an unexpected development, one Florida state elector has announced that she will cast her vote for Luanzi and Everett. One minute. She is Yana Menses, a

Republican Party official who lost her entire family in last week's nuclear devastation. In her words, 'This cannot happen again. I cannot vote for a party that brings traitors and enemies into our midst.' Can she do that, Paula?"

"Of course. There is one precedent. The outcome was not in the balance in that case, but the contestation in the state government and courts ended in support for the man who went against the party vote. *No Constitutional provision or Federal law requires electors to vote in accordance with the popular vote in their State.*"

"We'll be back after a short break. At this moment, the Democrats win it all."

None of them believed it, not yet. FAF had to have something else. The other shoe.

By 02:30, there was no further news of importance. The now 'frayed four' gathered in the Lodge to consider the world, basking in anticipated relief while shaking at the thought of what lay ahead.

Phil smiled. It was good to see everyone a shade more light hearted again.

"We have a small army working on all sides of NOAbots, Damien and Rana on the science, the citizen networks on transparency, now military intelligence on the leads we find. We're in the middle of all the core networks except FAF's We've got eyes almost everywhere. It's hard to imagine what more we could be doing."

Kat's frown was strong enough to put a crease through the room.

"Not enough. If we watch and respond, we're probably dead. We need to think further ahead. I've asked Dylan to look into it. He and Rana have the most unencumbered minds when it comes to jumping outside the box. No offence, Phil and Sandover — you, too, but you have a lot of other things on your mind. Rana's FAF connections are still a worry. Worse perhaps is that she and Damien are making independent plans."

"Surely they're on our side."

"No doubt, Phil, but they're also free spirits, slightly intoxicated by the power that flows from their knowledge. You can feel it in subtle changes in our conversations. Conspiracy is not easy for the good hearted to cover."

Another fly in the ointment, Beya knew. Sandover asked the question on the tip of her tongue.

"What about sending Orion?"

"Time to put that on the front burner," Kat asserted. "Lock and load."

"We've got a perfect shot at doing it," Phil added. "Are we sure it's the right thing to do?"

It was a question they'd asked a hundred times, but these were the real times coming.

"I don't know the answer," Phil signalled with some shift of body language that they all recognized by now. "We've always had two main possibilities. Orion came from some advanced group of beings or from the future. Pyramid/Visitors or inter-place-time. If it's Pyramid/Visitors, there never was inter-place-time communication and there's no reason to try to replicate the Orion transmission. If we do, we'll just attract more attention and magnify the target already painted all over us. But here's the rub. Do the real message senders want us to resend? Presumably yes, or why would they have planted the idea in Orion and given us the technology leads to try it?"

"Do we trust them?"

"Very good question, Kat. At this moment, yes. They haven't led us astray so far. Ironically, there is no such thing as inter-place-time communication in this view of the world but we try it nevertheless because that's what we were told to do. I don't know why the senders would want inter-place-time opened up as a technology at this point in human history. Did they fear it would be discovered by others? Was it just a ruse to get our attention? Will they tell us more when it comes to the crunch?"

Sandover asked the inevitable question.

"What if Orion did come from the future?"

"If we find the last pieces of the technology," Phil replied, "there's the possibility that we send Orion and simply complete the loop, complete the healing of place-time that started right after the tear was made that night in Merimbula. In that case, mission accomplished, no harm done."

"But?"

"But there's also the possibility that we open a new slash in the fabric of place-time. This is where it's hard to escape our insistence that one thing must happen before another. Linear time."

Kat looked very dubious.

"Given that we did receive it, doesn't that mean that it was in fact sent? That there is no need to do it again?"

"I agree, Kat. If we're doing OK, we shouldn't take the risk. But we should push ahead and be ready to try, maybe soon, if we find we have to. Frankly I don't believe in inter-place-time communication — no such thing, and maybe no Visitors. Just us mice, as my uncle used to say. But we may need the capabilities we find while we're looking for inter-place-time. Someone went to a lot of trouble to plant the idea. Until we know why, we'd be foolish to drop it."

"And others may be looking," Kat added. "If they find it and open a new chasm, everything we know disappears."

Sandover looked oddly relieved as he turned to Phil.

"We have a little time. I'll get all I can from Pyramid while you fast track the R&D with Ben. How is the security at Seaside?"

"We can keep it quiet a while longer."

"Still, better not to take chances. I'll mention to friends that a discreet watch would be prudent. What about Ben?"

"Inter-place-time is in many ways an extension of pinpoint technology. That and curiosity keep his attention. Scientists are really just detectives without the hats. We'll figure it out if it can be done. We may not know for sure until the last moment."

"Security will be the key," Kat rejoined, "FSA, PAD, and Pyramid."

Five weeks later, on a frosty December 17, Saba and Beya stood before a bleacher full of America's top leaders and journalists, facing a commander and a company of athletic-looking men and women.

"By the powers invested in me, I hereby commission the United States Naval Space Command and appoint Admiral Luisa Stollery to the post of Chief of Naval Operations, responsible to me as Commander in Chief through the Secretaries of Naval Operations and Defense. I look forward to working with you. Godspeed, Admiral Stollery."

The startling jade eyes of the decorated astronaut and space pilot who was now in charge of USNAV focused for an instant on Beya. She would be a strong leader for the PAD forces in space. She smiled as she received her papers from the president, her stern demeanour softened, perhaps a momentary nod to human frailty and the vagaries of fate and fortune.

Phil was this moment headed up Spacelift, with encrypted notes drifting back like postcards from on high.

Beya, Sandover, Kat

It's still a hard-ass haul, after seventy-five years of people in space. Lovely place to be but it bloody well could be easier to get around and survive. No point complaining, and the view is spectacular, Earth down the gravity well, 'below' as they used to say on old Earth. Fuller and Bucky above, space tugs working construction, ships and vessels of all shapes and sizes coming and going, a small cosmos in motion.

The base at Banks already seems a faint memory. The vertigo eases after the first few miles up as the internal feeling of an airplane replaces that of a rail-less platform looking fifty thousand feet straight down. Earth fades and the feeling of something impending grows like a starburst. Four thousand kilometres is a long haul in a tiny cabin hanging on a thread.

Admiral Stollery guided us neatly through the predictable stages of alarm with illuminating accounts of the history of the Lift, the core of astronauts from many nations, and the new space navies. I feel out of place, my first mission, as we marvel at the Lift and the stories. I'm happy now that Dylan talked his way into our party. He's as much at home here as Stollery.

This 'evening,' Admiral Stollery lulled us with a long tale, a deliberate ruse as the first carbon digestor shot by the viewport. We whooped in fear nonetheless, until assured we were not being attacked by an armada of flying saucers. The mammoth apparatus spreads like mushrooms on three platforms from the elevator shaft out into the upper atmosphere. Placed every half-kilometre, these three-leaf clovers and their core make the beginnings of a tree-like structure. Yggdrasil came to mind, a memory from the story of a quest through space to Earth on giant, warp-drive Dyson trees.

Systems have engaged and our quarters are locked down as we approach vacuum. Silence and black above. An exquisite incandescent layer of atmospheric envelope stretches out below our feet, the carbon cable spread out in a long bow when you dare to look straight down at the slowly widening planet underneath, rotating and changing for our viewing pleasure.

Admiral Stollery put an end to the show by telling us to get some sleep. We would be going much faster now and arrive in the morning. Of course, there's no morning out there, but it'll be morning on our body clocks, and the Admiral assured us that rested was the only way we wanted to arrive."

We didn't shoot out the top of the Lift, Sandover's nightmare. Instead, we decelerated and coasted into EOL Station. End of the Line gave us the first full view of a magical vista. First Fuller, dark and violet amethyst with its burgeoning complex of carbon structures and diamond windows. On arrival, the transfer tube had a clear strip in the top, with the curving face of Fuller filling the view above us. In the Welcome Lounge of the main complex, the world changed again. Full Earth lay 'beside,' the sun rising around it's right edge, no more 'down' or 'below' except for a modicum of gravity that kept us on the 'floor.' Out the other side of the lounge loomed Bucky with its micro settlements spotted over the smaller light grey surface of the orb, rotating slowly.

Straight ahead in the upper horizon spin the wheels and quaint Rube Goldberg structures of the last generation of orbiting space stations, Freedom's Child and Mirage, first after Earth to enter 'the Dance' in orbit. Behind lie the partly clothed skeletons of the new habitats. Stellepharm's structure is almost ready. Svarga's first contours imitate the bulbous temple peaks of ancient Rajasthan. Beyond lie endless seas of dark and not so dark matter, unconcerned about our tiny perch on the edge of infinity, waiting politely if aware of us at all. Somewhere out there are billions of intelligent species, if theories and speculation can be trusted. Somewhere far or near are the Visitors. Are they watching? Can they see my exhilaration and my fear in this tiny rendezvous in the void?

Admiral Stollery brought us back to the present.

"Gentlemen, I must take your leave. May I introduce you to Ariel An, your assistant while you are here. She will be in touch with me on a regular basis. Follow her advice on everything. I need not remind you that small accidents are big accidents in this miniature armada of structures and ships we call home."

A white-suited brunette approached, a slim Asian silhouette moving with cat-like balance, giving Dylan an appraising stare and looking as though she could take out the lot of us if we twitched.

The brief tour of Fuller was spectacular. First the hotels with the best-stocked shops and restaurants under the sun, room rates running to yearly incomes for the grand suites looking out on the Dance. Then the labs, and the compact offices for people who come for a while but don't own. On the other side of EOL Station, the splendid offices of the big players: companies, countries, religions, and other interests, hive-like behind hexagonal fronts of diamond. No doubt R. Buckminster Fuller would have been proud, R. Daneel Olivaw no less so.

Within the see-and-be-seen quad, when we reached its halls and tunnels, were friends and enemies alike, FAF and PAD, businesses and governments, residences and mansions, churches and mosques, none more majestic or expensive than the elevated platforms and windows of Stellepharm's structure. There, sparing no expense, Édouard Moreau has built his pied en haute, where he hosts FAF's ventures on Fuller. His NOA labs hang out into space, connected by a long coiled tunnel.

The void suddenly felt colder as we realized that both friends and foes were in tight elbow-to-elbow contact on this awkward ark. Once in private, Ariel An gave us a quick rundown on security procedures, then on who was who. FSA has a big presence, backing Luisa and USNAV. Stellepharm already has occupants on Freedom Force, its half-build habitat, while building a second tier of NOA labs in case its operations on Fuller are disrupted. Golgotha and Mathias Abbott's cronies help Torbido to keep the old man well guarded. P-TEK escorts Jean-Christophe on his frequent trips to Freedom Force. The graceful towers of Svarga are protected by contracts with both FAF and PAD.

"Two friends are better than one," Ariel observed, "but friends talk too much at the wrong times. The chosen among the temple of Dilwara are pushing ahead with food and energy technologies for the long trip to their new world. Cryogenic freezing, too. This is your field, Dr. Rush. I don't think all of this can be done without NOA. They've had enough shipments come in by direct launch to have fully operating NOA labs."

"It sounds like no one is safe."

"Put briefly, gentlemen, there's a 'no nukes, no NOA' agreement here in the void, but it's impossible to enforce. Within PAD, there's an agreement that anyone using nuclear or NOA gets obliterated. We have advertised this as a deterrent. FAF has done the same. I advise you to move very carefully and always in the company of USNAV. Day to day, don't move without me."

"The Iranian Faction ships and habitat form a strong force by themselves. Add Stellepharm, P-TEK, and the naval mercenaries of the other FAF powers, not to mention the absolute absence of any agreement on mutual inspection, and we're in a very unclear situation concerning intelligence and security. Lack of clarity, gentlemen, is precisely what we all want least but what we have in abundance. To be honest with you, it is what I enjoy most in this otherwise severe perimeter of human survival."

Severe was only one of several words that sprang to mind in connection with Ariel An.

'Shuttle service,' when we got to the departure bay for the short trip to Bucky, was a misnomer of some proportions. There were no ships immediately available given the extreme press of demand from the now dozens of government and business inhabitants. Even with override priority from the admiral, it took some hours before launch. Worth the wait.

The docking bay looked strangely like a scene from Star Wars. Dylan turned to me and bowed formally.

"Trust the Force, the Force will be with you."

Even the no-nonsense Ariel smiled at that as a huge bay door slid shut behind us.

"Don't worry, Dr. Rush," she interjected smoothly. "We're snug here. But I should mention that a our flight was watched by a P-TEK yacht, in appearance not unlike the Imperial fighters of old.

Life hates coincidence. We act out our flights of fancy.

Portals

Dylan brushed a finger along the polished brass bar, alone with Ariel An in a shadowy vault on Bucky.

"The gym and recreation area, Mr. Rush, Every habitat needs one. You will find in low gravity that you require vigorous workouts to keep your muscles from wasting away."

"Dylan, please. It's a beautiful gym, but how do you use it? I don't see any machines."

"They come up from the floor. There are three gravity settings for the room. We call it the 'pool.' Would you like to know why?"

"Is it like the pool that Ender's squad trained in?"

"It can be. But it can be much gentler. The highest gravity setting is Earth-normal, which it is wise to use most of the time. Right now we are at Bucky-normal, about 70 percent less. You can move in long slow arcs, as you've discovered. You can move around the pool like a dancer or an acrobat. Excellent workout, but start slowly. When ready, a session in zero-g is the right way to map whole routines and drift through their movements the first few times. Here, I'll show you."

Ariel flipped a lever, and the little feeling of weight that remained seemed to drain from the pool like water, leaving their feet resting lightly on the floor. Pin lights provided soft illumination. Through the diamond side of the room shone the stars and the stardust of galaxies. Floor changed to ceiling as the sense of being outside in space became almost overwhelming. A sound track from the new Hopes and Spheres album drifted gently into the mix.

"To do this properly, Dylan, you must shed your heavy outer garments."

Ariel drew a fastrip down her body from left shoulder to right ankle and stepped, in a most gracefully weightless move, straight out of her jumpsuit, revealing along the way that it had been her only garment. In another seamless sequence of fluid movements, she removed Dylan's jumpsuit and the thermal comfort suit beneath. He didn't resist.

"Now you must catch me, Dylan, but don't be too impatient. You must move slowly, with the music."

She turned in a spiral arch and lanced across in front of the metres-wide window. This isn't space, he thought, I've wandered into paradise. His interest was beginning to show rather firmly. A moment of schoolboy bashfulness dissolved. Curiosity and desire weren't going to be denied.

"Don't worry, the space window is one-way. We are by ourselves in the universe."

He pushed toward her, trying to be careful and trying to look at least a little graceful. Ariel smiled.

"Not bad."

She touched the wall beside her and approached him from underneath as he crossed the space before the window. Her hand brushed his leg and saluting soldier while her other fingers guided his hand across her body and breasts.

"Incentive is important. Music is master. Trust the force, Luke"

Her smile lingered for the winking of an eye before her hands tugged his ankles in passing and her slim curves flipped impossibly up above him, then drifted back across his plane. He turned on his side and reached up, catching the inside curve of her waist for a second and pulling her toward him. Her inside rotation brought her body next to his, holding his hips tightly against hers, brushing her lips across his smile, disappearing in the same supple spin.

"Enjoy. We have time. The scientists are pouring over their test results. Let them summarize for us later. I'll be notified if there is anyone in this vicinity, but I think we will not be disturbed. Push gently off the walls. When you approach another surface, do something different each time. Flip, twist, brush, bend, arch. Follow the music. We will see where we meet again."

Every contact of their bodies was a thousand lives and a thousand deaths as he began to get into some sort of flow, some rhythm. When he was breathing hard, she matched orbit and slowly docked. Holding his backside firmly and rotating hers soothingly, she looked into his eyes, the depths of her own flecked with starlight.

"Let me show you something I've been working on."

Her toe touched a surface beneath them and they were off in a slow spiral, glancing off the next corner and tumbling in a slow roll. Pike position. He had never fully appreciated all the dimensions of that metaphor. As the music rose very slowly to a crescendo, she took him through a classical martial arts tapestry, always together as one, always moving her hips in subtly changing swirls.

Wave over wave of pleasure. All the bonds he might have had with consciousness vanished into the inviting stars. Still together, Ariel wrapped both arms around his neck and brushed his ear with her lips.

"Welcome to the four-thousand-mile club, Dylan Rush. It is very good for me that you learn so fast. Practice makes perfect."

He couldn't imagine greater perfection, but purely for the purposes of scientific enquiry he was willing to practice. There was more to Ariel An than met the eye, hard as that was to imagine. She held real power with ease, perched on a precipice, a pinnacle. To what was her soul committed? How would he know?

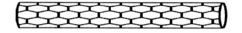

Ismael looked upward along the surface of Bucky, thinking of Emir Ahmad Mohammad's words, happy to be meeting Giza Weiss from Mossad. The old enemy was the new ally in PAD. They had talked on occasion since their last meeting during the Netwar.

Eleven o'clock high and halfway out from the main docking bay was the zone belonging to *Pinpoint Corporation,* a small warren of tunnels above the exit doors, with the labs on the left and living quarters right of the central diamond window.

"You might ask what they're doing out here that's so important, given the costs. Why are they protected like newborns by USNAV and all the PAD space navies? What do you sense, Giza? You always had the best sniffer."

"Saved our skins a time or two if memory serves."

"You don't buy the line that they're only here to test far-space communications, to see if second and third fortunes can be made in space?"

"Mossad buys it officially, and I am Mossad."

"But that doesn't mean you *buy* it?"

"It doesn't explain everything, Ismael. This nose I inherited from generations of Jewish mothers is sceptical."

"We meet too infrequently these days. Where did those years go?"

"Vanished in the mists of time."

"Look what happened to Abraham, Giza. Once ours, now head of FAFIST. That's a job he can have! Too many crooks spoil the broth."

"*Meshuggunas,* another turncoat, it honestly surprised me when he strayed."

"Surprise can be addicting in this dreary business!"

"Notwithstanding, Ismael, if you look right around the globe, a lot our people support FAF — your people, too. Devil you know. What about you — any doubts?"

"None. The emir is my life. What he believes makes me proud and hopeful. Of course, if I had any doubts, I wouldn't tell you."

"Of course."

"And you?"

"All my roots are in Israel. Like the Americans we hold to PAD by a slim but persistent margin. If I had any doubts, it would be about the sharpening of the terrorists' instincts for finding the best targets."

"Sad but true. The emir is not invincible and the 'Gulf of Islam' is deep and unforgiving. Nevertheless, we are both humanists before survivalists, Giza. No doubt it is the humanist in you that has brought you all this way to reminisce about old times."

"I wish. Pure sympathy for your lonely life here in the heavens."

"Heavens no, but lonely yes. It's the first time I've been lonely in the midst of pandemonium, constant communication but no one to talk to. It was easier when we were just fighting over wealth and power. We say we've changed but if someone can gain the power to dominate, will they still adhere to the credo of 'freedom'?"

"Of course not, Ismael, are you mad? Some would use these NOAbots for humanity. But, in a pinch, you would put the Islamic Alliance first, and I Israel."

"Trust is a fragile friend with bad balance. Yet we have come too far to jump lemming-like into the unknown. We are richer and healthier because of the NOAbots. Almost everyone is using highly over-designed safeguards on NOA reproduction. They haven't failed us yet."

"I don't like the sound of *almost* and *yet*."

"Indeed, that's where the trouble lies. Everyone who matters has plunged ahead with NOA. Unfortunately, not all are sane. But what can we do? If we all find the holy grail simultaneously, the first to act will win it all. If anyone survives. Their version of intelligent life will eliminate everyone else's."

"When the moment arrives, will we have any trust for each other? Even you and I, Ismael, how can we?"

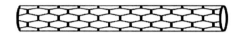

Kat gazed across the chimera. There was something deeply calming about sunlight on rippled water. It had followed her all her life, from the Minch to the Hudson and Potomac, but nothing could match a gentle evening sun on the bay south of Manitou. The quiet thrum of the old solar-cell engine briefly interrupted the scamper of birds and other wildlife, seeking a last meal, calling stridently or sorrowfully to mates and offspring.

Ellis drove in silence, both of them lost in the beauty of the moment. A loon whooped a long fading summons. The world could wait, but it couldn't seem to wait long. Reading her thought, Ellis looked ahead to the graceful ark of the Manitou listening station and the labs that huddled under its wing.

"Danielle's fine, Kat. Complete recovery, but she can't do it again. Just so you're forewarned."

"Understood, Ellis. I didn't come to apply any pressure, but it is true that I came to ask your advice on some important matters. There's pressure built into that, so you should both feel free to just say no."

"It's tempting to ignore the battles all around, but in the end that's like stealing time, only to find it was no more than a loan."

"*Bonjour*, Danielle!"

"Kat, welcome back to Manitou and our humble abode. We'll chase away our dark memories. Park your pack thataway, big cabin — you remember. We'll find wine and meet you in the courtyard."

There was nothing humble about the zillion-dollar view that met her eyes as they looked out from the glass-walled living-room at a red ball of fire in its last dive toward the waves, vermillion clouds ablaze in its wake. Danielle brought snacks, the kind that never survived on a plate for more than a few seconds.

"*Santé*! And thank you, Kat, for making the long journey back to our remote corner of nature. You've been gone too long, busy since the Netwar — Phil, too. Ellis and I follow events from a distance these days, only the trends as they pass. Ellis is getting impatient. I think he's been waiting only until he was sure I'd be OK."

"It's a joy to see you up and around, Danielle. How are you feeling?"

"Good. One hundred percent. But I'm not sure about endurance. Weird feeling, strong on the outside but soft in the middle. I don't know how fast it could be triggered if I got into that kind of pressure cooker again. But I don't think that's the kind of help you want from us."

"You're right on that. Someone else will be the point person next time around."

"Who will it be, Kat?"

"Well that deep-ends, as the divers say. Lord, I'm beginning to talk like Phil. Much remains to be seen. It's certain that we're coming at an unknown velocity to another crisis point. As you will have divined."

"Yes, and we understand it's generally about who's going to saturate the world with NOAbots, the kind that would occupy other life forms, perhaps change life irreparably."

"Excellent description. There are, of course, more details on who's doing what, who's ahead, where the threats lie. We have good intelligence and instincts, but that's not nearly enough. You have a gift of insight, Danielle. It's coming to the point where we need that input again."

"How long will you need it?"

"Until something tells us we've won. Or lost."

"I'm sure you've thought of the obvious, Kat. Be first at any cost. If you can't do that, help whom you trust to be first at any cost. Your worst threat is your worst enemy, the person you trust to act without any principle. Or the person who is most insane."

"What if someone does beat us to the punch?"

"I'd say there are two main ways to saturate Earth's ecology with these NOAbots. One is to release them from many points Earthside using wind and water and transportation systems as carriers. The other is to release containers space-side and have them open in the upper atmosphere. Seeding from space is a lot quicker, so concentrate on that. The space option is appealing for other reasons, principally the lack of effective order up there. I could go on a little further, but I'm sure you know the drill. What am I missing and what's the timeframe?"

"Good questions, good analysis. The bot killers, boticides and molecides, have the same seeding challenges. The timeframe is months."

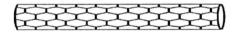

Phil studied Luisa Stollery as she glared at the small audience from the front of the conference room.

"Gentlemen, I am sorry for the abrupt invitation, but we have just apprehended three members of the Phoenix who appear to believe that the afterlife, or *al-akhirah*, should be experienced now rather than later. They came in on three separate maintenance crews and were in the late stages of assembling a small nuclear device in a tunnel just above EOL

275

station. The bomb components had been well disguised as maintenance equipment. They might have succeeded in separating the cable from Fuller, and you can imagine the rest. Your son, Dr. Rush, tipped us off to tighten security around EOL, and I would like to hear from him how he knew that an attack was imminent."

Somewhat stunned, Phil looked around at Dylan.

"I didn't actually know anything, Admiral Stollery, it was the logic of the situation. The only thing that would bring down the cable is a nuke. For three decades, it hasn't been a question of who has the most nukes but who could put one in a backpack. It would be easier to assemble a nuke at Fuller than to do it Earthside or lower down the cable."

"And?"

"Circumstances also pointed to this moment in time. Neither FAF nor PAD would support or tolerate such an attack, since both have too much to lose. But true fanatics with enough organization could try. I took a chance by telling Ariel — Ms An, that is — about my theory. Good guess, it appears."

Phil again felt old. At twenty-six, Dylan was making his presence felt on the world stage. How did he zoom in and out like that, focus and soar? James Joyce would be proud. Proud and humble was a good feeling for a father.

The long silence bordered on awkward as each considered the implications from their own angle. Luisa Stollery shrugged, perhaps at the unpleasant prospect of further interrogating one of her own personal guests. Ariel An had also morphed into a somewhat defensive stand, consciously or not.

"Well, good guess it is, then, and damn lucky for us all," Stollery conceded. "You can be sure security will be cranked up to full throttle at this end of the cable. Down below, too. There are only two or three other packs of lunatics who could try something on this scale. Their strength wanes and their chances diminish as we build more and more of a base in space. They begin to turn their eyes skyward to find distant worlds where their dictates will find no opposition. Good riddance."

"Do you think they will go?" Dylan asked.

"If you want my opinion, we've got another decade or more before Earthbound militants move out or die out enough to let us get a decent night's sleep up here. So you feel free to talk to me any time, Dylan Rush. And that goes for all of you."

She looked at Ariel as she spoke the last words, as if to say 'there are no divided loyalties here.' Ariel's shoulders straightened another improbable notch and a hint of colour touched her long cheek bones.

Dylan eyed the two with a wary smile as Phil realized he had probably been overlooking something there. Pay more attention, old man! He didn't actually think forty-nine was *that* old, but it was a kind of dividing line. Ariel An and Dylan warranted more attention. He was sorry to be returning to Seaside, notwithstanding their success in lining up R&D plans for the next tests of deep-space communications. Tentative arrangements had also been made for accessing the micro black hole lab being built by the Shandong and East Asia Trading conglomerate on their growing ark-shaped habitat named *Prism*. As he looked past their small gathering toward the broad oval viewport, Phil wondered again if the Visitors were watching.

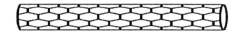

Dylan wished time would stop. His last night on Bucky was all urgency, lengthened to the point of exhaustion and beyond. The tank was almost dark against the galaxy that lay just outside. They went at their movements with something close to fury, to spite the long universe of time that was inching its way between them. Though his intuition told him he would be back, he was walking out of heaven with no clear reason. This is what men do, he sensed — leave perfection in a foolish attempt to save perfection, a little roundabout, one might argue. He was angry at himself until, on a rapid transverse flip across the weightless room, Ariel's arm caught his and they twirled in a fierce embrace. Then she was off in an explosion of torque and motion. His heart skipped a beat. She was attacking her own furies with a power he hadn't seen before. But even in her wildest rage she was exquisitely otherworldly. Effortless poise and discipline. He pushed his self-absorption away and dove across the universe toward her. They flew in a high-speed chase in which every pattern of approach was foreseen and eluded, countered and reborn.

His muscles were beginning to rebel when her body drifted very slowly past, feet first, face to face for a second, a feather's distance between them. He encircled her legs as they passed and looked up her taught stomach toward her firm, extended breasts. She arched backward in a crescent of arousal as he inched slowly upward, savouring her lithe beauty. A long and lonely cry escaped as they joined together. Slow undulations, gentle nibbles lip to lip, ascending to a pinnacle of abandonment. Music filled the world long before Ariel activated the amps. They moved toward a climax, an ending of all things. She bit hard on his neck as he grasped her even tighter.

"Don't forget me, Dylan Rush. We have more to do together. You will be back and I will come to you Earthside if I can."

"Time is on my side."

"You wish!"

He knew what she was saying, asking. It was more than just the two of them. Their lives were joined by larger forces. Although he was not the only centre of her life, they would not be apart for long. In his unworthiness he felt deeply grateful.

Édouard Moreau allowed himself a satisfied smile.

"Light a cigar, Maurizio. You deserve an hour off. It goes well."

"I will take you up on the cigar, *mio amico*. But there is no rest for the faithful and less for the wary. By misfortune of birth, I am both. But, yes, it goes well. The production lines are all doing famously. Medicine, agriculture, eco-remediation and terraforming. Precision equipment, too, and tailored NOA applications for our preferred customers in FAF. Yet herein lies the problem, Édouard, as someone famous may have said, for the NOA horizon is suddenly looming so much larger that it could soon block the sky."

"I hope most sincerely that you are too pessimistic, Maurizio, but I agree we must be the first to be ready if life-altering NOA is going to be released. I've put Jean-Christophe on it."

"We have some further problems regarding the selection of the most worthy candidates for the first habitat. The demand for a berth on *Freedom Force* is unexpectedly large and insistent, a small culture having come together around the notion that the first of us to meet the Visitors will be blessed among men."

"As long as the main players are on board, Maurizio, please decide on the other inhabitants as you wish. Ask me if you have doubts. This group of people will pack a punch. With a full range of NOA labs, *Freedom Force* will be a law unto itself. If things go badly for Earth, we will still survive and prosper."

"You are going, then?"

"Not on the first mission, my friend. I will leave that to J.C. and his friends, suitably supervised by your hand-picked staff. No, I am thinking of a second habitat that we can market as a direct approach to the Visitors. We will seek them out, travelling, of course, in luxury as the occasion demands. I will call it *Quest*. If all goes well here, we come back. If not, we find the next-best home. Will you join me?"

"Perhaps, Édouard, though I fear that the job of making the best of what remains will take my attention away from such a voyage, however tempting. Why not plan to build several more habitats as long as the demand remains strong? I could join the exodus if the mother ship were truly sinking."

"Excellent idea! We can market our terraforming labs as part of the package."

"A new home awaits, far from the madding crowd. I need to ask you one question, Édouard, about the wisdom of so much responsibility in the hands of your son. He is brilliant, without doubt, but he has a ruthless streak that makes me nervous. We use violence when we must while he bathes in it. His relationship with Gregor cannot be healthy."

"Keep an eye on him, my friend, but don't worry, I know him to the core. Like Hamlet, he could rise above his indecision were he not so addicted to it. Though the slings and arrows pierce him cruelly, he will not take arms against his sea of troubles."

Pinnacle

Phil gazed across the waves as they broke over reefs in their long march toward the shore at Seaside. A frown crossed his starboard brow.

The things that should frighten us fail to do so until it's too late. He feared for Dylan in a way he hadn't since the kidnapping. You have to let the children go, a voice reminded him. They have an armour of intellect and inexperience that lets them relish the unknown.

"Penne for your thoughts," Kat ventured.

He gazed a moment at leaves swirling outside the window, tossed up by the fresh May breeze like a salad into the purple-orange bowl of the sun as it eased slowly onto the platter of the Pacific. A very old tune massaged his memory.

Under my feet, the grass is growing
Time to move on, time to get going.

Fear was a fierce driver. This was the calm before the storm. He sputtered a weary reply into a lengthening silence.

"I'm worried about Dylan, Kat — not his abilities but the responsibility that rests on his shoulders. I'm worried about NOAbots and everyone losing their identify or their life, worried, if we survive, about the mid-terms next year and what happens if Saba loses the House or Senate, worried about trying to transmit the Orion message, although the closer it gets, the more sure I am it can be done."

"I think it's time to tell the kids the whole story, Phil, even if they decide we're crazy."

As if on cue, Dylan and Lara sauntered in their direction. Lara was reconciled to doing university studies at home, given the dangers they all faced. Despite Dylan's frequent absences, they'd stayed very close and it meant a lot to both of them to be together.

"Hey, gang!" Kat signalled.

"I haven't heard that in years, Mom. Hey, Dad, tell us one more gang story."

They all laughed at Dylan's imitation of his own nine-year-old voice. Phil could never resist a story, and the best were those that sprung unplanned from the imagination.

"OK, but I have an appointment at the fridge concerning a wayward lager. You start."

Both were momentarily startled by this undemocratic reversal of roles but rebounded with the speed of young minds.

"I'll start," Lara ventured. "I need practice for my creative writing courses. Once upon a time, or maybe twice as the tale unwinds, there was a small group of friends who listened to the stars and heard something that only they could understand. Something of themselves. The message they heard set their lives on a different path and gave them tools."

She had definitely caught their attention.

"As they came close to the moment when their life's mission would be gained or lost, they realized that whosoever had sent the message did not know the exact nature of the danger they had described. They now understood it better themselves, because they had been warned, and because the steps they had taken since they heard the message had changed the way the picture developed, the path by which the scourge was nurtured.

"They had powerful friends and powerful enemies. The most feared were the most reckless of their fellow men. They gathered together their true friends and even recruited their children who, till that time, had known only what they guessed. They stood firm. When the time came, all that history records is that something entirely new began. The end."

Lara paused and looked around. Dylan barked out a laugh and they all dissolved in the mirth of nervous release.

"Wonderful story!" Kat exclaimed, "Such an imagination!"

"Can't imagine where she got that," Dylan added.

Eyes turned to Phil. It was clearly his turn to ask some tricky question. Given the pinpoint insight of the story, it was going to be hard to be crafty, but in for a penny….

"So, what do you think they did, in order for history to be recorded in such a manner? Closer to the point, the pinnacle if you wish, what might have been their options? Did they actually have any influence over events or were they just pushing food around the plate for someone else?"

"Nobody knows, of course," Lara answered. "Accounts of this chronicle are sadly scarce and have a tendency to change without notice. Nevertheless, from the few scholarly references that can be examined, it would appear that some good god had set them on a course with somewhat better odds than a fart in a windstorm. 'Why not?' was their conclusion."

"The options were likely few," Dylan continued, "but they could consider a multitude of paths, including, it would appear, a message to the past."

Phil and Kat gaped at Dylan as Lara resumed.

"Yeah, we guessed it. Process determines outcome. Dylan and I figure that a universal dose of NOA is by far the worst possibility. The world can probably survive anything else."

"NOA saturation may arrive by many paths," Dylan continued, "and the way to proceed is to be on all those paths with an ambush. Finding them all is, of course, the hard part. Because this is so improbable and so important, you need insurance. You need some paths of your own."

They were like a tag team. Kat and Phil could only watch in fascination.

"Damien and Rana are at the heart of both ambush and insurance," Dylan pushed on, "so I've set up links with them.

There was a need for technical expertise that none of us has. No offence, Dad, you're the closest, but this needs the top guns. Besides, you have your hands full with Ben and, might we assume, the task of transmitting the messages you received nine years ago."

"That's right on the money, Dylan. We seem to have underestimated how much you two would figure out. We'll show you the Orion transcript now. The cipher is one that Sandover invented, after his family told him to."

"Pyramid?"

"No doubt. We know what Orion says, but we don't actually know if it was sent from a future time as claimed. Or, as the rest of the world seems to think, by superior humans or the Visitors. Ben and I are the only ones working on the inter-place-time science and tech as far as I know. It's a dangerous path whose death toll could be worse than NOA, a lot worse."

"Which brings us back to tactics," Kat jumped in. "We've identified fourteen emerging sources of a NOAbot cocktail. That includes countries, sects, and a couple of maybes. It's a large number. We have Earthside countermeasures in place with a backup saturate that will kill all NOA. We don't want to use that. The number of people depending on good NOA has skyrocketed to almost ten million. But better that than risking the loss of all humanity, or its change beyond recognition."

Phil stepped into the silence.

"The worst danger is space-side delivery of a new NOA life-print. We're going to need some muscle topside, some real fire power on Fuller and Bucky."

"Got one idea on that, Dad," Dylan offered, "but we'll both have to be topside to make it work. We have to go back soon. Time and tide wait for no man, as the Bard observed."

"On such a full sea are we now afloat, Cassius. We take the current when it serves, else lose our ventures."

"You made that up."

"Busted."

Phil thought back to the startling conversation with Dylan and Lara, now weeks ago. Ben Singer raised a toast to faith and hope as the transparent cabin rose slowly up the Lift toward the first fifty-kilometre platform en route from Banks to EOL. Dylan had gone ahead. The big wall screen on the cable side of the habitat showed their progress on a globe, with the atmospheric layers in changing colours. Troposphere, the first ten kilometres, stratosphere, and mesosphere the next forty- and fifty-kilometre layers. Thermosphere the next three hundred, and exosphere the last insubstantial band of particles beyond six hundred kilometres.

Their cabin would keep them at normal pressure another hour, before suits were donned and the remainder of the journey became a less comfortable test of adaptation and endurance in free fall. They were still woefully unsure of what was going to happen if they tried inter-place-time connectivity. Neither the feasibility nor the accuracy was assured.

"What do we really know about Pyramid?" Ben enquired as they sipped the customary mimosa on entering the thermosphere.

Phil decided to approach the subject slowly to see if Ben had any hard information to add.

"Cells and a 'pinnacle,' is about all I know, Ben. Also, they've been very helpful to my family and more so to Beya and Sandover. We think that's on account of Sandover's father, who is thought by some to have had an important role in the earlier days of building the structure. The members of the Pinnacle are so carefully isolated that their identities are only rumoured. Some of the rumours are undoubtedly wrong. Do you know anything reliable about them?"

"Not really, Phil. Only supposition. What I think of as the true pyramid has four identical triangular faces. The tetrahedral pyramid has four points and six edges. Here's a picture of one."

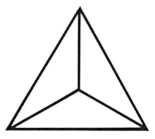

"That's very interesting. And very abstract. How could it work in an organization?"

"Be patient; a little more abstraction. This is not the usual kind of triad structure. Each point or person is directly connected to three others — a cell. Now imagine a larger pyramid made of thousands of smaller cells, Pascal's pyramid."

Ben flipped another diagram onto his monitor.

"I still don't see."

"If you are at any point in the structure, you are connected to the other three points of your own cell, and *also* to one point on each of three other cells. Beyond that, you have no knowledge of the rest of the structure. If there is one cell that is the Pinnacle — say, the top one — these four points connect to the rest through a cascade of interconnected cells. If the cells are linked by near-instant communication, the structure can act almost as a whole."

"So the Pinnacle is four."

"If my speculation is right, yes."

"Who would they be, Ben?"

"I don't know. Maybe the obvious thing globally would be Asian, African, European, and North American."

"Any idea about identities?"

"None at all. The real world has never been my *forté*. I'm sure there are plenty of people out there who could fit the bill. If they were eliminated, any other designated cell could take their place. Whole levels could be added to expand the organization. This organism has coherence, speed, redundancy, and growth. Do you know the identity of any in the Pinnacle?"

"No, Ben, but whoever they are, it looks to me like they're probably going to run the world, if they don't already. Whether for good or ill, I don't know. I suppose we have to give them the benefit of the doubt. But it's still running the world, and I don't recall that humanity has done particularly well in its flirtations with oligarchy."

Later, they dozed. Phil woke suddenly to a deafening thud that echoed through the cabin. Two men jumped to the floor from the overhead hatch. Thank God we put our suits on, Phil thought, then realized the foolishness of his relief. Two armed enemies. One closed the hatch and the room began to repressurize. The other held them at gunpoint as he spoke in an accented voice that came clearly through their suit coms.

"Gentlemen, welcome to the Thermosphere."

It was Torbido!

"Remain in your suits. We will travel the next few kilometres together, no further than Genoa to Cinque Terre, a pleasant ride along the coast via Portofino, if you will."

"Who are you?" Ben spurted out. "Where are you taking us?"

"That depends on you. Nowhere in a hurry, but if you don't give us your NOA specs before we climb much higher into the sky, you may have an accident during your ascent. Very regrettable, but such things are bound to happen sometimes in these pioneering days."

NOA specs. Phil's mind raced. They think we're headed up to release a saturate, change the world. How's that for luck? Not in our mission at all. Ben knew enough about NOA to get them into trouble, so Phil jumped in.

"Señor Torbido. Maurizio, if I may. Our trip has nothing to do with NOA, nor do we have specs. Nor does either of us have any useful information about NOA, technical or tactical. We are here to pilot-test a technology for deep-space communication. The specs are topside, as we were advised for security reasons to bring nothing with us. In any case, you don't have the right to steal commercial technology. Monsieur Moreau will surely not look good if he breaks the code of conduct of his own Freedom And Faith alliance."

Code of conduct, who was he kidding?

"Perhaps, Señor Rush. In which case, you and Doctor Singer have lost your usefulness. A tragic accident that sadly derails your monopoly over space comtech and yields the field to us. That would still preserve great benefits for mankind."

Pi grande tazza di merda! He'd talked them out of the NOA into the fire. OK, to borrow a page from Ellis, when all else fails, lower your standards.

"Perhaps we could discuss this new space-point technology, Maurizio. A joint venture could be attractive."

Torbido regarded him with clear disbelief, but what did he have to lose?

"We do have some time to spare, Señor Rush, though my patience is limited. What do you propose?"

They were by now almost weightless, with only the upward push of their tiny ecosphere holding them to the floor. Phil thought of lunging for the loo, locking the door, and using the floor hatch. But he'd be a sitting duck much too long, and that seemed an unfitting end. Not to mention Ben. 'Better play the game,' he thought, as he framed an answer.

"Fifty-fifty on profits, same on the venture capital up front. Future spinoffs negotiated."

Phil had Torbido's attention at least, and his blond-haired companion seemed to ease slightly the pressure on the trigger.

"You're stalling, Rush! You're here because of NOA, just like the rest of us."

"I am a close follower of all that concerns NOA, Señor Torbido, but not a player. For those, you have to go higher. On pinpoint and space-point, I am in a position to offer you something valuable."

The next second they were flying upward through the capsule, which itself was screeching to a halt. The back of Phil's head and shoulders hit the roof. He caught a glimpse of vast space outside as his consciousness failed.

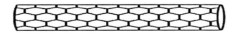

Beya took out her frustrations on the first thing at hand.

"It's just all bass ackwards, Sandover Lee! The whole world should be healthy, happy, and prosperous. We have the means."

"But?"

"We're on the brink of extermination by overheating, NOA and other forms of war."

"Maybe, Beya. But this will be the first year of actually taking carbon out of the skies, after decades of long-winded discussion. Maybe we'll dodge that bullet."

"Don't forget your own oft-quoted words that we've still got a long way to go. The impacts of global warming will increase for another decade before cooling actually begins. It takes that long to turn around the cumulative forces already built up."

"How did we fail that test so badly?"

"Aside from greed?"

"There was something else, Beya, something most people missed, though not all the scientists and environmental activists. Nature isn't linear. At the turn of the millennium, we didn't have fifty years of gradual climate change ahead, as most predicted. Nature is geometric, flying off and accelerating in every direction, everything balanced only by all the other things flying off in opposite directions. We removed key balances when we heated the planet's surface. We triggered tipping points in every facet of our world, from earthquakes and volcanoes to bacteria and viruses. We're lucky we're still here to tell the story."

"And now we're running hell bent for leather into a NOA meat grinder in the hope that the hamburger is better than the cow. Is there no one who can stop this?"

"I don't even think there's time for a timeout."

"Would anyone actually do it? Release a plague? Risk humanity on untested tech?"

"Not you or I, Beya. But, yes, and not just fanatics. In the end, any power that *can* do it may have to, just to avoid losing the race. Look at everyone's reaction as the world slowly learns of this new dread. Leaders preach and implore while most of us cling to some hope or faith, frozen in our inaction.

The Church of the Ultimate Survivors has millions of new recruits."

"If faith could keep the plague outside the chapel doors, I'd be the next to join. Maybe the Lord will protect us if our faith is strong enough."

"You have a lot more faith than I do, Beya. You always have. Faith or not, our job is to go on doing what we are being advised or warned or guided to do."

"But surely you don't have to go up there!"

"I've heard directly from Pyramid, or so the messenger said. Eng Kai is asking me to take this case up the Lift. They say they can't trust anyone else. It's the last place I want to go, believe me! But I'm told it's not too dangerous. If there's any tampering, the contents of the case will self-destruct without blowing up the room around them. Getting the contents to Fuller intact is clearly not the last resort for whoever is sending me and whatever is being planned."

"You think it's a NOA saturate, that Pyramid is asking you to deliver the plague we were warned to prevent?"

"Could be. But what choice? I have no idea if this case contains NOA, or something that can destroy NOA, or is a feint or something else entirely. If I don't do it, somebody else will."

"Bad turn of phrase. That line's from a musician who was referring to stealing away his best friend's girl."

"Maybe I'm taking a *good* plague to prevent the *bad* ones. Whom else can we trust, Beya? Phil agrees."

"Sounds to me a bit like you've just run through the five great lame excuses of history. What choice do I have? I don't know what will happen. If I don't do it, somebody else will. It might be a good deed. Whom else can I trust? Still, I can't say you're wrong. Except on the 'whom can we trust?' part. We also have to trust Phil, Damien, Kat, and our allies in Washington and PAD."

"You're right, of course. But you agree that I have to deliver this package?"

"I don't like it. Too dangerous and you have crippling vertigo. If there's no other way, if you can't reconsider, of course I'll put it in gear with Luisa Stollery and the navy."

"Wait a day. I'd like to have the next WEO Council meeting on Fuller, to finalize agreement on the rules of the space economy. Several Council members are already up top. This will give me cover for a trip that's hard to explain otherwise. We've got a bit of time yet."

"And have you forgotten that November is when it's all supposed to hit the fan? When the Orion message claimed it was sent?"

"No, my love, that's hard to forget. Why am I not surprised by the timing?"

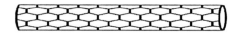

Phil was looking at someone he knew as breath came back and the world reappeared.

"Nigel Montgomery, Mr. Rush. A former colleague of your wife's. We met once in New York. For reasons not unrelated to your good wife's concern for your safety, we've been keeping a casual eye upon your progress. Thought you might appreciate a spot of help. Sorry about the bump on the head."

"You caught Torbido?"

"Regrettably he perished in the skirmish. Moreau and FAF will not be happy. Did they let anything slip about their plans. And what did you tell them?"

"Just the truth. That we aren't involved with NOA. Under threat of death, I said we would cut them in on the next generation of space coms."

"Good. This will put FAF on the defensive. The Royal Navy is at your command, Dr. Rush. We are ascending again, assuming you wish to continue your journey. Dr. Singer, as you can see, will be fine. We're just patching up the shoulder where he hit the roof."

"How did you..?"

"We dropped an operative onto the cable a kilometre above your location. He went into the security shaft and activated the braking system as you passed the platform marking the thermosphere."

"We're very grateful, Nigel. You've come in the nick of time."

"Our pleasure. Did they tell you anything about NOA? "

"They were very insistent, seemed very sure we were involved with NOA. I take it they are worried about losing the race — a race we also watch carefully. We're hoping the good guys win, whatever that means."

"Quite. And there was no mention of plans for FAF adventures in NOA?"

"No, but their urgency spoke volumes, now that I think of it. They were ready to toss us out of the Lift. Whether that comes from desperation or a very hard bluff, it says they are seriously worried. Maybe they think they're too far behind in the race."

"It could also signal that they're not that far behind, that something is coming soon, a possibility we are investigating with considerable vigour as we speak. For now, you should get some sleep. If you would put your helmet back on, we will depressurize the cabin. Call if you have any reason."

Phil drifted off, sending silent thanks to Kat for her friends in MI8. But the game was far from over. Now they were going to Fuller and Bucky with NOA war heating up fast. Someone was whispering in his ear 'don't despair, almost there.' Someone else was telling him he'd almost died twice in the past hour.

Sandover had that faraway look again, as if he glimpsed a different reality.

"If you had one wish, Beya, what would it be?"

"I'd wave a magic wand and violence would stop. Better still, violent acts would boomerang on the villains, leaving the victims unharmed."

"What about doctors and surgery, or athletes?"

"If their intent is healing or sport, fine. If it is injury, they can go to hell with the butchers, terrorists, and wife beaters. While I am humiliated to admit this, seeing them all pound themselves to death would bring tears of joy to my heart."

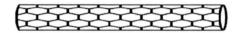

Phil woke to a blurred vision of shadowy figures gliding around the weightless cabin.

"Nigel, is that you?"

"Good morning, Comrade Rush. Your friends are still unconscious. When they wake up, they will discover that they are unarmed and then we will talk. You will talk."

His bruised brain couldn't take it. His second-to-last thought as he slipped again into oblivion was that he'd been transported down some kind of rabbit hole. Not his finest day, fainting in the moment of crisis, but Sandover had said that it's sometimes best to disappear.

Junction

Sandover held Beya, hoping time would stop. Whoever said that parting is sweet sorrow had it half-right. Life, loss, loneliness, love. In moments like this, we meet each other alone together, infinitely vulnerable, with the certainty that the death of the other would be the death of the soul.

"Come back."

"I will. Keep the faith."

Sandover stepped back and the Lift door rolled shut. A face looking up. The love of a lifetime. The reason to live.

As soon as his body realized what he was doing, it retaliated and left him shaking. Thoughts raced through his mind in an attempt to block out reality.

No worries, mate. Just a little hop up from the ground. Best look up, not out. Why are we always made to do what we want to do least? OK it's just like *1984* with the guy in the cage with the rats. You just have to close your eyes and ignore the fact that thousands of the most repulsively imaginable creatures are crawling over every part of your body. Thanks to encounters of an early kind with the rat population of Asia for not having that nightmare to deal with! No different with heights, right? I'm just in a room that is perfectly safe and happens to be rising into the sky on a rope hanging from nowhere. No, no. Unfair. Hanging from man- and womankind's burgeoning scientific and technical might. Regrettably often not matched by burgeoning enlightenment. But the Lift is guarded well enough to keep this bubble going up. Nothing can possibly go wrong…that's a good one! Can't avoid a peek down. Damn! Can't rationalize this fear away. OK, focus on the emotions. Have to feel them, let them out, celebrate them. Oops, not a good idea. If I fall out, I'll have a long reflective descent with historical slideshow before I suffocate or hit the ground. I should know which. Up higher I'd freeze. Easier. It gets better with time and I have time on my hands. Ha, ha. Literally.

OK, I'm going to have to fight this the whole way up and down. While I'm up there, too. I have to rest, avoid exhaustion. Dangerous. Breathe. And what if I were free falling. Would that be so bad? Well, aside from the death part? What was it in my past that put a lock on my trust of heights? That's all it is. I can find the lock and release it, shoot it off, beat it into a pulp with a crowbar. If I could share the panic. If only Beya.... No, Saba and Justine both need her more than I do. Far too risky anyway. Shouldn't have said that. Sharing is good, and bad. Mostly we're completely self-centred, my vast experience of human nature, ha ha.

Rambling. Good. People do good things when they're free of demons, free of want and free from madmen, free from hunger, disease, persecution, boredom, envy. Maybe there'll be much longer lifetimes by the time I get to ninety. Another good one, let's get to thirty-eight first. I won't press the panic button. I'll leave my coms off till I hear from Captain Glavin or the Lift operator. No need to show them my psychosis unless I have to.

"All's well, Professor Lee. You OK?"

"A bit woozy Captain, thanks. Not good with heights."

"Bummer. Potter principle. Least desirable is most likely. I come apart at the thought of giant spiders. Can't imagine that ever happening, though. Never had vertigo, but I can sympathize. Spacelift must be the perfect nightmare!"

"Hopefully ending with a safe return, Captain. My nomadic ancestors would be ashamed of me, but a foot on the ground is an ocean of relief for me. Never even liked second-storey balconies."

"Well, your sense of humour seems to be returning, so I'll take that as a good sign."

"I think I'll be OK. I may need some help at times."

A new voice sounded behind him.

"Further reinforcements, Dr. Lee?"

The man who walked in from the operator's cubicle looked familiar.

"We met long ago in New York."

"My god, Lianshen!"

"In the flesh."

"Chuanli said you had died!"

"I am afraid that news of my demise was premature. A line from your Samuel Clemens that I've long wished to use. The time was right for me to depart the scene. I am deeply sorry for the pain that this deception may have caused. In the interim, I have been following your striking career. My employer is a major partner in Spacelift, so when he invited me to join the venture, I was more than happy to agree. It has its ups and downs."

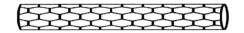

Phil stared down the barrel of a nasty-looking weapon.

"You're running out of time, Rush!"

No kidding. What do you say to a mad Russian? Everyone was wide awake by now. A staring contest with a high-tech stunner has a tendency to do that to you. Phil had always got through by temporizing, but time looked to be running out.

"I won't insult your intelligence, Gregor. I told Torbido the truth and I assume he shared our conversation with you. I don't know NOA. I am, however, a specialist in the physics and technologies of communications. Ben and I are exploring some new areas of long-distance communication in space. We have no NOA specs, plans, or documents, with us or anywhere else. If it is NOA you are after, you have chased the wrong ambulance."

"They killed Maurizio, a very good friend."

"There was a skirmish. I was speaking with Torbido about a partnership in comtech. We are useful to you in this. We will sign an agreement now if you wish. Nor do you have any reason to harm the British naval unit. After they responded to an unprovoked attack, Torbido fought to his own death."

"Good story, Dostoyevsky, but the bear is not fooled by the antics of the deer. Let's pop you outside a while and see if the tune changes. If not, we'll cut the tie and let you fall. We still have the eminent *Doktor* Singer as our valued partner. Seldom does the bear torture its victim, Philamon Rush. When it does, the pleasure is that much more acute."

Arms grabbed him around the chest as a Russian commando moved to open the overhead hatch. Gregor grinned behind his face plate, but his smirk turned sour as his second-in-command slumped and dropped to the floor. Phil felt suddenly very woozy. Not again! His eyes swept across Nigel as he passed once more into oblivion. Nigel was smiling.

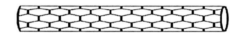

Sandover pushed back the demons, focused on Lianshen's sombre face.

"But to the present, Professor Lee. I have some good news and some bad news. Do you have a preference?"

"Good news!"

Neither his stomach nor his head could withstand bad news at this point in their endless upward crawl.

"Good choice. The good news is that your friends were rescued. Philamon Rush and Benjamin Singer."

"Wonderful. I mean excellent, of course. But rescued from what?"

"That's the bad news. They were attacked on the upper half of the Lift. By Maurizio Torbido, who was killed in a rescue by Nigel Montgomery and the British Orbital Navy. Unfortunately, they were then attacked by Gregor Sokolov and a pack of P-TEK commandos. We listened in up to that point, before they found our bugs. PAD forces are on their way."

Bad news, indeed. And if Phil and Ben were targets, it wasn't hard to guess who was next on the list.

"We need to seal our suits now, Professor, and stay that way. You will be less comfortable, but it may help with your vertigo. The captain and I have worked together before. He will undoubtedly look after you with his customary diligence. I will keep you informed of what I learn. Belt up. We may avoid trouble if it runs itself out of steam above us."

"Forgive me if I don't bet the farm on that!"

Phil floated in a state of limited occasional consciousness. There was a moment when he thought he was awake, and then that he was awake in a dream. Salvador Dali clocks oozed around him. Salmon chanted evening. Nigel fought a bear. The ghosts of the fantastic four flew toward him. FAF squadrons locked them on target. He couldn't get free of his suit to warn them — look behind!

"Phil?"

This time, when his eyes opened, it was not a smiling Nigel but a scowling Luisa Stollery. Scowling or not, she was a sight for sore eyes.

"I'm not sure what you find amusing, Philamon Rush. But you're welcome. We came down the Lift on Track B and shifted into the security track just above you. Hopped on the side of your car, used gas — something we've been working on. Still, you were lucky. If they'd been using their suits for air supply, they'd have come back shooting. Good chance you'd be full of holes or worse."

'Worse' seemed a bit academic to Phil, but he never thought he'd be so happy to see anyone, especially an admiral.

"Sandover is on his way up?"

"Right, we've informed him of your safety and we've redoubled security. That's not all that's afoot. Another plot has just been unearthed. Members of the Zurmani faction have brought explosives to Fuller, slowly, 'brick by brick.' There was an almost successful attempt to set off an explosion that would push the asteroid toward Earth. Our only response to an explosion on the 'dark side' of Fuller would have been to set off an equally large one on the light side, blowing up most of what's been built and probably everything living. Even then, the Lift would crash and we'd be lucky to salvage Fuller."

"How did you stop them?"

"Your son was instrumental in identifying the threat, once again by logic, he claims, rather than inside information. We won't be caught again without a backup plan and the punch to carry it out. If you want my opinion, we may be very lucky to get through the next month in one piece. Gentlemen, welcome to the war zone!"

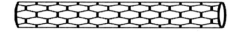

Sandover dreamt of Beya. When you close your eyes, it's the curve of a neck that fills your vision. The bow of a breast, the shadow of a thigh in the moonlight. The touch of knowing, the pleasure of home. Slowly, the passion finds you, a memory of a dream, a moment, a life time, a shower of rain, a glimpse from a distance. In the end, there is nothing, only the crescendo, only the climax, only the gentle embrace. In the morning it is gone, but it was real, is real. Much stronger than reality, the softest touch of love. Beginnings and endings are illusions. Some times stand out, some times lie in wait.

Lianshen's voice invaded his reverie.

"Good news, Professor! Admiral Stollery and USNAV took out Gregor Sokolov and the P-TEK commandos. All are sedated, a reprieve, but we are not there yet. Suits stay fastened."

Lianshen gave a curt salute and turned back toward his cubicle. His eyes froze as they swept past the clear dome of the cabin's ceiling. Sandover followed his gaze. Three high-altitude fighters were coming at high speed. A flash of light, and a shower of shards punctured their bubble. Floating toward the shattered wall, Sandover saw the captain's suit torn and red. Lianshen was diving toward him. He had to grab hold. Nothing but glass. He was going through.

"I have your boot. Don't move."

Glancing down he saw more fighters. Sky war. Lianshen on a tether, rubbing against the sharp glass. He was going to fly off into the sky. Lovely. Don't ever say it couldn't get worse.

"Get ready to move!" Lianshen's voice crackled in his ear.

His feet were moving back through the dome, Lianshen somersaulting out into the sky, his tether cut.

"Grab hold! Now!"

Sandover got a handhold. Three fingers. Four fingers. Fingers moving. Good sign.

"Lianshen!!"

"I am here. On com. Falling. Hang on. We have a moment. OZ-NAV is driving off the attack. Rescue will come. If you make it and I do not, may I say that you have a habit of being my nemesis. Your life has been my life. If it ends, it could end in no better way for me. Farewell!"

Silence. Echoes of his useless howls. A life for a life! Would he? Beya would. Must tell Beya. Have to move. Can I move? 'Tubby or not tubby,' that's the rub. Track too far away. Think! Tether still attached inside. Might get it, tie it on. Please, body, don't abandon me now. Just like the movies, close your eyes, hold on, now look up, twist slowly, my God, half the world beside me, too far down.

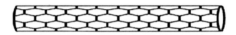

Phil winced, longing for respite, for the brief spot of sunlight to keep shining on his loved ones.

"Trouble below, gentlemen!"

Luisa Stollery barked at them as she listened on headphones, shattering the relief they'd felt on reaching EOL.

"Iranian fighters shot up Dr. Lee's cabin. Aussies and Kiwis drove them off, and we're right behind. One person flew out and is gone. Attempting to contact any survivors."

Come on, Sandover, you have to make it.

"Why would they attack the head of the WEO?"

"Relationship with Pyramid, Phil, and he was carrying something. They would assume it was NOA. On top of it all, he has crippling vertigo. Say some prayers for him!"

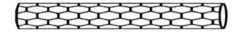

Damien heaved a sigh of doubt as Rana introduced the AI gene and protein managers into the nonorganic structures, the bots.

"Almost ready!"

"I'm afraid, Rana."

"We would be fools otherwise. What choice? We have improved on PAD's cocktail, 'plus plus,' in the jargon of the streets, plus tolerance and patience, as much as we've had time to inject these complex traits."

"It will take weeks to diffuse everywhere."

"Then let us pray."

"You first."

"Very funny. We have no gods."

"So who are we to say what humanity should be?"

"Don't overcook it, Damien. We're just in the wrong place at the right time. Whether or not we're the right people remains to be seen."

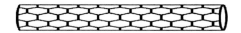

Sandover felt the last traces of gravity fading away. Not really felt, of course, in the pressure suit, the body just knows what's happening. Weightless in near-space in a thin costume of nano fabric and diamond. Above, the first glimpse of Fuller and Bucky. Below — don't go there. Tied in, all snug, rescue coming. Maybe. Aha! Signal on suitcom, a voice. Stollery.

"What happened, Captain Wesson?"

"Lift car detached from the top of the shaft, Admiral. It toppled over slowly in the low grav. Someone's been flung out the bottom on a tether!"

My luck, Sandover rued, no outgoing signal, mum's the word. When you have a panic attack, take the advice of the experts: don't panic. Tether will hold. Tether is rubbing over shattered diamond. Pull back in. Slowly.

"Admiral, the tether broke!"

Sandover fell slowly. This is it. The end. The beginning. The whole panoply in a layered snapshot. Not yet in vacuum, falling out of the sky. Slowly at first, how reassuring. How much time? Enough for the five stages of grief? I'll be saved! You bastards! Just one more chance? I was worthless, anyway. Oh, well. Vertigo gone, some consolation, can enjoy the finish without panic. That's funny. Been there, done that! A laughing maniac in a spacesuit headed for air. Not the life-saving variety, the suit-burning kind. Fiery death if I last that long. Maybe the suit jets. Get to the cable. Too far. Too late. Why not? Fear is gone, the last to go. One jet kaput. One discharge left. Aim well, William Tell.

Phil listened for Beya's voice on the secure channel patched together by Luisa Stollery's very efficient team.

"What's happening, Phil?"

Beya's shrill tone was heart stopping. Beya was never shrill.

"Dylan and I are at EOL after two attacks by Torbido and Sokolov. We're with Stollery, about to leave for Bucky with Ben. Nothing yet on Sandover's rescue. The attack was Golgotha and the Iranian Faction. They think Abbott was behind it. Old enemies fighting together to rule the roost, all under the banner of freedom."

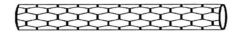

Sandover felt a slight sensation of weight.

Must be entering atmosphere. Draw legs up, ha ha, fat lot of good that'll do. Stopping. What the...?

"Good to see you again, Doctor Lee! Ewan Wesson, Auckland Command and the good vessel *Whale Rider* at your service on this nice fall day. Hang on, be right out to bring you in."

As he turned around, he saw the viewshield five metres away with a helmet behind it. On each side of the shield protruded girders twenty metres long, with a fine mesh net between them. He had been caught in a front scoop. A hatch opened just above the net.

"Sorry if we alarmed you there."

"I owe you my life."

"Pleasure. Not the easiest manoeuvre I ever flew, but no worries. Good as gold. Still on the lookout for more trouble, but I'd say you're a lucky man. Our success rate catching people in free fall so far is one out of two, including you. We can fly faster than you fall but normally we only get one pass, maybe two. Had to drift up behind and match your descent rate. Like ladling a wanton out of a falling soup bowl."

"Who attacked us?"

"Crazies. I checked with USNAV: three fighters from Greater Iran and the Christian extremists in America. Sad day. One had a big cross above the cabin. Followed 'em up from Banks as they seemed suspicious. To me they looked like stoats — you'd call 'em weasels, but a weasel is so weasily identified where a stoat is stoatally different. We put a few holes in that ship, my mates did. So, where you headed now?"

Good question. Million-dollar question. The case he was to deliver had gone out with Lianshen. Maybe it was a saturate and had spread through the atmosphere. He wanted to go back to Earth, but that was an old itch and by now it was pretty much scratched to death. He had a WEO Council meeting in two days.

"Up, I guess. Can you get me to Fuller?"

"Hold on. Benson, this tub good for Fuller?"

"Sorted, boss. Bit chancy but I'm not fussed."

"Rattle your dags, then. And tell Admiral Stollery we caught the duck and we're headed her way. Strap in, bottoms up!"

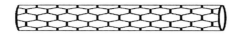

Dylan sprinted down the central passage of Bucky.

"This way. Faster!"

He strained every muscle to follow Ariel as she catapulted through the tunnels. Breathe. Relax. Think ahead, react faster. I can do this. Ariel's voice echoed in his helmet.

"Admiral Stollery, do you copy?"

"Copy. Status?"

"We're in a firefight in the Bucky tunnels. Headed for Pinpoint labs. Bogies ahead of us. We're gaining. You can hear them on system. Pharmacon troops out to capture the labs and revenge Torbido. We can't reach Rush or Singer inside the labs. Get to them however you can. Tell them to seal up tight and hide."

"Roger that. Fly well!"

Dylan redoubled his resolve. If Ariel could fly and think and talk at the same time, he could at least fly.

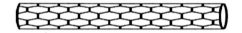

Phil stared at a bank of com screens, all dead.

"Sandover's OK, Ben. Thank God for that. But our coms are out and that can only mean trouble. We're completely isolated here in the lab."

"We're about ready to send at any rate, Phil. Black hole alignment is as fine-tuned as we're going to get, given the equations and the equipment. Now or never. Let's do it."

Phil and Ben were ready to test the deep-space pinpoint transmission equipment. They were also ready to attempt the Orion message transmission if necessary. Phil had the message ready in Sandover's cipher. Ben understood that some things are better left unsaid. They looked out over the growing inner-space colony.

"What's that?"

"Flashes, Ben. Must be signals."

"Lord almighty, it's Morse code. It says, just a minute... 'Rush seal up double. Disappear. Now'."

Phil knew if they sealed down, Dylan and Ariel would be caught outside. There had to be some way to contact them. What would Dylan want him to do?

"Sealing down the perimeters, Ben. We have no choice. Like it or not, with only very slight adjustments, our transmitter is now the most powerful weapon in space. We can get high-precision targeting with just a tweak to the math and the gear. I've put it in place just in case."

"Then we have to equip this weapon with a dead-man's switch and a remote we can operate from hiding."

"I did that, too, Ben, Dylan's suggestion. And I know the perfect place!"

"Exemplary preparation, my friend. After you."

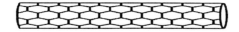

Dylan dodged, floated weightless, rebounded, just as in the tank. They were inside the inner perimeter, twenty-five metres behind the Pharma troops, five of them travelling fast but not fast enough. Close, but close only counts in horseshoes and hand grenades.

"Lock 'n' load, love." Ariel fired. "You know what you have to do. I've got right three, four, five. One and two are yours. We might get two passes but go for one. Put it in your head now and don't stop till it's over."

With that she launched like a spinning arrow, hit bogey one with her hand laser, flattened bogey three, and fired back into his suit as she flew past. Dylan, close behind, kicked bogey two hard in the head and fired at four. Both went down. He stopped and spun. Five was targeting Ariel as she launched back. Dylan fired as he hit a wall, missed. A bright red spot appeared on Ariel's skin-suit. In a breath, she pivoted, missed the second incoming shot, pulled a repair patch from her suit and slapped it over the hole as she twisted to launch. She passed over Dylan's head in a giant, inward-spinning arc and broke the neck of the last enemy with a kick that Dylan could feel through his suit and the vacuum.

"I'm OK, love. Laser caught the edge of my thigh. Don't beat yourself up. Remember this. You're not a killer. You did what you had to do, to live and save others. I know you know, but it's hard the first time."

Dylan saw Phil and Ben ahead He could hear them, the com block as dead as Torbido's ex-goons.

"Thank God, Dylan! Ben and I dead-switched the transmitter and came here to hide. You took out all five!"

"I had a little help, Dad. We're a good team. You too, nice job. Let's get back into the lab. Ariel needs some med and who knows what's next with these maniacs?"

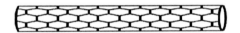

Ismael spun and marched back across the small room for the thousandth time as Giza Weiss followed his pacing with a bemused frown.

"So, it comes to this, Ismael."

"As we predicted, Giza. And where does the Jewish consciousness find itself on the eve of destruction?"

"Very close to the precipice, Ismael. Very close. Perhaps as we speak."

"I had heard rumours. We are also on the verge of launching our NOA cocktail. I wish I knew what's going on out there."

"We'll find out soon enough. Does it matter?"

"No, we launch our cocktail the second we're ready."

"We, too — there is no preventing it."

"If we win, if you and I survive, let's stay friends."

"I have hope that both of our authorities would insist on diversity as one characteristic of the NOA we spread. Tolerance of other varieties is critical for coexistence if not survival."

"It is done soon, my friend. We'll see what tomorrow brings."

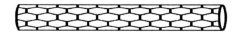

Phil paled as he gazed out the viewdome of the lab on Bucky. The voice of Luisa Stollery's rear admiral sprung from the speakers in the lab.

"Red alert, Admiral! Look at *Freedom Force*!"

"Lordamighty. It's moving toward us. Status!"

"Replaying, Admiral. They fired a seven-second blast on the rear booster jets. Building to two kilometres per hour. STATS, give me the exact course!"

"What's their target?"

"Us, Ma'am. Or very close. Too close for comfort. Sixty-one minutes and counting if they don't hit the gas pedal again."

"Prepare weapons and call in every ship that's close enough to make a difference. Tell STRAT that I want all options laid out in five minutes. Talk to Dylan Rush. Now give me com on all channels. Be ready to broadcast worldwide."

"On full, Ma'am."

"This is Admiral Luisa Stollery, US Naval Space Command. I address you, *Freedom Force* habitat and Jean-Christophe Moreau. Change course or face our full attack. Respond!"

"Admiral Stollery, nice to hear your voice. Before you shoot me out of the sky, or one of your belligerent allies saves you the trouble, please be advised that I have released an

NOA saturate that I have named Freedom Forever. It rests in a force field that will take you hours or days to find. The force field is kept activated by this habitat. If you destroy me, Freedom Forever is released and reaches every hectare of Earth in a few hours, every cell and atom soon after. If you cooperate, I will tell you the location so that you can retrieve and destroy it. Otherwise, I will release it from its bonds when we meet. Shall we say your place, one hour?"

"You're a madman, Moreau. What could be worth risking all humanity? What do you want? Tell the world, they are listening."

"It is you who are mad, who are risking humanity. Freedom Forever will make everyone more independent, more opposed to your brand of smothering, your tiny vision of human destiny. We will all move ahead faster. The weak will fall by the wayside but that is always the price of progress. Fear of failure makes us strong. Freedom Forever accentuates that fear, changing nothing else, making us survivors."

"Have you no humanity left?"

"It is precisely humanity that will be left, Admiral. Changed by Freedom Forever, you will join me in my cause. We are going to the stars, a tough enough road for the strongest, and who knows what we will meet along the way. Your limp-wristed brothers and sisters will never make it, never take the risks, never win the victories, never pay the price. What I want is simple. A treaty signed by PAD giving us full freedom to operate as we please on Earth and in space. We make our own rules, you leave us alone. The times have forced me to act. I will not lose. If you do not agree, Freedom Forever will be the first and only NOA cocktail the world will drink. It will kill any others that come later, in the bud, like picking off deer with an Uzi. I will leave you to consult with each other. Time flies."

"His transmitters are off, Admiral."

"Good God. He *is* mad. But this is not our call. Open the conference coms with all the PAD leaders. Include Ariel and the Pinpoint lab."

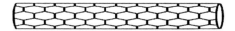

Édouard felt anger rise up his gorge. That *espèce de merde* was going to ruin it all, the boy he had raised, brought to the halls of power. He opened the channel to Freedom Force.

"Jean-Christophe, this is insanity. We are strong enough. Don't release the plague! What if your scientists are wrong? What if it destroys everyone?"

"You have turned into a PADDIE stooge, Father. What has happened to your famous courage, your contempt for danger? We have tested Freedom Forever on humans. It was pleasant to watch. Only the derelict few at the bottom of the barrel could not survive it. Everyone else grew cunning, broke through the boundaries, fought, killed, performed perfectly. The world will be recreated in our image. Your image, Father. Or the one that looked back at you from the mirror before you became an old fool."

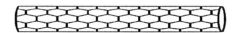

Phil swallowed another gulp of panic. By now the glass was looking more than half-empty, the minutes ticking down, Freedom Force growing larger in their view.

Stollery looked at him with an accusing glare.

"You've tangled with J.C. before. What's your advice? We haven't got much time. If the PAD leaders come back with their verdict, whether it's call his bluff or sign the deal, what do *you* say? What is our responsibility? More importantly, what do we do if PAD does not reach consensus in time?"

"Dylan and I are talking to Kat and Beya as well, Admiral Stollery. None of us is a psychologist but we think he'll do it. He has always had a demented streak. And the certainty that others will release NOA cocktails makes him a trapped animal. He worships the vision of humanity as wild hunters."

"And how bad is the cocktail, in your opinion? This vision?"

"Fanatics always make a good case for their visions, Admiral. The flaw in this one is not in the motive but in the method. Ultimately, in the feasibility."

"Explain."

"The odds for the ruthless are appealing. It is not hard to understand what drives Édouard Moreau, Mathias Abbott, or Gregor Sokolov. Like J.C., they know full well that when they are cutthroat, their own world goes well. So it's easy to extrapolate that, if everyone is cutthroat, humanity will thrive. Fallacy of composition."

"Could you put that in its simplest terms? Time is short."

"Murderers prosper in a world of sheep. In a world of murderers, the brutes will kill each other off. Human history will end or go off on a wild tangent."

"He will not see reason?"

"Jean-Christophe is governed by hate and by the enjoyment of death and destruction. Absent is the logic that would stop him short of suicide, let alone xenocide."

"So you think we should blast him to smithereens?"

"Regrettably no. For humanists, the deal J.C. is proposing is better than the alternative. We don't think he's bluffing. It's not in his character. Freedom Forever will either kill everything immediately or make us all cold-blooded killers. I'd say 'make the deal,' look for the containment field, play for a little more time. Someone else may use that time to release their NOA concoction, but we think not. I believe PAD is very close to having one ready in a pinch, but they need more time to be sure of its effects if released."

"Then they might want to consider how sure they can be in five minutes. And how prepared to act."

"I hear you, Admiral. I will tell Damien Benedykt immediately. I'm coward enough to hope that PAD has the wisdom and the balls to decide for us. I'd rather be a spectator for this last act. And a survivor. We'll help where we can."

"Thank you, Philamon. Wisdom guide us — balls are never enough."

Ariel's com broke into the conversation.

"Incoming, Admiral. It's a Captain Ewan Wesson, Auckland Command. He's got Professor Lee, picked him up in free fall in a skid. Got to be the luckiest man alive. They're headed our way, just past zero-g. Reporting an uncharted anomaly in their path. Investigating."

"You thinking what I'm thinking?"

"Yes, Ma'am, could be the containment field holding J.C.'s NOA salvo."

"Sandover, can you hear me?"

"Here, Admiral. Some static. Please speak slowly."

"Listen, we think what you're approaching is Jean-Christophe's NOA cocktail in a containment field. Can you mark it for our targeting? What do we have to throw at it folks?"

Silence.

"Don't all speak at once. One moment, gentlemen, we have a message incoming."

"No decision from PAD, Admiral. They're asking you to stall for time."

"I am afraid that time has run its course. How long until J.C. gets here?"

"Seven minutes, Ma'am."

"Admiral, there may be a way."

"Phil?"

"No, Dylan here. Our deep-space com launcher is linked to the black hole lab on *Prism*. We may be able to take out the containment field and everything in it. But we'd be lying if we claimed we knew exactly what would happen. Our blast could possibly launch the plague into the atmosphere. We'd need a com hotspot on the target to have any hope of accuracy."

"Wesson, you hear that?"

"Roger that, Admiral. Crew is on it, but not enough time. We'll get there a minute before Moreau hits your position. We can get into the field but not out again. We don't have the firepower onboard to wipe out the NOA for certain. Bad timing, friends. We're going to be your hotspot. We'll detonate what we have at the same instant you fire."

"Wesson, Sandover, no, you can't do that."

"Don't get maudlin on me, Phil." Sandover's calm voice had steel underneath. "I may be the unluckiest man in the world, but you'd do the same. No one is forgotten. We change the people around us and what they do. Our ripples diminish but don't die. They form the tapestry of place-time. How could it be otherwise? How else could we become different from the prophecy of our past?"

Jean-Christophe's voice broke the silence.

"Five minutes, Admiral, till we meet and Freedom Forever is released. Have your impotent masters instructed you to yield? No? I thought not! How can you believe in them if they can't cooperate when their lives depend on it? Time to roll the dice, my friends. Let the games begin!"

"Jean-Christophe, wait! I am entering the containment field."

"Sandover? Sandover Lee? How delicious! You will be scattered over the Earth with Freedom Forever, the first convert, the first fatality, the first to follow Maurizio. I will enjoy that very much. You have been nothing but trouble!"

"Such is life, J.C. Though you've given up on the human miracle, you live on, while we die for its future. Nevertheless, it is a small sacrifice to me. Time, Dylan. Stealth is not enough. Ask Beya to keep the faith — she'll understand. Ask everyone to forgive me. Thank you for your time."

Dylan's voice was almost a whisper.

"Now it starts."

Sandover's response trailed off into the universe.

"One more time."

Kat sat with Beya at the com, a half-dozen screens showing the view from Fuller, Bucky, and *Whale Rider*. They watched in horror as *Prism*'s giant reflectors focused an energy beam on *Whale Rider* and the containment field. The whole image evaporated into swirling patterns of light as the field simultaneously imploded from within and vaporized under the constant fire from above. Then there was nothing, not a ripple, not a sign of containment field, NOA, or *Whale Rider*.

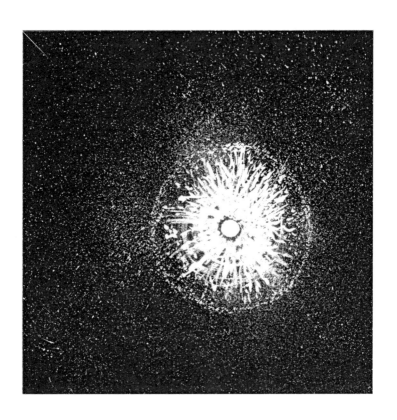

Aftermath

"Search the area!"

The snap of Luisa Stollery's voice brought them back to the present, when Kat wanted nothing more than to stay in the past.

"Get samples! Analyze the energy patterns! I want to know what happened down there, ladies and gentlemen and I want to know now! If the cocktail survived, it could be headed anywhere. We won't find it unless we know exactly what became of *Whale Rider*. Questions?"

"One minute to impact from Freedom Force, Admiral."

"Moreau, that was your containment field we just eradicated. Your threats are empty now!"

"I will escape in a pod, Admiral, while you die in flames. I'll make another cocktail, you fools!"

"That tells me all I need to know. Goodbye, Monsieur Moreau. Gentlemen, fire when ready."

Seconds rolled by. Were the weapons jammed? J.C.'s voice penetrated the silence.

"Father, don't abandon me! You can back them down, use your power."

"There's nothing I can do, Jean-Christophe. They will never trust you again. Why did you do this?"

"You of all people should know. Tomorrow you will be saturated by a form of NOA that is an Iranian or Russian vision of life. Ours was better!"

"If you must lose the war to win the battle, isn't that a line you cannot cross?"

"Others cross it. Where is your backbone? You don't even know if we'd lose the war."

"I feel it, Jean-Christophe. Wolves live on caribou. A world of wolves has a lovely ring but we wouldn't stop until we had torn each other apart. There is something about the possibility of the future that appeals to me."

"To an old man fat on his fortune. I thought as much. You, who taught me to win at any cost. You, who never loved me!"

"It is a hard thing for a father to say to his son, but there was never much to love."

"You never looked! Always the chairman of the board, never the father!"

A series of flashes bridged the gap between Fuller and *Freedom Force*, hitting the enormous habitat on its edge, pushing it sideways and starting a slow spin. Kat and Beya watched from afar as they listened to the coms.

"Message incoming, Admiral. Pinpoint Lab on Bucky sent an energy beam. Black hole facility on *Prism* directed it at *Whale Rider*. There was briefly some kind of link between *Prism* and *Whale Rider*. Then 'puffs of nothing,' Ma'am. That's how the techs describe it. The vacuum reclaimed the space, empty as a monk's purse."

Freedom Force closed in on Fuller as Stollery barked back.

"There can't only be empty space, Captain. Mass of vessel and crew, Moreau's cocktail, dark matter, grey matter — it all matters! I want to know where it went. Yesterday! Dylan, your analysis, and exactly what kind of weapon did you fire?"

"Admiral, the launcher was designed to test the sending of high-speed long-distance communications through space. To do this, we routed the transmission beam through a miniature black hole created by *Prism*. Our plan was to aim the beam toward your USNAV lab on *Outreach*, in the asteroid belt, where we could measure any significant gains in velocity over normal transmission speeds. We fired it at *Whale Rider* instead."

"What happened? Your best guess."

"The physics says that 'distance' may be compacted in the immediate region of a black hole and in the ripples it creates unceasingly through the matter of all kinds that makes up the known universe. Our best guess is that the link was caused by this effect, amplified by Pinpoint's new technology as it travelled through the region."

"Are you saying that the containment field and *Whale Rider* could have been moved to some other place?"

"That would be getting ahead of ourselves, Admiral. We're not actually sure how the beam would behave with the containment field, but it could have pierced it."

"Causing the implosion of the field?"

"Yes."

"Keep me posted, Dylan. Captain, anything from the salvage fleet?"

"No, Ma'am. I mean, they have just arrived and have so far found nothing."

"Nothing?"

"Nothing, Admiral. Not yet."

The rear end of *Freedom Force* passed above the central window of USNAV headquarters. The forward tip swung slowly toward the corporate sector of Fuller in a final suicide arc, toward Terrepharm HQ, where Édouard Moreau stared out through the transparent diamond dome.

"Accident, Captain?" Stollery barked.

"No, Ma'am. We held our fire long enough to calculate the best place for *Freedom Force* to hit Fuller, best among bad choices."

Édouard's voice broke the silence.

"Your urge to destroy did not come from me, Jean-Christophe, nor from your mother, rest her soul."

"Then farewell, Father. You will not live to see the results of your cowardice. Freedom forever!"

A ball of fire inflated out the side of *Freedom Force* as it struck the face of Fuller, the face of Édouard Moreau staring in helpless rage.

Phil patched Beya and Kat into a secure link with Dylan before asking the question topping his list.

"What did you do, Dylan? What was the beam you sent. Was it the Orion transmission?"

"I modified it."

"What would that do?"

"I have to study this further. It was an impulse. I'll tell you more as soon as I have anything solid."

"Could this have saved Sandover?"

"If you want the truth, I think it's one in a million. Not good enough odds, but a chance."

Kat looked at Beya, her head bowed. Sometimes a chance can make a lifetime worthwhile, no matter what the odds.

"You did the right thing, Dylan." Beya choked.

"I'm so sorry, Beya. No other choice. But that doesn't make it any easier. You've lost everything."

"Don't beat yourself to death with the guilt," Phil urged.

"I know. I got debriefed by the pros earlier today during the short interval between slayings. They tell me I'm not a killer. But I am, that's the problem. We weren't ready for J.C.'s kamikaze stunt and we couldn't save Sandover."

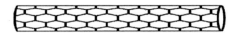

Damien procrastinated, frozen in the headlights of time.

"The time has come, Damien. Which will it be, my love? The PAD vision or ours?"

"Ours is more positive, Rana, lighter on obedience, stronger on cooperation. But can we sanely launch either? To be or not to be. If we do, isn't it our sworn duty to spread the vision of PAD?"

"Are you a revolutionary, Damien?"

"I wasn't before I met you. Now? It is the ultimate arrogance, but we know the tech best, the possibilities and the margins of risk. Better to err on the side of innovation than condemn the future to some mindless conformity."

"If it works, no one will remember that PAD's intent was more cautious. We will just be different."

"Less human?"

"More guided by creativity."

"And we play God."

"Do you think anyone else will do better?"

"Not in time."

"Then anchors away. Even with the world on red alert, we can substitute our brew into the PAD launch sequence and have it reach every corner of the Earth by nightfall. We'll know within hours what happened, if we're still around, if we can just remember to ask!"

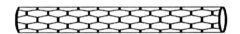

Next morning, back in the command centre with Luisa Stollery, Phil waited, hoping against hope.

"Admiral, the president is patched in."

"Admiral Stollery, Saba here. I'm with the joint chiefs of staff. Kat Rush and Beya Lee have joined us. What have you got?"

"Good morning, Madame President, and my deepest regrets to Ms Lee. We're still looking, of course, but so far the area is as empty as if nothing had happened. I have Phil and

Dylan Rush connected along with Ariel An, whom you have met."

"Good morning to you all. Firstly, my warm thanks for stopping Moreau, if we have indeed stopped him from spreading the Freedom Forever plague. Second, the silence surrounding the impact of our own saturate is as deafening as the void that swallowed Sandover Lee. What is your assessment, Philamon? We need to know what's going on."

"Greetings, Saba. Dylan says he has new information, so I'm going to ask him to start."

"Good morning, Madame President. There is one admission I have to make at the outset. We had already launched a saturate. By we, I mean myself, Ariel, and the Seaside team."

Silence.

"We understood at the time what your silence now confirms, that our action was one of arrogance bordering on treason."

"What could you possibly have been thinking? And more to the point, what does this saturate do?"

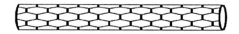

Damien watched as Rana scrolled through multiple monitor images.

"Nothing?"

"Still too early."

"But we should be starting to get signs of permeation. All we've got is some unexpected pattern in the NOA monitors, something unknown. Could someone else have launched a cocktail before ours? Not good, Rana. It's going to be a long day."

"We have all the time in the world."

"Right, maybe a second or two."

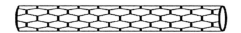

Dylan responded in a tone Phil had not heard before, weary and humble.

"It came from a conversation with Justine Lee, Ma'am, Beya's daughter. I believe you know her."

"You bet the fate of humanity on the tale of a seven-year-old?" Saba Luanzi's outrage cut through space like a knife.

"Not exactly, Ma'am. And no offence, but the world has been in the hands of adolescents since I was old enough to notice. Present company excluded."

"I'll ignore that. Proceed."

"Justine is a story teller, and my sister Lara is her friend. We asked them what they thought of the stories about plagues that they were seeing on the ViDs, and they said that, in a story of this sort, it's best to decide how the ending should turn out, then proceed from there. We asked what ending they suggested. They answered that Sandover always said, when uncertainty prevails, make yourself invisible and lie in wait. So we made a saturate that lies in wait, but we added a wrinkle. We wanted to prevent all other saturates from spreading. So we made a sidekick that kills all the others once they have arrived and lowered their guard. Anyone who launches a cocktail will be looking for impacts. They will find none. Ours remains in the shadows, almost invisible. Its passivity is its shield. It comes out of hiding only to kill the NOAbots launched by others, then slips back behind its veil. We call it Stealth. It remains in place throughout the world at this moment."

"You have taken an unpardonable chance with human life."

"We understood the consequences of Stealth, Madam President. It changes nothing fundamental. It leaves us with all our human warts and blemishes, our grand aspirations and lethal loathings. It was the worst of all possible solutions, except for all the others. In the circumstances, we could find no better ending to this story and many much worse."

"Heaven preserve us! And when did you let it go?"

"Just over a week ago. It was tested secretly in our labs and it was easy to launch. We simply sent courier packages to every corner of the world, contaminated with Stealth. Sandover unknowingly seeded a final batch into the atmosphere when his lift capsule was attacked."

"And who produced this Stealth?"

"The team at Seaside did most of it. We stole the idea from Damien Benedykt and Rana Myagdi when we spotted some work they'd done to embellish the PAD saturate. We stole a sample of their NOA. As it turned out, they had made a change that caused the saturate to be more *Bohemian*, if you will."

"Bohemian is not exactly the word that comes to mind from the little I know of those two."

"They're much less formal underneath, Ma'am, believe me. So we took the same technology and extended it to the point where Stealth simply drops out of sight. Adapting it to destroy all other NOA cocktails was a relatively simple problem. We just had to make sure it didn't also kill the bots being used in medicine and life support."

"You never cease to astound us, Dylan Rush. Your actions were indefensible, to say the least, but so far you've managed to save our bacon."

"My pleasure. Ma'am. I had a lot of help, as I mentioned. Lara also figured out how to find Zhaolin on the nets. Zhaolin won the Imputer War on exactly the same strategy: get there first, lie low, and kill anything with the power to destroy. 'He' helped us with the AI side of our saturate. With Stealth out there, it's unlikely we'll be at risk again for a spell."

"Would you care to define that a little more precisely?"

"Yes, sorry. Years, maybe a decade. No more."

"May I ask a difficult question?"

"Of course."

"If you knew Stealth would work, why did you need to destroy *Freedom Forever*, and Sandover along with it?"

"We didn't know, Ma'am. Although lab tests said Stealth would work, the first real-life test didn't come until now, with the launch of the PAD saturate. When Moreau made his move, we had no certainty, no evidence or proof. Sandover knew this, in his words, 'Stealth is not enough.'"

"May I ask the obvious, then? Are you also connected in some way with Pyramid?"

"Aren't we all? The interesting mysteries that remain unsolved seem to me to lie around the nature of our connections."

"And you will let me know if you stumble across any more critical facts?"

"Of course."

"And you would agree to that even if you had no intention of doing so."

"Yes, Ma'am. But I would honour my agreement to the best of my ability. We all would."

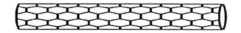

Kat was leaving for Beya's place when Phil and Dylan called from Bucky.

"I'll come down soon," Phil promised. "Beya needs our help."

"She'll be OK for a while. Work will keep her mind off Sandover most of the time. There's going to be a lot of rethinking going on by the powers that brought the world to the brink. She'll be in the middle of it."

"I hope you're right, Kat. And she's got Justine to look after along with Saba and the White House."

"She has PAD to serve and frontiers to explore if she survives the shock. Justine will need you and Lara, Dylan."

"We stay close, Mom. We talk all the time."

"And you'll stay up there a while?"

"It's where I should be, with the lab and Ariel."

"I'd say you're a lucky young man, but luck is never far from insight, so congratulations from one of your biggest fans."

"Thanks, Mom, that means a lot. It was friends more than luck that showed the way, if I have to be honest. I've been lucky to learn from the best. Keep an eye on Justine."

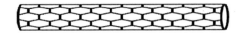

Kat gazed out a window of Beya's spacious parlour, now too empty. Beya motioned her to sit, and offered a question into the late afternoon air.

"So, we saved the world?"

"Of course. But probably not."

Beya laughed. A welcome sound. A soft snow dusted the trees and the valley out over the river. The far silhouettes of the capital's monuments disappeared in a soft blanket of white, enclosing them within a warm cocoon in the sunroom. Silence descended with the snow. A scarlet cardinal danced a moment on the balcony rail outside before leaping into a world beyond their sight. Heading home. A silent tear rolled down Beya's cheek.

"I can't seem to walk a straight line between one moment and the next, Kat. I take a step and the ground is firm. Then it dissolves and I'm falling. I don't even know who we are. Is it you and I or the ghosts of our former selves, banished into the mists of time? Maybe Justine and Lara will write our story and find an ending."

"I don't know, Beya. But I think back to the people we were in Merimbula. We've learned so much about the world and a bit about ourselves. What we spend most of our lives doing is getting to know the person who stares back from the mirror, our vessel, and our mask. Maybe in the end we learn to see ourselves from the outside, through the eyes of others, just in time for it not to matter anymore. Yet the adventure obliterates boredom and offers some salvation, the chance to learn long after the body has failed and the mind is perched on the rim of oblivion."

"*Flowers for Algernon.*"

"Funny, Phil always saw that story as a tragedy. A boy was given brilliance, rose from obscurity to become a human powerhouse, then lost the spark at the peak of potency and fell back into insignificance. I always saw it as just the cycle of life. A time of anonymity at the end. A taste of peace without life's burdens and woes. But you're too young for that, Beya. And the world still bangs on your door. You need time, but we need to talk, too. About what we know."

"I know one thing, Kat. Sandover is still alive. I know it sounds crazy, like I'm in some misshapen state of denial, but I have dreams that are more real than life. He asked me to keep the faith. The rainstar keeps an eye on me, its power grows and wanes. I'm a fool, but I know it in my heart."

"Nothing I know says he isn't alive."

"Does me little good, though. I have to face what's left of life. I have Justine and work to do. But so much sadness. So perfectly infuriating. So absolutely Sandover. We were always like sister and brother, Kat, along with the passion, so there was a hint of incest there and a small part of him that stayed private. Perhaps he went somewhere to die, to save us the pain of his passing. What good does it do to speculate?"

"I don't know, Beya, it might. The Machiavelli in me says the game isn't over. Phil and Dylan agree, Lara too. And probably Justine."

"She's been quiet with me lately, protective. In her words, 'The end is the beginning, what is true in the moment is true in the fullness of time'."

"You've earned her love, Beya. A battle was won at too high a cost and the war goes on."

"And?"

"You know me well. For one thing, *Prism* was active at the moment Dylan fired the Orion transmitter, more active than just producing the black hole. *Prism* also shaped some form of emission that no one has yet been able to identify at all precisely. This complicates the picture no end. I have almost no idea what Pyramid may know regarding Sandover and Stealth. I was hoping he might have told you something more, shared some knowledge that would give us a clue. Any clue at this point."

"Nothing I can think of, Kat, and I've been searching my memories for even the feeblest shard. There *is* one thing that sticks in my mind after missing it for so many years. Sandover has an almost-perfect memory, more than photographic. He could keep the Orion cipher in his head and a hundred more. He has a mind that records everything, even the underlying thoughts and mood."

"I know what he meant by 'stealth is not enough,' Beya, but what did he mean by 'one more time'?"

"You think I haven't asked myself a million times?"

"Sorry, just trying to understand. Sandover invented the Orion cipher back in Merimbula. Given his relationship with Pyramid, we've always figured they knew it pretty early in the game. But maybe he was telling us they were the senders. If they had remote satellites out there, or the help of the Visitors, or inter-place-time communications, for that matter, they could have sent Orion immediately on creating the code.

For someone looking for a safe way to speak to the past, such a language would be a gift from heaven."

"You mean we were set up, and Sandover played dumb?"

"I'm not sure, Beya. Maybe it wasn't quite so calculated, but it's a good guess, my best guess right now. It fits with many things."

Beya stood up after a long moment of reflection and drifted into the kitchen, returning a few moments later with steaming hot coffee.

"My brain is full, Kat."

"I know the feeling."

"What about the Orion transmission. Did Phil succeed in resending it?"

"Apparently no, Beya. Dylan and Phil say they didn't dare. Maybe they could have altered history in a way that would save Sandover. But if it worked, they could also have undone everything that's been done to avert the NOA plague."

"Then what was the beam that passed through *Whale Rider*?"

"Phil doesn't know and Dylan isn't saying. Pyramid, as always, is silent. We may know soon enough."

"You have an idea?"

"If you were on *Prism*, Beya, and knew that Sandover was in the line of fire, what would you do?"

Beya suppressed a helpless shrug.

"I'd try to get him out of the way."

"How? Say you had no physical way of removing him."

"Send a message? But where, or when?"

"Exactly. To the recent past, if you could do it. To alter history just a little, enough to save *Whale Rider*. A long shot, but you asked."

"At least that murdering deviant didn't survive. May he rot in hell!"

"You can count on that, Beya. The debris of J.C. and *Freedom Force* are headed toward the asteroid belt in the general direction of the Southern Cross, at a good clip. Stollery took a beating for the execution of Édouard but no one has turned up the heat. So much for FAF solidarity. "

"Fitting. The path in FAF is sink or swim, dogma eat dog. Good to see the last of that twisted family. What about Abbott?"

"Crippled in the dogfight after his attack on Sandover. His bird slipped away in the fray so USNAV can't touch him. He's angry and injured, going to cause us a lot of trouble. The Christian Right is furious. Gregor Sokolov faces criminal charges under the new Inner Space Accords. The penalty for such an attack is banishment from Earth. Abbott has sided with Sokolov against PAD's takeover. But for now they are both up against the wall. Pharmacon is in disarray."

Some trick of afternoon sunlight lent a soft luminosity to the snow-flaked mists outside. They watched the ViD awhile. Beya took two calls from the White House and fidgeted in little ways when she wasn't working. Desperate to be busy, to hope, not to think.

"What about trying another experiment, Kat? Something that might tell us if inter-place-time transmission can work?"

"Ah, yes. Dylan and Phil have been working on that. They are ready to try a message to the near future, aimed at the USNAV lab on *Outreach*. That way, it wouldn't be picked up by the listening stations Earthside and start another round of dislocation."

"When will they try?"

"They want to leave things alone a bit longer while relative stability prevails — mission accomplished, for the moment. You have to think twice about the consequences. They also say the odds are near zero of doing anything that could help Sandover, if he's alive. Nevertheless, it would solve a *lot* of worries to know if any form of inter-place-time connection is possible. They'd like to know what we think."

"I'm in favour, Kat, but that's just wanting to know what happened to Sandover."

A ray of sunlight found a hole in the frozen mist and fell prism-like through a stained glass panel, dressing Beya for a moment in rose-blue and deep purple splashes.

"What else do we know about Sandover, Beya? I know this is hard for you."

"You mean, could he have known more about the whole shebang? Maybe. It's hard to believe, but, as I said, there was a part of him he could or would not confide."

"Yet his actions were beyond commendable."

"I know. So, without thinking about it much, some part of me assumed he had a good reason for downplaying his perfect memory. Maybe he was protecting us. Just a feeling I had. We all did, I think."

"You're right. It was a little too convenient. We accepted on the one hand that he was a valuable element of Pyramid, but on the other that he was cut off for his own good from the organization and the Pinnacle."

"Which is whom, by the way?"

"I don't know, Beya. We didn't ask these questions sharply enough because we believed his story. Concealing is not easy to do over the long haul. You'd have to be a special kind of performer to pull that off."

"That's true in most things, being great is people not noticing your effort or even that you're there. He did at times seem like a desperate actor, Kat, as though time was running out. Another feeling I had, like he was looking back and ahead at the same time."

"Mmm."

"What are you thinking?"

"The good news or the bad news?"

"Good."

"Good choice. My best guess is that Pyramid was formed in the teens and twenties. In retrospect, who could have created Pyramid? Who would have been both strong and cagey enough? China for strong. Thailand and maybe Singapore for cagey. Likely all three, with a core of Chinese families taking the lead. As this story goes, Pyramid created pinpoint and sent the Orion message from a remote satellite they'd sent out for that purpose."

"But why go to all that trouble? Something we've always wondered."

"It's not so much trouble if it was done over two decades. Orion was a wakeup call. Even with no understanding of its meaning, the world began to believe that someone was sending warnings."

"OK, but what about the fact that we four were the only ones who understood Orion and the rather odd matter of inter-place-time communication that it claimed?"

"Easy, from one or two perspectives. Pyramid was engaged with Sandover through Eng Kai. Maybe Sandover was a rising star."

"Why was he in Merimbula?"

"Pyramid would have wanted to keep close tabs on the listening stations and technologies even while moving ahead on other tech, including NOA. Merimbula and the other stations had the best AI tools of the time. Pyramid also needed a basic familiarity with the equipment to be sure Orion would be heard loud and clear. Makes sense to send Sandover."

"And he found me."

"Yup. Then composed the cipher. The Orion message followed shortly thereafter. Then he played the roles of Pyramid foot soldier and global chief economist, helping us get on with innovations in science, helping build the alliances that might stave off an impending catastrophe."

"Which Pyramid was predicting because…?"

"Good question. Brings us back to Pinnacle. They would have a clear view of the dangers of emerging technologies. They could very easily have come to predicting something like NOA cocktails."

"So everything is explained, with no need for inter-place-time communication. And Sandover was just basically blown to bits."

"Occam's razor. But there may be a few nicks in the razorblade, Beya, quite aside from our feelings and memories."

Justine arrived with hugs and a backpack full of stuff, mostly books.

"Hi Kat. Essay due tomorrow, Mom. Talk at dinner."

Gone in a flourish. Beya mused as she started putting together a meal.

"And the bad news, Kat?"

"I thought you might have forgotten. It's not really that bad, just a scenario with more dark alleys and angles. As I said, there are questions unresolved by the most logical explanation. Why would Pyramid raise the possibility of inter-place-time communication and put us on its trail if there was nothing to it? Maybe they were developing it, say, in the twenties. According to Phil and Ben, it is in many ways an extension of pinpoint thinking. Paired particles, separated either by distance or by time."

"But Pyramid would understand its dangers, if they were developing it. Why let it out to anyone else?"

"I'd guess they mainly wanted to send the wakeup call, but then they saw a way of engaging some people they thought they could trust."

"You're leaving something out."

"Ah, you know me *too* well. Yes, well, if I were Pyramid in that position, I would have understood that, if all else failed, a last-ditch option would be to try to contact the past with information that would change history. Change it enough."

"So they put us on that track, and we succeeded. We saved the world."

"Of course. But probably not. The likeliest explanation is still that inter-place-time was always a fiction, but it motivated us, helped produce a team that could stop the NOA plague. Our children, in particular, as it turned out. The world was lucky, but there's still no need to accept inter-place-time connectivity."

"You believe that?"

Justine arrived, ate, and vanished in a flash. After dinner, Beya fidgeted, a question clearly on her mind.

"There's one thing I've wanted to ask you," she ventured, after a shadow passed, some wayward cloud drifting by the last rays of sunlight.

"Fire away."

"Well, you've always been the best of us by far at looking into other people's minds. Couldn't you have learned about Sandover and the cipher from reading his thoughts?"

"If you can believe me, no. I can gauge people's motivations most times, sometimes predict what actions will follow. But I don't have the kind of insight you'd need to sort out a puzzle just from seeing traces of it in someone's thoughts or emotions And while we're being candid, can I ask you one in return?"

"Be my guest."

"And a grateful one, Beya. So, with as little indirection as possible, what brought *you* to Merimbula?"

"Now that sounds more like the Kat I know. And yes, your instincts serve you well. In retrospect, I think I may have been recruited in very small steps, almost without my noticing, until Merimbula. While I assumed I'd got there because of my own abilities, it wasn't only merit, looking back. The competition was fierce. Probably everyone there was the choice of one powerful group or another."

"But Sandover never said more? Like, who told him to create the cipher or what role he played in Pyramid?"

"No. And Pyramid certainly didn't tell me either. You might have thought they'd have kept me less in the dark — I guess that's their way. What you don't know won't kill you. I accepted that Sandover was in the same mode. I went on believing that for so many years, but I wonder."

"What makes you wonder?"

"That part of him I've never known."

Presentiment

Night set in. The ViD featured the new PAD-FAF Accords on cooperation in inner space. Beya beamed when Kat congratulated her, confirming how much she'd put into the process.

"Strike while the iron is hot, Kat. We knew we'd lose momentum the moment FAF stopped bickering amongst themselves and started seeding discord again. And it's a lot easier to bargain with Stealth on your side and the ancestors of Zhaolin on the Nets. But you never really answered my question. Do you believe inter-place-time connection is possible? Or, if you prefer, what's the outside limit of reality? You've never suffered from an underactive imagination."

"I'll take that as a compliment. OK, perhaps they pretty much go together, outside limit and inter-place-time. How's this? Sandover went up the Lift prepared to launch a benign NOA cocktail in order to test Stealth. He also had Stealth in that case, to seed. He had it worked out with Dylan that, if anything went wrong, Dylan would try inter-place-time transmission as a last resort. They were always close, Beya, two of a kind. Getting caught in J.C.'s debacle and the way it ended was an accident. J.C. was just bad luck."

"A fitting epitaph!"

"On the positive side, they destroyed *Freedom Forever*."

"Which might have changed us all into wolves?"

"Yes, though we'll never know for sure. In the last moment before *Whale Rider* vanished, you heard Sandover say 'one more time.' That was the signal to fire. *Freedom Force* was destroyed before it hit the Earth."

"It didn't?"

"I don't think so, Beya. Any sudden urges to go out and tear out someone's throat?"

"Not lately, no. So Sandover's death stopped Freedom Forever, which in turn might or might not have been wiped out by Stealth?"

"Exactly."

"So, he saved the world."

"Of course. But probably not. Probably Stealth did the deed."

"And where exactly did Stealth come from?"

"It's a longish story, Beya, but basically from Dylan, working with heavy backing from Pyramid."

"You've known this long?"

"I've had a sense of it for quite a while, but nothing concrete, so I didn't pursue it. Like your feelings about Sandover. There were changes in all three kids that were way too rapid without some outside support systems. I'm a first-time parent, like all of us, destined to have it all figured out by the time it isn't needed anymore. I saw it, but I didn't see it."

"So that explains what Dylan said to Admiral Stollery about all of us having connections with Pyramid."

"Exactly. Dylan must have been contacted when he first went to university. I have little doubt that Lara also has direct connections. Maybe Justine."

"I think all three are tight, Kat. They may even be in it together. You must be proud of Dylan."

"You should be, too, Beya. You and Sandover are his younger parents, Lara's, too. Like Sandover, Dylan had a lot of help. Ariel An didn't materialize out of nowhere to become one of the great tacticians of the day. Ariel An, who, by the way, is about to wed Dylan."

"Congratulations!"

"They're very young but the die is cast. She looks a match for anyone. He has that very unusual portfolio of cognitive abilities, including my intuition. She has the kind of eidetic memory you describe for Sandover, which makes me wonder if it might be teachable."

"By Pyramid? Or the Visitors?"

"Maybe we don't need the Visitors, at least not yet. Let's say Sandover and Dylan both learned from Pyramid how to remember everything in technicolour. That they were groomed for the tasks they would face is one way of looking at it. But who exactly did the grooming?"

The ViD interrupted their deliberations. Saba was speaking to the Nearspace Forum of the Council of Nations. Already, there were signs of discord and corridor deal making. It would be a long haul to get the benefits of space into the service of all humanity. For the first time in a decade, however, there was a sense of possibility, of what might come, a hint of something new.

"So, what was a nice girl like you doing in an odd place like Merimbula?"

"Ah, good question, Beya. Are you asking about the odds of a retired British paramilitary operative's being married to the scientific head of the station?"

"Something like that."

"Sheer coincidence?"

"Plausible."

"OK, when I think back now, I did marry Phil because I fell in love with him. But I could have been led into meeting him quite easily. There are a couple of people I suspect, looking back."

"He's such an idealist. But not really naïve."

"No. Well, anyone who's an idealist has got to be pretty naïve, but he's well aware of how ridiculous it is to be idealistic, so he isn't exactly being duped."

"How is he connected to Pyramid?"

"He may not be. He could be the only one we know who isn't, despite being our leader in the conventional sense of the word. There would be advantages for Pyramid in leaving someone like him to pursue his own hunches."

"And backing him up with someone who can demolish a small army if the need arises."

"Something like that. And connecting him to an absolutely first-rate scientist to develop the pinpoint technologies."

"They're a pair of idealists, those two, though Ben is less adventurous when it comes to danger. Less bravado."

"So let's assume I was recruited by Pyramid to support Phil and look after tactics. That recruitment took place in the period between the Visitors' patterns and Merimbula. Quite feasible. They were rounding up the posse during those years."

"But who was?"

"OK, since you ask. Sandover. Head of the Pinnacle."

Beya looked both dumbfounded and riveted at the same time, so Kat plunged on.

"And now, once with feeling, the scenario I'd bet on. Ready?"

"Was I ever?"

"Pyramid took shape in the teens and twenties. It was the work of a brilliant human, or someone contacted by the Visitors."

"Pyramid was in with the Visitors?"

"Or the Visitors were an invention of Pyramid."

"I see. What do you think?"

"I think there may be only one person in the world who knows the answer to that question, Beya, whether Pyramid invented the new tech or got it from aliens. I'll come back to that. Meanwhile, back at the ranch, the Orion message catapults the world onto a new course and changes our own lives completely."

"And?"

"And it worked. The plague has been stopped. But Sandover was caught. The case he carried was lost, orbiting Earth. So there was no test of Stealth and no certainty it was spread everywhere. J.C.'s cocktail had to be destroyed. There was time for one more act. As a result of Phil's tireless work over almost a decade, inter-place-time transmission was ready to try, as a last resort. Rana Myagdi had found the last piece of the puzzle. In that final moment, Dylan and *Prism* sent a message to Sandover, back in time but not far back. It warned him what was coming. That changed the intervening history. When the beam was fired, Sandover and *Whale Ryder* were not there. No trace has been found."

A silence followed before Beya timidly asked, "Doesn't that mean we're all ghosts?"

"Afraid so."

"I'm a bit confused, Kat."

"Understandable."

"So now they are…?"

"Living that final loop."

"I'm too much of a flesh–and–blooder, Kat. He has to be somewhere. Or nowhere, if he's dead and gone. In the words of God, 'Nietzsche is dead'."

"Hard to argue. And I believe you're right. I can't explain it in linear logic, Beya, even though we've had nine years to think about what occurs after inter-place-time communication."

"Which never happened."

"Not before, not until now — if it worked. Dylan modified the equations to send a message to Sandover, let's say two months ago. Given the range of error, it could have reached him two weeks or two years ago. It told him briefly what happened with J.C. and *Whale Rider*."

"Slow down, Kat, how could he get a message to Sandover without the world hearing it?"

"I'd bet he sent it to *Outreach*, Beya. I'd also bet there's someone from Pyramid on *Outreach* with a cipher known only to Pyramid and Dylan. So Sandover gets the message, say, two months ago, and does everything identically except for the very last part. Wesson takes him somewhere else. It would have been easy to arrange. In the reality we saw, *Whale Rider* was obliterated. In the reality Sandover experienced, they weren't there."

"That's hard to swallow."

"I know, but sudden changes in reality are what we actually experience in life, alone and together. We're a species that insists on living in the crosshairs of the larger forces that mould us. Tipping points are common. Some are small moments in a life, some are huge fulcrums in our known universe. We experience the certainty, too real to be fabricated, that reality is changing completely around us, that we were expecting something much worse or much better, that the cast of the die has been altered."

"That still doesn't tell me where he is."

"In our world, he's hiding. Once you knew the secret of Stealth, wouldn't that be what you would do? You would get there first and lie in wait. In the other reality, he is living in Washington, saying goodbye to you at Banks, going up the Lift, and getting attacked. If all goes well, some weeks or months from now, the new 'us' will displace the 'you and I' that are here talking. We will not know the difference when the merge occurs. Sandover will be back and we will accept that as naturally as rain in April."

"So we sit back and wait?"

"Quite the contrary. Our job is to make sure the world is still alive and well at that time. That'll be easy for all of us to sink our teeth into, especially you."

"When will he be back, Kat?"

"That's what I'd bet Dylan is trying to figure out, whether it worked and how far back the message went."

"If there's any chance, that's enough."

"I believe we get second chances, Beya. Things change. You have a lot on your shoulders. What we do now matters for what we consider to be the past. The present and near future have to jibe with their antecedents, mustn't be allowed to pervert them. Otherwise, whatever he did and whatever we succeeded in doing will be lost."

"Do you think he's in a safe place?"

"I'm not enough of a scientist, Beya. Or a romantic. But, yes, that much is clear to me, whichever reality he is in, *gone* is definitely not the word that jumps to mind."

Late night drowsiness spread like a warm caress from the slowly dying embers. A fire tells a story, of ignition, passion, potency, decline, and farewell. Each story is different, the embers reflecting how our own stories interact with the intricate changing patterns of the flame. Some embers change like fireflies, some larger coals ebb and flow. Their fire that night had burned with a flourish, then formed into a cauldron of glowing cinders, a window into Mordor or Hades.

"You're not comfortable with the multiple-reality story, Kat. You like it, but there's something else."

"There are the brothers, the family, and the extraordinary talents. I have a story there and I don't know if you know it all."

"An alternative view of events?"

"Partly. It's the one angle where the Visitors may have played a part. It goes like this. Sometime in the early part of this century, Visitors approached Earth, looked around for quite a while and decided the species was on a pretty good course for extinction. 'Not uncommon,' they observed, 'for might to outstrip wisdom at critical points in the growing-up of a species.' They looked for solutions. They saw Pyramid slowly building an effective global operating structure. They contacted Pyramid, offered the power to enhance a group of humans to lead the way. Sandover and his brothers — not really brothers, orphans under the care of a master tactician named Zhǔ. You've met many of the brothers — Chuanli, Lianshen, Enlai, others — in passing."

"Enhance?"

"All have superior memory and mental quickness. I believe those are the only characteristics that were changed. They use more of their brain, have more mental power. All share the humility of hard work and early poverty."

"You know this is true, this enhancement?"

"You know it, Beya. You've known that Justine has some different physiological characteristics than other children. She has added protein patterns that are slightly reminiscent of some patterns we've seen around recently, in the Visitors' messages, in the beam that hit *Whale Rider*. There are clues to follow."

"How do you know this?"

"Well, that's the tricky part. There was a friend working for that family of orphans, a friend of England and MI6, as it was called back then. Chance but not chance. I was on the team that went in to find out what was up. We were attacked. I took out several of the enemy in a kind of slow-motion rage, allowing my team to escape. But I was captured, out cold and near dead. I was given the treatment, enhanced. It turned out differently in me because of my age and personality. It amplified my powers to perceive and absorb the thoughts and patterns of others."

"So, Dylan and Lara are...?"

"Enhanced, yes, the same genetic and protein patterns. They are family with Justine in this sense. The first generation was Sandover and his brothers."

"And you."

"Yes. And the second generation is Dylan, Lara, and Justine. I do not know if there are others, children of Sandover's clan."

"Sandover knew about you?"

"I was sent home, Beya. When I came to, there were no obvious changes. I kept quiet about sensing thoughts, some instinct. Pyramid may have thought the enhancement hadn't worked. I didn't meet the brothers until later."

"And?"

"And I was pregnant, had been impregnated. Phil is Lara's father but not Dylan's. Lara is a mixture of enhanced and not. Dylan is pure enhanced from both *parents*."

"Phil knows?"

"He knows I was pregnant but not the specifics. He senses the similarities between Dylan and Sandover, Lara and Justine. He never asked, and I've left him in the dark for fear of knocking him off balance. He's a good man, Beya, he doesn't deserve this. But he signed up for the adventure. I'll have to tell him now."

"Justine is different, Kat, a combination of analytical and emotive strengths that's more like Sandover."

"She may have the most powerful mind yet — you have to face that possibility. She made it look easy."

"She saved the world?"

"Of course not, but probably. She saw it all, knit everything into a big picture, and then invented the strategy for Stealth. Our kids are close to running the world."

"And Dylan's father?"

"I don't know."

"Could have been Sandover?"

"Very unlikely. Though I know it was a medical procedure that changed me and caused my pregnancy, how it was done and the identity of the other genetic partner are secrets that I've never learned. That was 2015, Beya, twenty-six years ago, Dylan's lifetime. At that time, Sandover was twelve. I don't know if he and his brothers were enhanced before or after birth. I think after, as boys or early adolescents. Sandover would have been too young and unknown in terms of his eventual capabilities to risk as a parental partner. More likely it was the person who was also the genetic father to Sandover and his brothers."

"The one person in the world who knows where the enhancement technology came from."

"Yes, and his or her identity is the best-kept secret in human history."

"So, you are Sandover's sister."

"In that one sense, yes, and Justine's aunt. We've all been enhanced."

"And Sandover is an uncle to Dylan and Lara."

"In the same sense. They always had an easy way of talking. In quiet moments, I think he taught them how to use their abilities, how to zoom in and out, what key question to ask in any situation. Sandover showed them how to use their mental agility and power."

Distant lightning caught the colours around the room, intermittently highlighting the bold shades of the rainbow, probing the more imprecise hues of emotion.

"What again makes you believe Sandover was at the centre of the Pinnacle, Kat? Doesn't Mr. Occam say that Sandover was simply part of the development of Pyramid and the events that led to the NOA showdown, not the leader? Pyramid arose simply because some group of smart people saw the need for a progressive power base to counteract the growing fundamentalist claptrap. Pyramid shepherded humanity through a mid-life crisis by developing a human enhancement technology, likely their first, followed by pinpoint and NOA."

"Maybe. Occam gets my vote but not my heart. There were nine in the family. Six remain alive. He was the quickest, smoothest, most successful, Beya. Who else would you guess could have masterminded Pyramid's strategy? No one jumps to mind, no one else in the known world."

"So, we didn't save the world. He did."

"Of course not. But probably. It wouldn't have happened without him, where it might have happened without any of us."

"What about the Pinnacle, Kat?"

"My guess? Lee Eng Kai, Mosi Nkaidi, and Kenzie Moore."

"And Sandover."

"Yes, the four points of the Pinnacle."

"In front of our noses!"

"Why not, Beya? If they had pinpoint first, they could operate as a cell, the top one, with backups, no doubt, Ameena in Africa, Saba I'd bet, Sandover's brothers, Dylan and Lara, Justine one day. Don't forget the versatility of Pyramid's structure."

"And you?"

"In a pinch, Beya, but I have a wild streak."

"Yet you said these are guesses, about the Pinnacle."

"Yes, and whether he was the head of Pyramid or just a foot soldier, we don't know what kind of technology they could have brought to bear."

"And what *Prism* has in its labs and holds."

"And how Pyramid is run now with Sandover absent. If he's absent."

"If he planned this all, Beya, leaving us in the dark would be a thoughtful gift if the alternative was believing him dead."

"You do think he planned it."

"One way or another, yes. And if he survived, he will have arranged some ways to look after us, as he always did."

"Yet some part of you clings to inter-place-time. Why, Kat?"

"It fits the physics. It fits the shape of his absence now. It fits the mystery of his disappearance better than anything else. We'll know more when we talk to Dylan."

"Maybe the Visitors will enlighten us, Kat."

"The Visitors are clearly Occamian fiction. Nevertheless, it's a little curious how all this technology sprung forth at this exact moment in time. Explainable, possible, but still suspicious. I think they are here, or were here. Maybe they accomplished their mission and then returned to their prime directive, not to confront us further with their superiority. Maybe their knowledge is what left Pyramid effectively in charge. I can see them sailing off with a 'cheerio and have a nice googleverse'!"

Beya and Kat watched the night sky, now clear as crystal, the tiny cluster of asteroids and habitats just visible as a dot in the heavens. Where would their species go from here?

At 03:00, Dylan's com broke the silence in an uncanny reminder of that night in Merimbula.

"Mother, Beya, welcome to the future."

Kat was the first to reply.

"You sent a message to *Outreach*, to the future?"

"I didn't have to. The beam that passed through *Whale Rider* was a message to Sandover, sent back a few months ."

Beya looked at Kat with sharpened respect.

"Kat guessed that, Dylan. Do you know if the message arrived?"

"Yes, confirmed by a note that Sandover placed in WEO meeting minutes two months ago."

"Congratulations, that's brilliant!"

"Mostly lucky, Beya."

"It looks like more than luck to me."

"OK, a masterpiece of retrospective planning."

"So, he's alive?"

"I believe so, Beya. But there are no guarantees that he'll come through the next two months safely."

"Where is he," Kat cut in, "the one who escaped?"

"On *Prism*, at a guess, or *Outreach*."

"But he can't talk?"

"Not without destroying us."

"Who is in charge of Pyramid, Dylan?"

"In the absence of its primary leader, his alternate is called to fill in."

"An alternate who was groomed for the job?"

"Or that his mother was chosen."

That put a stop to Kat's questions, so Beya took up the inquest.

"And the Visitors?"

"Everyone in Pyramid believes that our first builders were contacted by superior beings. Who am I to argue?"

"Pyramid doesn't know?"

"One person keeps the secret. His name is known only to himself and his triad. He is called the gnome."

"Sandover's father!" Beya recalled her first impression of Eng Kai.

"When you say those words, Beya," Dylan agreed, "they have a ring of truth."

"But it makes no sense. He goes around unshielded."

"Just like Sandover, the perfect disguise."

"Can you really send a time message, and have it go only to Sandover, without risk that the world will hear?" Beya's voice carried a hopeful trace of disbelief."

"Yes, inter-place-time communication is by paired particles, in effect by pinpoint. Only his receiver picked up the message I sent him via Prism and the *Whale Rider*."

"But the Orion message was heard everywhere."

"It wasn't inter-place-time, "Dylan reminded. "Sent from a remote satellite by the Pinnacle of 2032. Old school. The Orion message foresaw the possibility of time-link and how it might work. We did the heavy lifting."

Kat's rejoinder was pointed but not unkind.

"Haven't you unleashed pandemonium, in saving the world from the xenocidal identity-theft of the NOA cocktails?

What will you do with this inter-place-time technology, Dylan?"

"Working on it, Mum, the time equivalent of Stealth and Zhaolin that would lie in wait in the time-fabric of place-time, to decline the twinning of particles instigated from outside. Something like time-amnesia."

"Why can't we talk to Sandover?" Beya whispered into the pause that descended on the conversation. "We're all ghosts in this place and time."

"Sandover is the fulcrum," Dylan replied sadly. "Because my message went only to him, any disruption in place-time around him would trigger explosive changes. Hang on. If all goes well, we've only weeks to wait."

Dawn found Kat and Beya lightly dozing, their hearts too full to let them sleep. Beya took up the book on her lap, then glanced down to read.

"'Snow was general all over Ireland. It was falling on every part of the dark central plain, on the treeless hills, falling softly upon the Bog of Allen and, farther westward, softly falling into the dark mutinous Shannon waves. It was falling, too, upon every part of the lonely churchyard on the hill where Michael Furey lay buried. It lay thickly drifted on the crooked crosses and headstones, on the spears of the little gate, on the barren thorns. His soul swooned slowly as he heard the snow falling faintly through the universe and faintly falling, like the descent of their last end, upon all the living and the dead.'"

"James Joyce?"

"*The Dubliners.*"

"'The Dead.' Oh, I'm so sorry, Beya. If brains were dynamite, I wouldn't have enough to blow my nose."

"I have to be a lot stronger than that, Kat, not the minnow that bolts at the slightest shadow. We live with the living and the dead."

"You have your faith and your daughter, Beya. You have time on your hands, time enough. Take your time."

"That's a good one. Take whose time? I thought I was taking mine when it was quietly taking me. Time to take it back? Thanks for that, Kat. I'll remember when the need arises."

"From time to time?"

"Every now and then."

影 You know me now. You knew from the start. History cannot be rewritten, but what is history? In the beginning there is no end.

Randy Spence is an author and economist who has lived and worked in many corners of the World, though not yet elsewhere.

Watch for Time Keeper..

CPSIA information can be obtained at www.ICGtesting.com
Printed in the USA
LVOW012143120911

246010LV00007B/2/P